W9-CAU-230

The Complete Penny Stock Course

LEARN HOW TO GENERATE PROFITS CONSISTENTLY BY TRADING PENNY STOCKS

First Edition

Jamil Ben Alluch

Foreword by Timothy Sykes

Millionaire Publishing LLC.
80 SW 8th St, Suite 2000, Miami, FL, 33130, USA

First Published 2018

First Edition

Book design by: Jamil Ben Alluch
Edited by: Lisa VanDyke Brown
Foreword by: Timothy Sykes

Ben Alluch, Jamil; The Complete Penny Stock Course: Learn How to Generate Profits Consistently by Trading Penny Stocks

Notices

ISBN 10:   0-692-99267-7
ISBN 13:   978-0-692-99267-8
eBook ISBN: 978-0-692-04560-2

Foreword

Foreword

As I write this, it's been one decade to the month since my breakout role in the first season of "Wall Street Warriors," a TV show that became such a hit that it was the #1 most downloaded TV show in the early days of the iTunes store.

Filmed over several months, viewers saw my crazy life as a stock trader and start-up hedge fund manager in New York City. I was only in my mid-20s, but had already made several million dollars, so I was living pretty well. Despite everyone telling me not to do the show, I figured at best it might get my story out there and at worst it might be fun, so it was worth a shot, but I had no idea that it would single-handedly shape my career.

Wall Street Warriors was a classic wannabe-dramatic reality TV show, but it was entertaining enough, and the producers also tried to educate viewers about the financial industry, which I appreciated. Within days of the show's first airings, I was pleasantly surprised to receive several emails from interested viewers, and within a few months it became clear that Wall Street Warriors was a hit as thousands of people contacted me wanting to learn exactly how I had turned my few thousand dollars of Bar Mitzvah gift money into millions, all thanks to the greatly misunderstood niche of penny stock trading.

At the time, my focus was on trying to grow my small hedge fund, but it was going nowhere fast as due to strict industry rules. My lawyer told me to ignore anyone who contacted me if they were not accredited investors, meaning anyone who didn't have a net worth of at least $1 million, excluding the value of their primary residence, or have income at least $200,000 each year for the last two years – ruling out just about everyone!

The good news was that something about that quirky little TV show really caught on and I found an ever-growing audience of sadly non-accredited investors hungry for more information about me and my stock trading strategy. So I had a decision to make: either continue to try to make it in the fast-growing hedge fund industry filled with the richest people in the world, or shift gears completely and go with the far more speculative option of teaching my stock trading strategy to regular people.

At first, I diligently obeyed my lawyer's warnings, doing my best to ignore the roughly 100-200 emails per day that were piling up in my inbox, which was an insane amount of attention for me, as over the previous three years in the hedge fund industry and despite all my hard work, I was averaging a mere 5-10 emails per day, so already this was 20x anything I'd previously accomplished. Because as I reminded myself, and everyone else reminded me too, these emails were from people who were the complete wrong audience for my hedge fund.

Then, both The New York Times And The New York Observer wrote feature articles on Wall Street Warriors, and both mentioned me in particular. The upstart HDTV network that the show was on lacked content (because HDTV was a brand new technology back then) and began re-airing the show up to six times per day, which led to me receiving 300-500 daily emails all basically asking the same thing: "Can you show me how to do this?"

Forget about the damn hedge fund industry rules; these people needed my help! Not to mention it made my blood boil that many of these people claimed my main strategy of short selling penny stocks was illegal and that what I was doing was impossible; that simply wasn't true! Incompetent brokers had lied to them to make up for the fact that they couldn't find shares to short on these stocks and didn't want to be exposed for their shortcomings, so they kept spreading lies. Someone had to step in and break this cycle of misinformation, and I seemed like the perfect choice to make it happen.

And so, I officially exited the hedge fund world and entered the financial education business.

It was a difficult decision to make, but it got easier the more I thought about it, as my $3 million hedge fund was "puny" by Wall Street's standards and I was fed up with the ridiculous rules prohibiting advertising my fund and performance in any way. Did I mention you had to have a "pre-existing relationship" with potential investors? For me, that was impossible because at the time I was just 25 years old and had spent the past few years trading stocks non-stop, not developing relationships with any high networth individuals like most other hedge fund managers. And worse, I hated schmoozing with the superficial wealthy elite at charity events, I've always gotten along with average people far better, probably due to my personality and the down-to-earth manner in which I was raised.

My hedge fund lawyer and many others thought I was insane to leave the fastest growing, most respected, and highest-paying industry in the world in favor of the notoriously shady industry of "stock market education," filled with snake oil salesmen who promised to make their customers rich, but never actually did. After all, those who can't do, teach, right?

But, as I reminded everyone, I actually could "do" and I figured I could also teach others how to successfully trade stocks, so I would have the upper hand in this industry full of scams. And as demonstrated by my overflowing email inbox, there was already a great demand for my teachings.

What nobody other than I truly understood was that my turning $12,415 into $1.65 million in four years and then roughly another $1 million in trading profits the next three years was a feat, not a fluke. My success wasn't based on luck or fraud, or any one or two big successful investments, or even a bull or bear market – it was achieved by following a very disciplined strategy of taking small gains over and over again, in every kind of market, and I had very specific patterns and rules that I could teach and help others become successful too.

And while my ability to make "only" a few million dollars over a few years didn't meet ridiculous Wall Street or hedge fund standards (which to this day still makes me laugh given that roughly half of Americans have savings of less than $10,000), I knew that making this kind of money was more than meaningful enough for the now several thousand people who had messaged me after seeing my TV show. And the fact that my strategy was real and replicable would give me an advantage over everybody else in the notorious financial education space that was full of liars, cheats and frauds.

It's also important to note that my hedge fund was sitting dead in the water, not just because of the industry rules and my lack of connections, but also because despite my three years of roughly 20% per year performance that had made me the #1 rated short-bias hedge fund manager in the industry, I had gotten greedy and undisciplined, ignoring my key trading rules (that I had not yet come to respect like I do today) of going for singles instead of home runs. I also invested roughly one third of my fund into my best friend's father's startup company that basically invented print-at-home ticketing and had won impressive contracts from AOL, Expedia and Six Flags Amusement Parks.

Can you guess how that investment ended?

Unbeknownst to me and my naive research skills at the time, despite their breakthrough technology and solid contracts, this small company was heavily indebted, mismanaged and on its way to eventual bankruptcy. My best friend's father got thrown out of the company and the new CEO sat me down to tell me everything would be okay, which made me feel better for a little while, until a short time later when he pushed the company into bankruptcy, wiping out all existing shareholders like me and my hedge fund.

But the company wasn't entirely dead. A few weeks later, that slick CEO bought the company in bankruptcy all for himself, somehow managed to keep all their contracts alive, and later sold out to a larger company for roughly $30 million, which would've made my fund and I several million dollars had we not been wiped out by his slimy bankruptcy move. It was a great lesson for me, and you, to never trust any CEO or company management!

It was a tough loss for a cocky young guy like me who had never had any big losses like this and was just beginning to get taken seriously, thanks to my fund's superior three-year performance track record and the popularity of Wall Street Warriors.

But all of that was over now after losing roughly one third of my fund on such an ill-fated investment. Credibility goes quick on Wall Street, no matter the details of what happened. It took me years to grow my few thousand dollars into millions, and after my roughly $500,000 personal loss and my hedge fund's roughly $1 million loss on the investment. While I still had several hundred thousand dollars left to my name and roughly $1.5 million in my hedge fund, my industry credibility, whatever little I had to begin with, was now shot. And my hedge fund, while not totally blown up as some suspected (with my overall gains now reduced to a measly 2% per year in profits, down from 20% per year in profits over 4 years), wouldn't be growing fast anytime soon.

While no investors were clamoring for their money back since they understood my stock trading strategy – not my long-term investing strategy – was still consistently profitable, I couldn't ignore this new opportunity that was knocking on my door. And more importantly, these losses helped crystalize my rules and they made me a far better and wiser trader and teacher, so my timing of getting into the teaching business couldn't have been better.

From the start, teaching others was far more fulfilling than managing my hedge fund and it truly felt right. Instead of focusing solely on trading profits, I greatly preferred trading, while simultaneously mentoring average people who had big dreams, but needed guidance over the superficial and moneyed, cocaine- and pill-addicted Wall Street crowd I'd previously dealt with.

In the beginning of my teaching career, I wasn't sure if I could successfully pass down all the nuances of my strategy to my students, but I was going to try my hardest to make it happen. After all, 90% of traders lost money so it wasn't a very high bar for me to overcome. And I figured any rules and discipline I could pass down were better than none, especially compared to the junk "guidance" that the many fakers in this industry were "teaching"!

Now 10 years later, I'm proud to say that I have successfully passed down my rules, patterns and lessons to my students, who now number in the thousands and hail from over 80 countries. In the process, I've created several millionaire students from scratch, along with dozens of students who have made six figures, and hundreds of students who have made five-figure profits, all within a few short years. More importantly, lately my students' success is improving quite quickly.

Remember, teaching success isn't based on student profits alone, as most of my students begin with just a few thousand dollars, and many don't even trade for the first few weeks or months while studying and getting used to my stock market niche. Knowledge truly is power, and it's been my honor to teach every single thing I learned the hard way over the years, without any mentor whatsoever, so my goal is to be the mentor to others that I never had.

Why did I go into so much detail about the beginnings of my teaching career? So you could understand the rushed circumstances in which I began and why there was never any time for me to organize my teachings and structure everything appropriately. From the get go, I've been playing catch up – with students asking me questions galore, all while I actively trade stocks daily, adding to my already solid multi-million dollar profit track record, during what has become the second longest bull market of all time.

In order to answer so many questions (and in an attempt to preserve my sanity), I wrote my best-selling book "An American Hedge Fund: How I Made $2 Million as a Stock Operator & Created A Hedge Fund" in just a few months, but it wasn't a very technical book because I simply didn't have the time or the training to make it so.

Since then, my teaching process has also been refined and optimized, as I have now made 4,500+ video lessons, 1,000+ webinars and 15 DVD guides that explain everything I've ever learned about penny stock trading. And it's not just me teaching my strategy anymore – several of my millionaire students now also help me mentor other students and we all give live stock trading webinars every few days exclusively for my Trading Challenge students. But despite our stock trading success, none of us have ever been formally trained in academia and our teaching is far from structured, and that's a shame.

Fortunately, just over two years ago, one promising Trading Challenge student named Jamil showed me how he had programmed all of my teachings, patterns and indicators into a software platform that would greatly optimize our daily stock research process. What used to be a very time-consuming process of having to check over a dozen websites for new data and information throughout the trading day (and nightly, too) could now be accomplished all with just a few simple clicks of a mouse. From the start, I was amazed at how solid Jamil's program was. Once I played around with his program some more, it struck me: This was definitive proof that I had successfully passed down my theories and teachings to Jamil, as there's no way I would've been able to create this software on my own. I'm forever in Jamil's debit for his talent and ingenuity.

More importantly, I knew that Jamil's program wouldn't just save me time, it would also help all penny stock traders, so I partnered with him to release this software called StocksToTrade.com, since it helps identify all the best stocks to trade in the fastest way possible, using all my indicators, charts and lessons that I've learned over the past two decades. And because I'm a perfectionist, it has taken two years now to build out StocksToTrade.com to my exact specifications, and we still have more features being released weekly, like the newly-released paper-trading feature (so students can practice their trading without risking their hard-earned money). But long story short, the amazing StocksToTrade.com software has made my stock trading strategy so much more efficient and understandable. It's truly a work of art and I am so proud of it. Most importantly, StocksToTrade.com goes a long way in helping establish penny stock trading as a legitimate financial niche like it should be.

On top of Jamil's supreme programming skills, he's also well versed in academia, and he took it upon himself to organize and structure all my teachings as only a martial arts trained engineer could. So this book written by Jamil is a welcome addition to the educational offerings my team and I have previously produced. I know you will learn a great deal from it and enjoy its well-structured approach immensely.

On behalf of my whole team that now numbers nearly 40 employees (including both of my parents and my first few millionaire students, who help me mentor other Trading Challenge students), I'm very proud to announce that we recently surpassed the 100,000+ trader milestone on our https://profit.ly/community, and little by little, we're cutting through the barrage of BS that exists on Wall Street, and more specifically in the penny stock trading world.

To be clear, there is no magical, easy path to riches anywhere in finance – especially in penny stocks. The vast majority of traders lose money. It's a little-known fact that most investors fail to beat the major stock market indices year-in and year-out, and even in bull markets, nearly three quarters of stocks drop in value each year. So in order to succeed where most fail or underperform, you must rid yourself of any assumptions and misconceptions and you must study harder than you've ever studied before. You'll also need patience and perseverance along the way, because making six and seven figures takes several years, not just a few days, weeks or months like most wish for.

The good news is that my success, and the success of my several millionaire Trading Challenge students, and future millionaire students, is real, and more and more students are learning to profit consistently in this hugely underserved niche. Not by believing the hype spewed by unethical Wolf Of Wall Street-like promoters, but by utilizing time-tested patterns and rules to profit from predictable patterns and volatility, taking it one trade at a time, never going for home runs, accepting and cutting losses quickly when wrong, and winning more times than not in order to grow even a small brokerage account exponentially over time.

– *Timothy Sykes*

Table of Contents

Introduction

Preface

Welcome to the world of penny stocks – the outcast in the field of finance and the stock market.

Often regarded as the black sheep of Wall Street, penny stocks are responsible for the financial demise of countless traders venturing in this wild west of highly volatile and unpredictable truth.

As such, trading these stocks has been labeled as a risky, unpredictable journey for anyone trying their chance with it... and yet, some people have managed to achieve insanely high levels of success.

"How is this possible?" an outsider may ask. *"How can you make any money with such random and fast-moving financial instruments?"*

The truth is that penny stocks have gained a bad reputation by being a misunderstood field of finance that leads to all-too-frequent losses for too many inexperienced traders. People often fear what they don't understand, which is a breeding ground for misconceptions.

Penny stocks are companies that aren't worthy of big network broadcasting. Since there's not much reason to talk about them, big Wall Street players don't mention them in their TV shows, so they aren't taken seriously as legitimate investments. The general public has no interest in worthless companies that often don't even have a real product or service; only gamblers looking for "the next Microsoft" partake in this niche.

Fact: People often confuse trading with investment.

Penny stocks are definitely a sideline niche. It's a niche ignored by the general population, but one that's surprisingly filled with consistent moneymaking opportunities, if you take the time to learn its intricacies. It's that dark alley in Wall Street where few dare venture, yet where a surprising amount of money has been made by flying under the radar of other, more established financial sectors.

Penny stocks are the Wild West of Wall Street, a land of opportunity for those who take the time to learn their intricacies. *Are you ready?*

Acknowledgements

This course is the result of myriad hours of personal study while participating in the Timothy Sykes Millionaire Challenge program. More importantly, however, it's based on structuring information and lessons developed and refined over the years by very successful multi-millionaire penny stock traders.

Since the core concept here is based on Tim's penny stock trading strategy, I strongly encourage you to buy his DVDs as additional material and/or join his Challenge program (contact admin@timothysykes.com for more information), which provides great support for your trading via mentors, a vast video lesson and archived webinar library collection, and access to real-time chats with Tim and his most successful students.

A major influence in my work here is Michael Goode (aka Reaper), Tim Sykes's first millionaire student. Michael is an excellent and dedicated mentor from the Trading Challenge program; he's a master of helping and guiding students through the hurdles of penny stock trading. Thanks, Reaper.

Most of the chapter on risk management is the result of adapting and developing the techniques offered by Michael W. Covel in his book, "The Complete Turtle Trader," (Covel, 2009) to the realm of penny stocks. Although it's oriented toward a completely different type of trading (trend following), you'll benefit from reading it.

Credit also goes to Gregg Sciabica (LX21, a trader who has detailed over $10 million in penny stock trading profits publicly, and has made several million more since becoming a private fund manager), who has, through his presentations at some of Tim Sykes's Las Vegas conferences (you'll find them on the Pennystocking Framework and Timline DVDs), provided me with a great deal of insight in the true psychology and state of mind of a successful trader. While his presentations are not technical in nature, his insight was invaluable in developing this course and pushing me to establish my own strategy.

Big thanks to my friend and colleague Timothy Bohen, for proof reading the initial versions book and providing great insight on part-time trading and creating viable daily trading routines.

Thanks also to Tim Sykes's second millionaire student Tim Grittani – who recently passed $4.8 million[1] in profits in his fifth year of trading penny stocks – for providing great insight in terms of research, entries and exits, and showing different types of strategies that can be applied to the realm of penny stocks.

---

[1] Tim Grittani has made around $4.8M in profits at the time of writing of this book.

On a personal level, I'm extremely grateful for the opportunities that Tim Sykes has offered me. You helped me make this course a reality. I'm thankful for the knowledge that I've gained from hanging around an excellent and dedicated group of people. Thank you for believing in me.

Very special credit goes to someone who requested to remain unmentioned. You know who you are; know that I am also very thankful for the opportunities and chances that you've given me throughout this project and beyond.

Last but most certainly not least, writing this book wouldn't have been possible without the continued support and patience of my family and friends, for whom I am deeply grateful.

My parents, who have indulged every single crazy idea I've had since I was a child, taught me that there is nothing that a person cannot achieve. I owe that knowledge and confidence to them.

More than anyone else, my fiancée Aleksandra and my daughter Maya have endured this whole book-writing journey and everything that revolved around it. They're the pillars of my life and the reason that I dedicate myself to achieving excellence every single day.

Who am I and why should you read this stuff?

Let me start by saying who I am not.

At the time of writing of this book, I have not yet become a wildly successful or fully self-sufficient trader. In fact, my overall trading record shows minimal profits... so far. While that's probably not a very encouraging start if you're reading this and were expecting a super-slick professional, *don't worry*. Here's why...

Partially to blame for my lack of great trading success is my recent all-encompassing dedication in programming the www.stockstotrade.com software, a game-changing venture to pair Tim Sykes's highly effective teaching with well-programmed software. I've spent a ton of time overseeing and ensuring the development of this software. Though I have little time to trade, I greatly enjoy this development project because I know how useful and crucial this stock market tool has already become, and many more features are coming soon.

So who am I? I have a bachelor's degree in computer engineering. I like to play with numbers. I'm extremely good at learning fast, and am even more skilled structuring seemingly complex ideas into simple concepts. I'm academically fluent in three languages. I've lived in over five countries, and have visited about 25 countries so far.

My life has revolved around problem solving and finding simple solutions to complex problems in all kinds of fields. I also have a degree in advanced computer security and hacking, which often helps me think outside the box. I'm addicted to efficiency and improving imperfect processes; whether it's system automation, mechanical systems, or trading, I like to improve and optimize upon existing concepts.

As a martial arts practitioner for over 25 years, I know the necessity of discipline and dedication required to be successful in any endeavor. I've spent many years as a martial arts instructor for children and adults, which has given me great experience in conveying the necessary information to my students in structured steps and a progressive manner. It has also helped me develop a strong analytic process for learning.

So why should you read this course written by a "nobody" in the field of penny stocks? Because this course is based on the collective knowledge gathered by those who ARE successful – those who have made several million dollars each, with tens of millions of dollars made collectively. And it's not based on luck or any one or two great investments, but due to thousands of trades based on strategy. And this collective strategy has never been properly conveyed in a structured manner... until now.

Bottom line: I'm an incredibly organized guy reviewing and putting everything in a far more structured, more academically adequate manner, compared to what these accomplished but non-engineer millionaire traders have already provided. I also added some personal touches and techniques in the process, as that's who I am.

Why should you read this? The answer's simple. I've dedicated a ton of time to watching and understanding the behaviors, processes, techniques and rules of highly successful penny stock traders, and all the most important information is organized and featured in this book.

Given that academic studies have shown that over 90 percent of traders in all financial niches, let alone penny stocks, consistently lose, comprehensive study is the best option for becoming part of the 10 percent of traders who consistently profit.

My goal with this course is to create a piece of learning material that can offer you the necessary knowledge to become proficient at trading on your own in a structured and progressive manner.

My intent is to show here what I wish had been shown to me when I started trading, and how I would have liked the material to be presented to me when I decided to focus on my pursuit of achieving wealth through penny stocks.

For me, day trading isn't a hobby or a game. I take this endeavor very seriously and I decided to learn it and approach it as I would with every other professional task in which I engage.

This course is the result of my ongoing learning process – the compression of thousands of hours of videos lessons, written texts, blog posts, chat discussions and personal procrastination on the subject.

This material is sound. And the credit truly goes to those who are successful and have worked for many years to develop these ideas, concepts and techniques. I'm grateful to be the engineering-minded messenger of these ideas.

Here, I share the knowledge of the masters with newcomers, although in a slightly different (read: far better) format than is currently available for this type of critical instructional material.

I hope you enjoy the ride.

LEGAL DISCLAIMER

Before you proceed with the course, make sure you read and understand the following disclaimer.

This manual is for informational and entertainment purposes only. The author is **not** an investment adviser, financial adviser, or broker, and the material contained herein is **not** intended as investment advice. If you wish to obtain personalized investment advice, you should consult with a Certified Financial Planner (CFP). All statements made in this manual are based on the author's own opinion. The author does not warrant or assume any responsibility for the accuracy of the statements or information contained in this manual, and specifically disclaims the accuracy of any data, including stock prices and stock performance histories. No mention of a particular security or instrument herein constitutes a recommendation to buy or sell that or any security or instrument, nor does it mean that any particular security, instrument, portfolio of securities, transaction or investment strategy is suitable for any specific individual. The author cannot assess, verify, or guarantee the accuracy, adequacy, or completeness of any information, the suitability or profitability of any particular investment or methodology, or the potential value of any investment or informational source. **READERS BEAR THE SOLE RESPONSIBILITY FOR THEIR OWN INVESTMENT DECISIONS. THE AUTHOR IS NOT RESPONSIBLE FOR ANY LOSSES DUE TO INVESTMENT DECISIONS MADE BASED ON INFORMATION PROVIDED HEREIN.** At the time of writing, the author has no position in any of the stocks mentioned in this manual.

By proceeding with reading this course, you affirm that you have read and understand the above disclaimer.

Section I - Getting Started with Penny Stocks

Chapter I.1 - Why You Need This Course

The Million-Dollar Question

Why do you need THIS course, specifically?

While there's a fantastic and overwhelming quantity of material available on *Pennystocking* (Timothy Sykes alone accounts for about 15 DVD sets; that's more than 100 hours of content, plus hundreds of webinars and video lessons available to Pennystocking Silver subscribers and Trading Challenge Program students), what's out there is rather unstructured and often overwhelming for beginners.

Basically, what's out there is gobs of over-exhaustive content that usually only cover the main strategy guidelines without providing a proper framework for newcomers. *"Here's the information. Learn everything and start trading when you feel ready."*

Countless times, I've seen some of the other students in the chat rooms mention that they just lost a significant percentage of their account by not following the rules. Almost as often, you see people asking questions that they shouldn't be asking if they're actively trading penny stocks with this strategy and rules known to them beforehand.

Personally, I found that there's an important learning curve to understanding all the intricacies of trading stocks – especially penny stocks – and that just providing the material in a do-it-yourself is not ideal for all the people who are trying to learn.

Unsurprisingly, I'm a big fan of Tim Sykes's Trading Challenge, as students get access to two to four live webinars each week from Tim and several of his millionaire students, along with hundreds of archived webinars from the past few years, which greatly aids in the overall learning process.

But having spent most of my life in educational institutions, I highly value the place of structured learning material and a proper curriculum that clearly states what the learning goals are and what is expected of the student at the end of the course.

The Complete Penny Stock Course aims to fill this gap that exists in the learning structure for getting acquainted with the realm of penny stocks, while maximizing profits and minimizing the risk to the novice trader.

In order for me to develop and optimize www.stockstotrade.com, I had to dive deep into all the core concepts of the strategy and rules of the game and get intimately familiar with its trading. This step goes beyond the simple act of keeping a journal and posting on a blog, it forces me to assimilate and adapt to the concepts at hand. So everyone wins here.

What To Expect from this Course

The main objective of *The Complete Penny Stock Course* is to teach you all the core concepts associated with developing a successful strategy for trading penny stocks while minimizing the risk to your capital.

This course is mainly based on the strategies developed by Timothy Sykes for trading penny stocks, as well as the knowledge obtained from other successful traders and adding some of my own personal touches and improvements to the content.

At the end of this course, you should be able to efficiently:

- Understand the various ideas associated with trading penny stocks and understand all the necessary trading terms.
- Build daily watchlists and state the reasons why you are watching those stocks or why you have dismissed stocks not present on your list.
- Perform in-depth research on a company and understand its worth and why you should or shouldn't trade it.
- Understand what pumps & dumps are and know how to exploit this knowledge for your profit – legally and ethically.
- Read charts, recognizing and predicting profitable patterns before they happen.
- Know when you should enter or avoid entering a position.
- Know when you should add to, lessen or exit your existing position.
- Report and analyze your trades, and research and track your trading performance.
- Develop your own trading strategy without external assistance and adapt to new trends in the market.
- Perform your own trades, based on your own trading ideas, without external influences.

Your goal here: To become self-sufficient and not have to rely on external sources to perform your daily trading activities.

When you face the market, I want you to have the answer to all your questions on whether or not you should enter a position and why you should or shouldn't do so. If you become totally self-reliant on your own trading skills rather than depending on others' tips and alerts, then I've done my job.

This Course Will Not...

It's important that you understand and accept these points straight out of the gate...

This course will not make you a millionaire overnight.

Anyone who tells you that you can become a millionaire overnight with a small starting capital is trying to sell you a pipe dream. This course requires a lot of dedication and a lot of intensive work in order to become a successful trader. Even Tim Grittani, Tim Sykes's top Trading Challenge student, who has now turned a few thousand dollars into $4.8 million in just over five years, took approximately nine months to become consistently profitable... and that's best-case scenario.

Don't expect to generate $100 million in profit.

While the strategy has been proven to work time and time again in the six and seven-figure profit levels, it is not scalable to Wall Street's eight- and nine-figure profit level standards; it's why penny stocks are ignored by the multi-trillion-dollar hedge fund industry – but for us that's a VERY good thing since all the smartest people compete there, leaving this niche open to far less intelligent competition!

This means that, while making over $2,000,000 like Michael Goode, or over $4,800,000 like Tim Grittani, or over $4,700,000 like Tim Sykes[2] is a potentially achievable goal within a few years, but expecting to generate much far more profit is probably a stretch (although not impossible, especially in this current hot market environment). At that point, it's probably time to consider strategies such as Trend Following or Options trading, which are more scalable and thus far more competitive, risky and also more difficult. Long story short, penny stocks are not the deep end of the financial markets; this is the kiddie pool.

This course cannot guarantee that you will be a profitable trader when you finish it.

As I've discovered throughout my own journey, trading penny stocks is based mainly on experience, layered on top of the extensive acquired knowledge and preparation. While the educational material is crucial to success, the experience factor is also very important.

You may know how you're supposed to act, but much like martial arts, the fact of knowing and the fact of performing an action are worlds very far apart. Remember that over

---

[2] Tim Sykes, Michael Goode and Tim Grittani current profits may be higher or lower as they are still active day traders; these were the published gains at the time of writing of this book.

90 percent of traders lose money in every trading niche, so profits are not a given for anyone.

You won't complete this course in two weeks.

The sheer amount of information and experience required for trading can be overwhelming. Expecting to complete the course within a couple of weeks is unrealistic.

Chapter I.2 offers you a suggested schedule for going through this course and achieving your penny stock trading goals.

Learning speed and assimilation vary greatly from one individual to another. It's worth noting, however, that some of the most profitable penny stock traders have only become profitable after six months to a year of full-time learning and active trading. Some of Tim Sykes's top students took a few years to become super-profitable, so you must remember to have patience and persevere, as you can't force overnight success and knowledge assimilation.

This course isn't kind to the uncommitted.

Life-changing success trading penny stocks requires commitment, dedication, and discipline. If you don't feel that you can fully commit to learning and applying these techniques, my advice to you is to quit now.

Doing otherwise will simply result in disappointment and losing some or even all of your hard-earned cash, and you'll be out of the game quickly enough. Try something else.

Why You Need This Course

Chapter I.2 - How to Read This Course and Suggested Schedule

How to Read This Course

Reading and Learning

The Complete Penny Stock Course is divided into four major sections, each regrouping a specific set of correlating subjects. Each of these sections is divided into chapters containing the necessary knowledge required for you to progressively become self-sufficient at trading.

Be sure to follow sections I through III chronologically, as the information contained within each chapter is dependent on previous chapters. Skipping chapters, or not following the chronology may result in confusion later on.

Section IV focuses on sample strategies, and reading these chapters doesn't need to follow a chronological order, but does require the completion of all previous sections.

It's important to take the time to read, understand and assimilate the knowledge contained within each chapter before moving onto the next one. Failing to understand and assimilate the knowledge may result in potential losses when venturing into a real trade.

Chapter Structure

Each chapter of this course has been divided in multiple sub-sections to facilitate assimilation, learning and understanding.

Overview

The chapter overview provides a brief introduction of the content that will be provided throughout the chapter. You'll only see this section in technical chapters.

Goals

The chapter goals summarize what you should expect from the chapter and what you should know when it's completed. You'll only see this section in technical chapters.

Summary
Bullets covering the main concepts covered by each chapter, when applicable.

Questions
Some chapters will offer this section, so you can test your knowledge after completing a chapter.

I strongly advise that you complete this section after solidly completing and learning the chapter material.

Exercises

Here's your chance to perform analytical tasks to improve your understanding of the chapter content.

I strongly advise that you complete this section after solidly completing and learning the chapter material.

Homework

Great opportunities to immerse yourself into real-life trading processes and situations and develop your ability to gain experience to practice real events. Repeat homework assignments as often as necessary until comfortable with the process.

I strongly advise that you complete this section after solidly completing and learning the chapter material.

Suggested Course Schedule

Here's your proposed schedule for getting through the course. Adapt as you see fit based on your learning speed.

Days 1 to 30

The first month with this course is the most crucial. It's intended to establish all the most basic concepts of trading and the mentality behind it.

This period of time focuses entirely on Sections I and II.

While the textual course can be read relatively fast, it's important to understand and assimilate the knowledge before attempting to trade. This period offers you this opportunity.

Progressively, through this period, you will be immersed in your platform and be able to start performing trades.

- **Week 1**: Cover Section I and assimilate the knowledge, which mainly focuses on the personal aspect of trading and getting into the right state of mind required to perform this type of activity
- **Week 2**: Cover Chapters II.1 through II.6. This will help you get acquainted with the basic practical concepts of trading and understand how to read and analyze the information available to you.

- **Week 3**: Cover Chapters II.7 through II.10. These chapters get into the meat of penny stock trading and provide you with the necessary information to actually start performing trades.
- **Week 4**: This marks the end of the core concepts and offers you the opportunity to put into practice the knowledge you've gained so far. By doing the homework assignments at the end of each chapter, you will progressively be able to start trading in a real environment while controlling your positions and limiting your losses considerably – this is the training-wheels conclusion to Section II.

Days 31 to 60

This period of time focuses on the advanced concepts associated with pennystocking as well as getting to know the most basic sample strategies developed by the most experienced traders. This includes Sections III and IV.

- **Week 1**: Chapters III.1 through III.3. This gets you acquainted with some of the core advanced concepts that serve as the basis for maximizing the use of the tools at your disposal.
- **Week 2**: Chapters III.4 through III.7. This allows you to get a good understanding of the more advanced techniques used in pennystocking and applying them in a real-life trading environment.
- **Week 3**: Chapter III.8 and Section IV. During this time, you'll learn how to develop your own strategies and discover existing strategies at your disposal.
- **Week 4**: Putting it all together. Here, you'll put all your knowledge into practice while taking very small positions in order to gain confidence and trade with ease while following the rules. The focus here is to help you assimilate all the knowledge you've acquired and gain experience while being subjected to minimal financial risk at any given time.

Days 60+

From this point on, you'll be able to perform trades and progressively increase your risk management strategy to match your comfort levels. I strongly advise you to make progressive changes and get acquainted with all the information before increasing your position sizes or taking bigger risks. I'm proud to report that one of the newest features on www.stockstotrade.com is the ability to "paper trade", to practice trading with fake/fantasy cash. It's great practice without the risk of losing your actual hard-earned money.

This period is the transition from a learning perspective to a practical and profitable perspective.

Here, you'll also progressively learn how to cope with financial loss, and develop your discipline and personal trading habits.

Chapter I.3 - STOP NOW!

Whatever you're thinking of doing right now, stop it...

At this point you need to take a step back from the romanticized fairy tale about Wall Street and trading that has been sold to you by the big players, Hollywood, big TV networks, etc.

Wall Street is full of scams, shady companies, even shadier individuals, promoters, furus (fake gurus) and myriad low-life wealthy individuals who don't possess a conscience, existing only to profit from inexperienced traders, such as you probably are now.

What does this mean to you?

Well for one, I'm willing to bet that your first idea when getting this course sounded a lot like:

"Hey, I got this trading course, let me start up my broker platform and see if I can make some trades while I'm learning this stuff! I'll just skim through the pages and learn as I go!"

PLEASE, STOP NOW!

From the point where you begin this course to the point where you're safely able to trade, about two to four months will have elapsed, depending on your learning ability and dedication level. Attempting to start trading without having all the proper knowledge will prompt the devil that is the market to claim some, most, or even all your trading money.

The market may lure you in and you may get lucky with some beginner trades; this will give you lots of confidence to keep on going. The next thing you know, you're betting all your capital only to realize that it's going the wrong way. End result: Your account is blown and you're out of trading, down $10,000 with a very unhappy spouse.

The purpose of this course is to train you to be self-sufficient. However, training takes a lot of time before you're ready to face the real world and risk your hard-earned money.

Another martial arts analogy here: It takes years of training, as much time spent on conditioning, and a lot of mental preparation before you ever begin to participate in tournaments or fighting competitions. The reason for this is because entering the ring unprepared will get you hurt. The guy in front of you has possibly been training for a long time before accepting the challenge of a real fight. If you start too soon with pennystocking, you are fighting the market with real money, unarmed with the knowledge that will prepare you and give you better odds of success on every trade.

Again, if you're thinking about opening your broker's platform and start trading right away, I urge you to immediately stop and cast that thought aside for the time being. Studying and preparing first before risking your money is the way to go. And remember that practice makes perfect, thanks to the new Paper Money practice account feature on www.stockstotrade.com.

The time will come soon enough when you'll be prepared to progressively enter the ring and start taking and giving hits in a manner that you can better control. Fact: The market is merciless, and will take you down without pity if you aren't ready to confront it.

Even the most experienced penny stock traders have lost considerable amounts of money by not knowing or not following the rules, neglecting the will of the market.

Always trade with caution.

You have been warned.

Chapter I.4 - Personal and Financial Requirements

Personal Requirements

You have decided that you would like to start "investing" and/or "trading" your money by becoming a penny stock player.

Here are some of the necessary personal traits that will help you determine whether or not you're ready to trade. You must possess or be able to solidly these traits, or you're probably not ready for this fast-moving world.

Discipline

First and foremost, a successful penny stock trader has a strong sense of discipline; the ability to follow a specific set of rules developed by studying successful traders and trades of the past. Without discipline, you'll join the majority of wannabe traders and investors who end up losing money and eventually blowing up accounts.

Emotional Stability

This is also a very important requirement for any individual venturing into penny stocks. Pennystocking is a rollercoaster, where, within a matter of days, hours or even minutes, you can end up with significant gains or losses.

The ability to keep a level head and control your emotions are absolute necessities when trading. Those who are prone to strong emotional swings will be the victim of unnecessary irrational reactions and decisions; that will lessen the likelihood of consistent profits and possibly even result in significant losses.

Balanced Level of Self-Confidence

This is a critical aspect in making quick decisions and entering or exiting positions well.

Too little self-confidence may force you to miss opportunities, and too much could also eventually result in significant financial losses. Excessive studying and preparation help greatly, as this skill can be learned over time.

Strong Sense of Determination

Pennystocking isn't ideal for undecided and non-dedicated people. In order to truly succeed, you must possess a strong sense of determination and perseverance with the proper mindset and awareness. It takes years to truly master this skill. This type of trading is for individuals who want to make money consistently in this undiscovered financial niche while understanding the inherent risks associated with all types of trading.

Conviction

Self-confidence and determination are both important factors, but the conviction in how you expect a stock to move is primordial to a successful trader. In order to succeed, you have to trust your strategy and have the conviction that you are making the right decisions even if these are wrong. Your conviction is bolstered by the more knowledge and preparation you have.

Acceptance of Being Wrong

There's nothing wrong with being wrong on any trade or investment, especially if you learn to minimize the losses when you're wrong. But if you can't accept that no matter how much research you do and how badly you want to be right, you will simply be wrong sometimes. You must accept that small losses are part of the game. You will lose big in the long run if you aim to be perfect and allow small losses to turn into potentially disastrous losses.

Successful traders accept their defeats and learn from them, and they learn to minimize them too. They adapt to every situation. Trading isn't a competition or a debate to see who can always be right. Your only opponent is yourself. Sadly, too many traders lose that battle due to a lack of proper preparation and guidance.

Able to Accept Losses and Forget About Them

Again, successful traders take small losses on a regular basis. What separates them from the crowd is their uncanny ability to quickly accept and control these losses and move on to the next trade without regret.

To become a successful penny stock trader, you need to feel confident that you can develop this counterintuitive skill. The alternative being that you will potentially end up with significant losses, a negative effect on your self-confidence that limits your capacity to consistently perform profitable trades.

Absolute Commitment

This is not a sprint – it's a marathon. It's not a game, so don't take it lightly. Pennystocking can change your life if you think about it like a full-time job where you need to perform your actions diligently and in a professional manner. Your hard-earned cash and potentially bright future depend on it.

Those who treat stocks as a "fun" casual hobby don't take it seriously, and almost always aren't prepared enough, causing them to lose money time and again. In order to become truly successful, you need to be able to dedicate yourself and commit to learning and researching your potential positions and learning to profit again and again.

Some people are able to do this part time, but even they take this practice very seriously. The scope of this course is for those interested in becoming full-time pennystocking day traders. However, if your schedule doesn't permit this, look up Tim Bohen, one of Timothy Sykes's Trading Challenge students who focuses on part-time trading, profiting roughly $50,000 per year while keeping a job and being a family man. Bohen also trains students on how to optimize their research and trading process using www.stockstotrade.com.

For more info about Bohen and/or Sykes, email admin@timothysykes.com

Bottom line: If you can't commit to spending hours upon hours of research and training BEFORE you risk your money on trading, and you fail to take on this endeavor in a serious and dedicated manner, pennystocking probably isn't for you.

Financial Requirements

Now let's take a look at what you need financially to become a penny stock trader.

Initial Capital

The capital that you will originally dedicate to day trading penny stocks is entirely up to you. Many traders start with completely different amounts, based on their savings, perception of the market, or a multitude of personal/financial factors.

Here are a few examples:

- Tim Grittani started with $1,500 of his own money. He also borrowed $11,500 from his parents to open brokerage accounts, but never used any of the $11,500 to trade. New low-minimum brokers now exist, with minimums of just $500 to $2,000 required to open accounts.
- Timothy Sykes started with around $12,000 (a Bar Mitzvah gift from his parents).
- I started with $12,500.

It's entirely up to you to decide how much you'll dedicate to trading penny stocks.

It is worth noting that most brokers require $500 to open an account and $2,000 to open a margin account that allows you to short sell. In the U.S., due to the pattern day trader rule (explained in Chapter II.1), accounts under $25,000 are only allowed three day trades per week (this is actually a good thing when you're first starting so you don't overtrade and blow up like too many people do. But you can also do unlimited overnight trades per week). We'll go over all this in this course.

Timothy Sykes himself admits he previously wanted more freedom from regulations for beginner traders, but after teaching for nearly a decade now, he views the regulations preventing overtrading as supremely useful given the problems he's seen beginner traders have.

Whether you begin with $500 or $2,000 or $12,000 or even $50,000, I encourage you to view all your beginning trades as simply practice and try not to think about the money, as you're simply trying to learn the ropes of this game and refine your process and discipline in preparation for if/when you trade stocks with larger amounts when the stakes are much higher It's not life-changing to make or lose $100 or $200, but it's a whole different story when you make or lose $10,000 or $20,000 or $100,000 or $200,000 later down the road. And if your account reaches such levels, you want to be FULLY prepared ahead of time, thanks to all your practice with small-account trading and www.stockstotrade.com paper trading.

Personal Savings

If you want to become a full-time trader, that means you're willing to quit your job and venture into the realm of penny stocks in order to generate your income.

In order to quit your job, you need to have money to survive and not be forced to make profitable trades in order to cover your living expenses. What does that look like?

The simple answer is that you probably won't become a consistently profitable trader in a month, two months or even potentially six or nine months.

Dedicated penny stock traders can become profitable after one or two years of intense dedication, commitment and learning, but usually not before. It's important to have the proper expectations so you don't quit a solid income-paying job in favor of becoming a professional and consistently profitable trader. It takes time. Eyes on the prize.

What this means is that for you to fully dedicate to penny stocks, you need to consider the possibility that you may not have any or much income for possibly a year or more. You need to account for this factor.

If you plan to trade part time, keep in mind that truly mastering this trade takes massive amounts of time and dedication. It'll be like having two full-time jobs, but it CAN be done. Many students have learned to study at night and on weekends.

Be smart: Calculate all your living expenses for at least a year and have those savings as your backup source of income throughout the process of becoming a consistently profitable penny stock trader.

Always remember that pennystocking isn't an exact science, and that you may not necessarily generate a steady income from trading. Pennystocking is a skill and experience field that relies on results to provide income rather than the amount of time worked (unlike any other job).

External Services

In addition to having your savings and covering for your expected monthly bills for living, you also need to consider the external services that will be associated with trading.

Trading is an expensive endeavor. The tools and information services are often expensive. These should also be considered in your monthly expenses.

Among the trading-related costs:

- Broker fees
- Data fees
- Software fees
- Courseware fees
- Subscription fees to news/gurus/chats/web applications

These fees add up very quickly, and cheap does NOT mean better. Cheap means your overall profits – and more importantly, your education – will suffer, so take this into consideration in your financial requirements. Those who do cheap out on their education realize the true cost of misinformation and flawed teachings is far greater in the long run, so choose wisely.

Chapter I.5 - The Psychology of the Penny Stock Trader

Overview

This chapter covers the psychology of the penny stock trader by exploring various aspects required in order to become a successful trader in this niche market.

Goals

The goal of this chapter is to give you a deep understanding into how psychology can affect your trading decisions, and how to manage your emotions when confronted with the unavoidable stress of trading highly volatile and liquid stocks.

In brief:

- Understand how successful traders think and process information in real time
- Understand what successful traders don't do
- Learn to adapt your thoughts to the necessary mindset of a successful trader

The Psychology of the Penny Stock Trader

A very specific mindset that exists in the head of every successful penny stock trader; it's developed through many years of experience, profits and losses.

Successful traders have learned to optimize their thought process in order to learn from their defeats and claim even greater profits from their victories.

Dedication is the Root of Success

Day trading penny stocks requires an unfaltering sense of dedication. To succeed, you must focus on learning diligently all the intricacies associated with pennystocking.

Trading low-priced stocks is not trivial; it requires an exhaustive amount of learning and is bound to the experience gained by the trader.

Fact: Undedicated traders will fail at understanding and mastering penny stocks.

The most successful traders are the ones who have dedicated their time, attention, patience and creativity to the pursuit of improving their trading abilities through intense learning and adaptation in both bull and bear markets.

They have followed their dreams and worked hard to achieve them, while others dream of having similar results, but don't do the work required to actually achieve them.

Of course, it's within everyone's reach, as long as there's a strong sense of focused dedication put into your studies from the start, as no one pattern, no one strategy and no one rule works for everyone. You must tailor your trading to your own personality, strengths and weaknesses and the changing markets.

"Trade It, Don't Marry It"

This concept represents what every penny stock trader should adopt as a motto when trading penny stocks.

As tempting as any one stock or their "revolutionary" technology or product may be, the vast majority with fail, so you absolutely can't allow yourself to fall in love and be unwilling to break up your relationship at the first sign of trouble.

As a penny stock trader, you're not a long-term investor getting into a serious relationship with a stock – this one-night-stand kind of situation. Crude analogy, I know, but it works here.

Successful penny stock trading is a numbers game, and while news and some fundamental factors may affect the behavior of stocks, success ultimately comes down to entering when profits seem likely and exiting if and when the position is in danger of no longer being profitable.

You need to learn to disregard the cheerleading from the company, the potential of the product and all the hype behind the façade. Your goal is ultimately to consistently profit from the price movement of the stock; the rest is just noise. Far too many people fail to follow this one concrete rule... don't be one of them.

Cutting Down the Noise

There's often quite a lot of "noise" that exists all around any single security at any given time.

To name a few: CEO and management assurances, analysts, newsletters, social media, chatrooms, breaking news, press releases, emails, promotions, and message boards. These are some factors that can cloud your trading environment with unnecessary clutter; think of it as information overload.

This clutter of information can significantly impede your ability to make rational decisions. Most of it needs to be filtered, and in some cases completely eliminated.

When starting out, it's easy to fall prey to everybody else's opinion on what stocks should be watched, which should be traded, the proper next move, and how to execute it. After all, this must be the case because you don't know any better... right? Wrong. Most traders lose, and most company managers, social media posters and chatrooms lie.

This forces new traders into a hive-like behavioral state, where everyone is trying to do the same move without necessarily knowing why. Often these picks will come from gurus, furus, promoters, TV analysts, and anybody sharing their "expert" opinion to anyone who's willing to follow.

This leads into our next rule...

Don't Be a Sheep

It's fine for beginners to follow the strategy and rules of legitimate trading gurus in terms of picks and plays, but successful traders need to ultimately become totally self-sufficient.

Picks and alerts are often time-delayed by seconds or even minutes, so you'd never be able to actually profit in the same manner as those who offer them. By the time you get the alert, it's usually too late to take a profitable and well risk-adjusted position. Do not follow alerts/picks from others – learn from them!

What this means is that the necessary mindset required for becoming successful in penny stocks is not one of dependence, but one of leadership and conviction in regards to trading decisions at any given time during the market session.

Successful traders don't follow what others have to say. They take everything in, and then trade by following their own set of rules, and sticking to them. Successful traders monitor their environment and intelligently filter the clutter of information in order to retain and zero in on the relevant bits.

This is an important skill, but difficult to achieve, as it's gained through experience. However, what must be present in your mind in order to achieve it is a strong sense of gradually learning how to think and act completely independently over time.

Use alerts and picks from a variety of sources ONLY as a way to learn and generate potential trading ideas in real-time, as within a few months and years you'll be able to learn what news, charts, companies, social media posters, newsletters, chatrooms and educators are best and worst to learn from.

Eventually, you'll rely on nobody but yourself, taking in information from others only for education (and entertainment), not reliance or dependence.

Discipline Isn't an Option

There are just as many successful strategies as there are successful traders in the market, but a couple of factors are common to all of them. One is an uncanny sense of discipline.

This is the kind of discipline that you find in martial arts and the military. Successful traders take their actions seriously and fully commit to their set of rules. So you must first learn these rules, then practice, practice, practice and refine, refine, refine over time.

Discipline is the most important factor for success in this industry, especially for new traders, as it allows you to limit the inevitable potential losses but also to maximize the potential profits over time.

There are simply no successful traders who don't fanatically stick to their set of rules as an absolute truth. Most will report that when they stray from the plan, significant losses occur.

Call it the Kung Fu of the penny stock industry.

Confidence vs. Conviction

Insanely talented penny stock trader LX21 stated during his presentation at the 2011 Las Vegas conference that trading is about conviction. (Sykes & et al., The New Rules of Pennystocking, 2011)

Successful traders need the conviction that their hypotheses are right and their reasons for entering trades are sound.

Confidence, on the other hand, needs to be managed and balanced. Being unconfident will prevent you as a trader from taking advantage of the opportunities that the market has to offer, missing out on a lot of potential profits.

On the other hand, it's been shown over time that over-confidence is often the downfall of every successful trader. Over-confidence pushes the trader to underestimate the will of the market and creates the false illusion that the hypothesis is factual.

With every trade, you must find a balance in your confidence, but also a strong sense of conviction in your trading hypothesis and resulting decisions.

Release the Illusion of Control

The market has a will: It is the collective will of all the traders that exist within its realm.

Just like in society, your own desires are meaningless in comparison to the will of the masses. In the stock market you are subjected to the same lack of control over its movements. No stock will ever care about your position – win or lose – so you must learn to react to stock price action.

> "You must be shapeless, formless, like water. When you pour water in a cup, it becomes the cup. When you pour water in a bottle, it becomes the bottle. When you pour water in a teapot, it becomes the teapot. Water can drip and it can crash. Become like water, my friend." – **Bruce Lee** (Lee, The Lost Interview, 1971)

Every successful trader understands that the market cannot be controlled, and so you must flow "like water" to adapt to every move and every change that the market performs.

Understanding this single concept is the basis upon which many traders become successful. Failing to do so, on the other hand, will only result in losses.

Dealing With Boredom

The stock market is often romanticized by Hollywood, books and even experts as a fast-paced environment where making a million dollars can happen in a matter of seconds. While there's some truth in the romanticism of stock trading, there are also periods where absolutely nothing happens (usually July and August are the slowest months of the year, although 2016 was an unusually busy summer).

This is where discipline comes into effect.

Sometimes there simply aren't very many – or even any – truly great penny stock opportunities offered by the market. Just like during some seasons, when you go fishing, even if you go to a pond full of fish, you won't get a single catch. Dipping in the pond to try to grab the fish at the bottom will only make you wet and possibly sick with a cold.

This is often referred to as "forcing a trade" or a "boredom play." These types of trades are usually losing trades that end up costing you money.

Successful traders avoid this type of behavior, and recognize that stock trading and its potential profits and need for action are addictive. They achieve this by simply taking the day off or dedicating themselves to other non-trading related activities like fitness, family time, etc.

Wait for Opportunities to Come to You

Building upon the previous section, successful traders try to wait for the right opportunities.

Being able to wait for a play with a solid profit potential is key in becoming consistently profitable over time. Those who became successful at trading penny stocks did so by developing the virtue of patience when it comes to choosing which battles to fight.

Patience is the essence upon which the best opportunities are caught.

Own Your Losses like Battle Scars, but Never Seek Revenge

Sometimes, you'll lose money during trading. It's the inevitable truth of the market. If you respect the market, it will provide for you, but it's nonetheless an untamable beast that can take from you just as well.

Successful traders own their losses like battle scars. They don't always remember their victories, but certainly remember the times when they've had losses, especially big ones.

Losing to the market is the reality of trading, a reality that must be accepted and managed and minimized. As a penny stock trader, there are times when you'll take losses, even if all the right moves have been made and you've done all you can to profit. There's such a thing as a "good loss", where a solid trade setup was there, but for whatever reason the trade didn't go your way.

It's okay. It happens to EVERYONE.

Successful traders document their losses and try to understand what went wrong with every losing trade. More importantly, they focus on the lesson from the losses rather than the loss itself.

To become successful at trading penny stocks in the long run, you need to learn how to deal with losses in a way that it doesn't affect your confidence. However, it's of the utmost importance to never seek "revenge" after a loss.

It's human nature to try to recover profits after taking a loss – but it's the downfall of most traders. Don't try to convince yourself that the price will go your way and the stock will do what you want it to do.

The market does what it does. It's an emotionless creature and doesn't care about your personal losses or profits. Successful traders remind themselves to be objective and move on by remembering the lesson about the loss, but never hanging onto the loss itself, nor seeking to recover these lost profits on the same stock unless the opportunity arises.

Trading on Cash, Not Margin

One of the most important aspects when trading penny stocks is to *only trade with the cash you have at hand,* and to never rely on leverage or borrowed money.

The idea is simple: What you lose when you trade with your own capital is your own money. What you lose when you trade using leverage is the broker's money; in other words, a loan.

This means that every loss that you incur while using leverage could potentially become a debt rather than just a loss that can be easily covered by your account.

Successful penny stock traders trade their own cash and grow their accounts gradually. More importantly, they don't try to borrow money to increase their gains and get ahead quicker, as losses can become very costly.

More importantly, you can't cheat the process of learning and refining your discipline as your account gets bigger.

Too many beginners mistakenly believe that they know everything about trading penny stocks in a very short period of time, itching to bet bigger in order to prove their knowledge and expertise. It doesn't end well for them, and they receive a very expensive reminder that education takes more time and patience than most people want to believe.

Never Bet More Than You're Willing to Lose

This is another line often repeated among successful traders. They're 100 percent right. Follow this rule, always. Don't ever bet more than you're willing to lose.

We'll cover this idea in great detail in Chapter II.4 when we examine risk management strategies.

Makes you realize why I keep repeating the concepts of discipline and being able to control emotional impulses, right?

Avoid Getting Into Bad Habits

A huge problem for experienced traders is breaking old habits that have been developed over time but aren't beneficial to trading, or have become detrimental to the process of buying and selling securities in order to generate profit.

It is important early on to spot bad trading behaviors and eliminate them from your trading process.

Once bad habits are acquired, it's hard to remove them, which may become a hindrance and/or lead to significant losses. Weed out these bad habits and focus on good habits from the start.

Foster the Rest of You

There's more to life than trading. Successful penny stock trading is a full-time job that requires intense dedication, deep commitment and unfaltering discipline, but it also allows you to truly live.

Beyond the dedication requirements, successful trading is often accompanied by a healthy mind in a healthy body.

As a trader, please value your free time and spend it doing other important things like exercising, enjoying your friends and family, and relaxing.

Penny stock trading is a mentally challenging activity intended only for those who possess the mindset to concentrate on the task at hand without allowing external influences to affect their decisions. Anyone can do it if they have the right state of mind and guidance.

Ultimately, it's a way to make money and create financial stability for yourself and your family.

Keeping a healthy and balanced life helps you become an even more successful trader because it allows you to focus on your goals like studying hard, prepping, practicing, finding your flow/process, and enjoying the financial benefits and rewards of your hard work.

Establish a Daily Routine

Day trading isn't only about techniques, patterns, strategies and risk management; it's also about managing your time and having a reliable daily routine to help you deal with every trading session.

Daily routines vary from person to person, but in essence, you should lay out and organize how every trading day should be, from the moment you wake up to the moment you go to sleep.

Organizing time and having a proper daily routine is how successful traders remain consistent with their results; it represents their day plan.

Such a routine should account for all aspects of your daily life:

- Meals

- Exercise
- Family/friends
- Out-of-office time (groceries, shopping, doctor, travel, etc.)
- Wake-up and sleep times
- Pre-market preparation
- Post-market research and next-day preparation
- Unexpected events and things to do
- Free time, rest and relax period

It is up to each trader to establish a properly laid out daily schedule to account for all these events, and adapt to things that may force you out of your daily routine, and out of good trades.

Planning your days complements planning your trading strategy, as it offers you a concrete expectation on how you should behave and how your process should be throughout the day.

In order to become a truly successful trader, you'll need a robust daily routine to help you deal with your day.

Here's an example of what that daily routine might look like:

- Wake up at 5:30 a.m. and have breakfast
- 6:30-7:30 a.m.: wake kids up, get them ready, take to school
- 7:30-8:30 a.m.: exercise
- 8:30-9:30 a.m.: perform additional research on potential plays and watch pre-market behavior
- 9:30 a.m.–12 p.m.: trading session
- 12-2 p.m.: lunch/relaxation
- 2-4 p.m.: trading session
- 4-5:30 p.m.: look for potential plays for next day
- 5:30-8 p.m.: pick up kids, have dinner, put them to bed
- 8-9 p.m.: prepare daily watchlist and next day plays
- 9-11 p.m.: rest and relax

While this might not apply to you, the idea is to have a baseline of how your day should look like when it comes to trading. Tailor your plan to yourself and your schedule. Make trading work for you!

Trade Like a Scientist

To become a successful trader, you need to treat all the steps of trading much like a scientist approaches a problem that needs to be solved.

Follow the scientific process using the concepts that will be shown throughout the course.

1. Define the question – what are you trading and why?
2. Gather information & resources – basic research, Chapter II.9
3. Form a hypothesis – based on research, Chapter II.9
4. Perform experiment & collect data – trade and see what happens, Chapter II.10
5. Analyze the data – track your results, Chapter I.6 and Chapter II.10
6. Interpret the data & draw conclusions that serve as a starting point for a new hypothesis
7. Publish results – comment your performance, Chapter I.6

Follow the Turtles' Core Axioms

You'll benefit from these excellent axioms from "The Complete Turtle Trader" (Covel, 2009):

- Do not let emotions fluctuate with the up and down of your capital.
- Be consistent and even-tempered.
- Judge yourself not by the outcome, but by your process.
- Know what you are going to do when the market does what it is going to do.
- Every now and then the impossible can and will happen.
- Know each day what your plan and your contingencies are for the next day.
- What can I win and what can I lose? What are probabilities of either happening?

Trading with 3 Accounts

You're now getting started with the various concepts and ideas of trading that will eventually allow you to become successful through hard work and perseverance.

As I stressed in the previous sections of this chapter, growing an account relies on unwavering discipline to achieve your goals. And yes, I'll keep mentioning this; I'm sure you're not surprised.

During the Trader and Investor Summit in Orlando (Sept 2016), Timothy Sykes introduced the concept of having two accounts when trading, and despite what the previous statement might seem to imply, these are figurative accounts. He referred to them as the financial account and the knowledge account.

After spending some time analyzing this concept, I concluded that there was actually a third account that came into play: the experience account.

Let's take a look at these ideas...

The Financial Account

This is by far the most obvious and concrete account that a trader will possess. It's the account that holds the money (whether you have one or many, we're keeping those as your account). This is the account that a trader ultimately works to grow exponentially to reach the desired financial goal and create a state of financial freedom.

This is the hardest account to grow over time.

The Knowledge Account

The knowledge account refers to the account that holds all that a trader knows about stocks and the market. Whether it is patterns, catalysts or trading techniques, knowledge is the basis for being able to trade to maximize profits and minimize losses.

Without knowledge, trading becomes a thoughtless gamble in the market that is no different from visiting a casino and playing roulette.

The knowledge account allows a trader to establish the guidelines for trading, and precedes entering and exiting positions by taking calculated risks and knowing when to exit a given position.

The Experience Account

While the knowledge account is of the utmost importance, the third and final account is, by far, the account that matters most when attempting to grow the financial account. The experience account benefits from knowledge, but knowledge without experience often leads to failure.

Growing the experience account should be the utmost priority for novice traders before truly focusing on growing the financial account.

Working with the 3 Accounts and Why It Matters

Now that we've established the three accounts, let's consider how they all come into play and connect to each other.

Growing the financial account is a trader's ultimate goal; however, it's impossible to simply start trading and become profitable overnight. The very first step is to focus on growing your knowledge account. This comes in the form of learning. Whether through the help of this course, a guru or other sources, you must start collecting knowledge.

As time passes, the knowledge account grows as you acquire information about the market and conceptually understand the ins and outs of how to trade stocks. Once your knowledge account balance reaches a certain level, you're then ready to focus on the most important part before attempting to grow the financial account.

Figure I.5.1 illustrates the initial step, which essentially consists of putting money into your trading account and starting to acquire the necessary knowledge for performing trades.

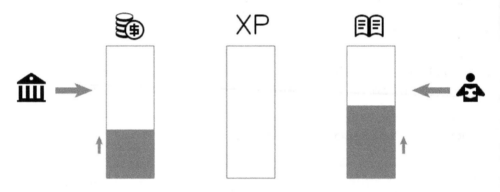

Figure I.5.1 - Growing financial and knowledge accounts

The most important part is to "transfer the balance" from the knowledge account into the experience account. Without experience, plain knowledge is worthless. You may have spent months reading this course and you may know every single thing there is to know about patterns and trading techniques, but without having applied the knowledge in a real environment, you'll always lack the necessary experience.

In martial arts, an individual may spend hours, days, months or years observing and re-peating the same movement over and over again. This is the acquisition of knowledge. When it's time to put this information into practical use, there's a completely different set of factors that come in, namely, emotions, reaction speed, physical fatigue, and such. The stock market is no different.

Figure I.5.2 illustrates the basic process of the "balance transfers" that occur when gain-ing experience.

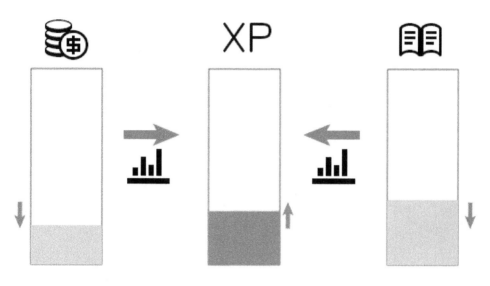

Figure I.5.2 - Growing the experience account

Growing the experience account typically results in a "balance transfer" from the financial account to the experience account. This is often caused by the losses that a novice trader experiences in the first few months of trading. This phase may result in both losses and gains, but what matters is to minimize these losses while growing the experience account. Don't let anyone else tell you otherwise: Gaining experience will cost you money; it's up to you to determine how small this cost will be.

Your knowledge account will also decrease as you gain experience, because practical experience will push you to question and re-evaluate the theoretical knowledge that you acquire over time.

The time frame for the figure above shows a process that lasts six months to a year, depending on how quickly you gain experience and adapt to the actions of the knowledge that you possess.

Finally, once the experience account and the knowledge account have both reached an acceptable level, the financial account will proceed to grow as you transfer your balances between these accounts. From this point on, all three accounts should experience a constant rate of growth, progressively increasing. Then three things will happen:

- You will have knowledge
- You will become experienced

- You will make money consistently

This is shown by Figure I.5.3, which depicts the interaction between the 3 accounts.

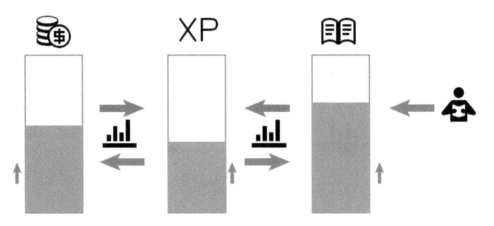

Figure I.5.3 - Continued growth of the 3 accounts

Note how the figure above still shows the external action of learning. This implies that acquiring knowledge is a continuous process that happens from both gaining experience and learning new information.

This is what ultimately allows a trader to transition from being novice to being successful.

Summary

- You are a *trader*, not an investor. Think about the numbers and not about the company.
- Cut down the information clutter and only retain the information you need to perform your trading tasks. Minimize chatrooms, message boards, Facebook, Instagram, etc.
- Don't be a sheep. Make your own decisions and don't follow what others have to say without having your own opinion first.
- Be disciplined and stick to your rules diligently.
- Choose conviction over confidence. Find the balance in your confidence level. If you think you're "that" good, you're going to lose, for the market always wins.
- You have no control over the movement of the market or the price of any given stock at any given time. *"Become like water, my friend."*

- Never force a trade. Boredom is a trade killer that usually results in losses.
- Be patient and wait for opportunities to present themselves. Don't go looking for them, as you won't find them if you're too impatient.
- Every loss is a scar. Remember the lesson it teaches you, but forget about the loss itself. Never force a trade in order to recover lost profits, and only trade when a solid opportunity arises.
- Don't get into bad habits, they are hard to correct and can become costly over time.
- Live a healthy and balanced life. Healthy mind in healthy body aids you in your quest to achieve consistent profits.
- Have a proper daily routine in place for every trading day.
- Follow the scientific process to trade.
- Remember the Turtles' core axioms.
- Learn how to trade and grow your three accounts.

Homework

- Identify and write down your personality traits and compare how these fare against that of a successful trader. Be honest; nobody is here to judge you but yourself.
  - Where are you comparable?
  - Where do you differ?
  - How can you improve your mindset in order to bring it closer to that of successful traders?
- Identify all factors that exist in your environment that could be considered as "noise" and affect your ability to trade.
  - How can you filter or remove some of these elements in order to improve your trading environment?
- Based on your lifestyle, establish a daily routine dedicated for trading and adapt it to your specific needs, accounting for all the necessities and responsibilities you have every single day.
  - Adapt as necessary based on how well it performs.

The Psychology of the Penny Stock Trader

Chapter I.6 - Your Journal

Overview

This chapter focuses on the various ways of keeping a journal in order to track your watchlists, your ideas, your learned lessons and your trading performance.

Goals

The goal of this chapter is to guide you through the steps for establishing a structured journal that will offer you a way to track your trading history.

How to Keep a Trading Journal

Over time, unwritten lessons are often forgotten. Most who remember are those who put their history in writing.

Here are some great ways for you to create and maintain various types of trading journals in order to track every action and event in your engagements with the stock market.

The Medium

There are multiple ways for you to take notes. Here are some of the media that you can use for this purpose:

- Blog
    - Offers a quick way to publish information on the internet and promotes transparency
    - Multiple choices available: BlogSpot, WordPress, Tumblr, etc.
    - Allows you to categorize your entries and is available online
- Profit.ly
    - Tracks your trades and generates trade performance statistics
    - Promotes transparency
    - Social trading platform that allows interaction with other traders
    - Imports data directly from most major U.S. brokers
- Notebook
    - Good ol' pen and paper approach
    - Easy access
    - More traditional
- Spreadsheet
    - Offers the possibility to perform calculations and generate graphs

- Word processor
    - Similar to the notebook, but on a computer
- Evernote
    - Quick notes from any device
    - Easy tagging and categorization
    - Online synchronization
- Video blog
    - Talk about your trades
    - Display media information and real movement of the stock at the time of recording

Each of these has its advantages. You can also use multiple ways to input your information in order to track your data in different ways, or to add redundancy to your journal entries.

The Watchlist Journal

There are a few types of notes that you should definitely have. The first of these is related to your daily watchlists.

A full overview on how to find stocks and build a watchlist will be covered in Chapter II.9, where you'll learn exclusively how to build daily watchlists. In this section we'll mainly just focus on the concept of note-taking that you'll apply to the watchlists that you'll create later on through this course.

Your watchlist journal will consist of simply a list of stocks that will be part of your potential plays for the following trading session.

This journal will contain the relevant information associated with every stock on your watchlist. Here are a few examples of the data that could be included in this type of journal:

- Stock ticker
- Average true range.
- Risk/Reward ratio.
- Profit goal in $/share.
- Rating (based, for example, on LX21's method for rating plays, or Tim Sykes's SSS scale outlined in his free http://traderchecklist.com guide and covered in Chapter II.11).
- (Key) resistance and support (we'll discuss this in Chapter II.5).
- Description of why this should be watched.
- Concerns about the possible price action of the stock.

- Applicable trading strategy.
- Anything else you can think of to help you make decisions.

Address these points in every entry on your watchlist.

A bonus here: You can add also stocks to your list intraday if you find anything worthy of a play.

The Trade Journal

This is one of the most important elements when tracking trading performance. The trading journal is an overview on the factual performance of a trade that includes all the elements associated with any given trade.

Here's some of the information that should be contained within your trade journal:

- Date
- Symbol
- Entry price, position and time
- Exit price, position and time
- Description of the trade
  - Why is it a profitable trade?
  - Why is it a losing trade?
  - What factors influenced the stock price?
  - What mistakes, if any, were made?
- Trading strategy applied to trading this instrument

You'll find a sample notebook entry below in Figure I.6-1.

Additionally, you may choose to make a more in-depth report for every trade you make.

Keeping a trade journal allows you to monitor your past performance and avoid repeating the same mistakes made in the past. It's used as a tool for personal improvement and also to track the performance of a strategy over multiple trades.

This, in turn, promote the concept of optimization to your trading techniques and allow you to become a more profitable trader with each iteration, as you gain more hands-on experience.

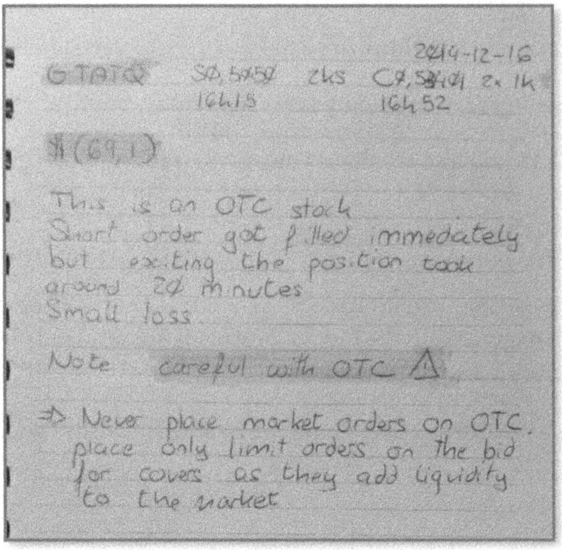

Figure I.6.1 Example of a notebook trade journal entry for a loss on GTATQ

As you see in Figure I.6.1, this trade, extracted from my own journal, reflects the various kinds of information that can be found in a trade journal.

Another example can be seen via Proft.ly in Figure I.6.2, which imports trades directly from a wide selection of brokers.

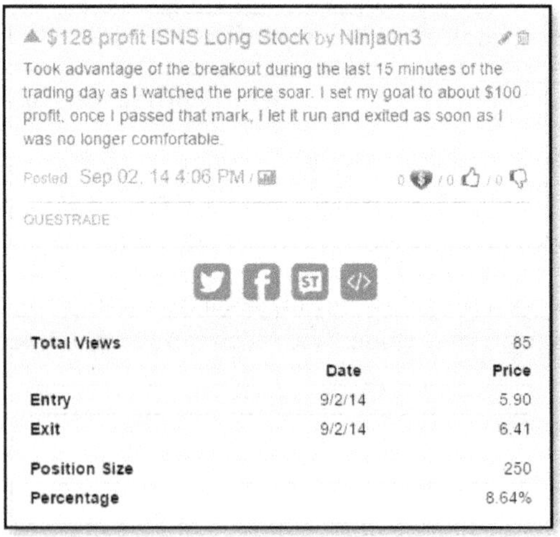

Figure I.6.2- Proft.ly trade entry for a profit on ISNS

You'll find another detailed analysis at the following address: http://www.redandgreen.ninja/trade-16-ninja0n3-vs-clrx-clrx-wins/

This represents a more analytic take on the journal entry, where all aspects of the trade are taken into consideration.

Your trade journal serves as a tracking tool to remember your successes, but more importantly your losses and any mistakes made.

Put simply, smart traders use trade journals to avoid repeating the mistakes of the past. Use a trade journal.

Strategy Analysis Journal

The strategy analysis journal tracks your strategy performance over time.

This results from your trading activities and reflects the results documented in your trade journal.

First of all, make sure that you give unique names to your strategies – names that you can easily recognize and differentiate for every other strategy in your trading book.

Tim Grittani is known to track his strategies' performance using spreadsheets and listing each of the stocks and their performance.

Here's how it works: For each of the strategies that you use in your trading activities, have a separate spreadsheet associated with that specific strategy.

Each of your strategies' spreadsheets should contain the following information:

- Strategy name
- List of stocks traded with that strategy
  - Symbol
  - Date traded
  - Entry and exit prices
  - Position size
  - Position value
  - Loss amount & percentage
  - Profit amount & percentage
  - Rating of how well this trade was executed within the strategy parameters
  - Notes on the trade
- Number of winning/losing trades
- Strategy performance in percentage wins and losses

- Average gains/losses
- Number of consecutive winning/losing trades
- Largest win/losses
- Average winning/losing trades
- The profitability percentage
- Gross profit/losses
- Any metric that suits your statistical evaluation needs

	All Strategies	Longs	Shorts	SBC	SBEW	SBDAS	SBON	SBEPD	SBMS	SBBO	SSBO	SSMP	SSPD	SSFPD	SSOS	SSOSRD	SSON	MSC
Total Net Profit	$267.77	$72.91	$340.68	$209.00	$16.50	$0.00	$83.30	$0.00	$0.00	$0.00	$0.00	$0.00	$271.26	$0.00	$58.73	$0.00	$0.00	$46.98
Gross Profit	$479.06	$389.00	$90.06	$228.50	$0.00	$0.00	$160.50	$0.00	$0.00	$0.00	$0.00	$0.00	$15.80	$0.00	$74.26	$0.00	$0.00	$0.00
Gross Loss	$746.83	$316.09	$430.74	$19.50	$16.50	$0.00	$243.80	$0.00	$0.00	$0.00	$0.00	$0.00	$287.06	$0.00	$132.99	$0.00	$0.00	$46.98
Profit Factor	0.64	1.23	0.21	11.72	0.00	0.00	0.66	0.00	0.00	0.00	0.00	0.00	0.06	0.00	0.56	0.00	0.00	0.00
Total Trades	21	12	9	3	1	0	7	0	0	0	0	0	4	0	5	0	0	1
Percent Profitable	28.57%	33.33%	22.22%	66.67%	0.00%	0.00%	28.57%	0.00%	0.00%	0.00%	0.00%	0.00%	25.00%	0.00%	20.00%	0.00%	0.00%	0.00%
Winning Trades	6	4	2	2	0	0	2	0	0	0	0	0	1	0	1	0	0	0
Losing Trades	15	8	7	1	1	0	5	0	0	0	0	0	3	0	4	0	0	1
Avg Trade Net Profit	$12.75	$6.08	$37.85	$69.67	$16.50	$0.00	$11.90	$0.00	$0.00	$0.00	$0.00	$0.00	$67.81	$0.00	$11.75	$0.00	$0.00	$46.98
Avg Winning Trade	$79.84	$97.25	$45.03	$114.25	$0.00	$0.00	$80.25	$0.00	$0.00	$0.00	$0.00	$0.00	$15.80	$0.00	$74.26	$0.00	$0.00	$0.00
Avg % Gain	6.38%	7.58%	3.98%	8.40%	0.00%	0.00%	6.77%	0.00%	0.00%	0.00%	0.00%	0.00%	3.78%	0.00%	4.17%	0.00%	0.00%	0.00%
Avg Losing Trade	$49.79	$39.51	$61.53	$19.50	$16.50	$0.00	$48.76	$0.00	$0.00	$0.00	$0.00	$0.00	$95.69	$0.00	$33.25	$0.00	$0.00	$46.98
Avg % Loss	4.41%	3.64%	5.30%	2.05%	6.67%	0.00%	3.42%	0.00%	0.00%	0.00%	0.00%	0.00%	9.02%	0.00%	2.27%	0.00%	0.00%	4.22%
Ratio Avg Win to Avg Loss	1.60	2.48	0.73	5.86	0.00	0.00	1.65	0.00	0.00	0.00	0.00	0.00	0.17	0.00	2.23	0.00	0.00	0.00
Largest Winning Trade	$127.50	$127.50	$74.26	$118.50	$16.50	$0.00	$127.50	$0.00	$0.00	$0.00	$0.00	$0.00	$15.80	$0.00	$74.26	$0.00	$0.00	$46.98
Largest Losing Trade	$178.99	$71.50	$178.99	$19.50	$16.50	$0.00	$71.50	$0.00	$0.00	$0.00	$0.00	$0.00	$178.99	$0.00	$64.24	$0.00	$0.00	$46.98
Largest Winner as % Gross Profit	26.61%	32.78%	82.46%	51.86%	0.00%	0.00%	79.44%	0.00%	0.00%	0.00%	0.00%	0.00%	100.00%	0.00%	100.00%	0.00%	0.00%	0.00%
Largest Loser as % Gross Loss	23.97%	22.62%	41.55%	100.00%	100.00%	0.00%	29.33%	0.00%	0.00%	0.00%	0.00%	0.00%	62.35%	0.00%	48.30%	0.00%	0.00%	100.00%
Max Consec Winning Trades	2	2	1	2	0	0	1	0	0	0	0	0	1	0	1	0	0	0
Max Consec Losing Trades	8	3	7	1	1	0	2	0	0	0	0	0	3	0	4	0	0	1

Most Profitable Strategy	SBC	$209.00
Less Profitable Strategy	SSPD	$271.26

Figure I.6.3 - Google Sheets - Strategy performance tracking

Ticker	Type	Strategy	Entry	Entry Date	Exit	Exit Date	Position	Comm.	Profit/Loss	Percentage	Cum. P/L
BDR		SBEW	$1.76	2014-08-15	$1.65	2014-08-15	150	$0.00	$16.50	6.67%	$16.50
MOBI		SBON	$8.48	2014-08-18	$8.27	2014-08-18	30	$0.00	$6.30	2.54%	$22.80
HPJ		SBON	$5.59	2014-08-20	$5.92	2014-08-20	100	$0.00	$33.00	5.57%	$10.20
JRJC		SBON	$10.23	2014-08-21	$9.71	2014-08-21	100	$0.00	$52.00	5.36%	$41.80
DGLY		SBC	$6.48	2014-08-21	$6.35	2014-08-21	150	$0.00	$19.50	2.05%	$61.30
DGLY		SBC	$7.29	2014-08-22	$8.08	2014-08-22	150	$0.00	$118.50	9.75%	$57.20
DGLY		SBC	$14.55	2014-08-26	$15.65	2014-08-26	100	$0.00	$110.00	7.03%	$157.20
ISNS		SBON	$4.45	2014-08-27	$4.29	2014-08-27	400	$0.00	$64.00	3.71%	$193.20
ISNS		SBON	$5.90	2014-09-02	$6.41	2014-09-02	250	$0.00	$127.50	7.96%	$230.70
ISNS		SBON	$9.10	2014-09-03	$8.814	2014-09-03	250	$0.00	$71.50	3.24%	$159.20
ISNS		SBON	$9.10	2014-09-03	$8.90	2014-09-03	250	$0.00	$50.00	2.25%	$109.20
AEMD		SSPD	$0.555	2014-11-26	$0.534	2014-11-26	1000	$5.20	$15.80	3.78%	$325.00
GTATQ		SSPD	$0.595	2014-12-16	$0.534	2014-12-16	2000	$11.08	$69.10	5.74%	$55.90
IMRS		MSC	$0.803	2014-12-31	$0.839	2014-12-31	1127	$8.79	$46.98	4.22%	$8.92
AMLH		SSPD	$0.2115	2015-02-03	$0.2484	2015-02-05	4500	$12.70	$179.99	17.47%	$170.07
CLRX		SSPD	$1.53	2015-02-06	$1.589	2015-02-06	590	$4.16	$38.97	3.86%	$209.04
GENE		SSOS	$6.33	2015-02-26	$6.40	2015-02-26	200	$1.73	$15.73	1.11%	$224.77
GENE		SSOS	$5.98	2015-02-27	$6.05	2015-02-27	200	$2.73	$16.73	1.17%	$241.50
RESN		SSOS	$11.054	2015-03-02	$10.70	2015-03-03	100	$0.89	$36.29	3.31%	$277.79
OREX		SSOS	$8.76	2015-03-03	$8.067	2015-03-03	200	$2.84	$64.24	3.50%	$342.03
OREX		SSOS	$9.11	2015-03-03	$8.73	2015-03-03	200	$1.74	$74.26	4.17%	$267.77

All Strategies	
Total Net Profit	$267.77
Gross Profit	$479.06
Gross Loss	$746.83
Profit Factor	0.64
Total Trades	21
Percent Profitable	28.57%
Winning Trades	6
Losing Trades	15
Avg Trade Net Profit	$12.75
Avg Winning Trade	$79.84
Avg % Gain	6.38%
Avg % Loss	4.41%
Ratio Avg Win to Avg Loss	1.60
Largest Winning Trade	$127.50
Largest Losing Trade	$178.99
Largest Winner as % Gross Profit	26.61%
Largest Loser as % Gross Loss	23.97%
Max Consec Winning Trades	2
Max Consec Losing Trades	8

Figure I.6.4 - Google Sheets - Strategy performance tracking, trade entries

Figures I.6.3 and I.6.4 show my personal strategy tracking spreadsheets that I use to establish statistics on my current trades.

By following closely how your various strategies fare, you'll learn to optimize your results and adjust your strategy parameters in order to maximize profits. Additionally, you'll develop a sense for which strategies you're more efficient at turning into profits and which strategies generate the lowest yield.

This also allows you to eliminate strategies that keep you from generating steady profits over time.

Periodic Performance Reports

Much like you do your accounting weekly, monthly, quarterly or yearly, you should also consider writing periodic performance reports about your trading activities.

These types of reports should highlight the trading events encountered during that time period and discuss your general performance.

This type of report should include:

- Reporting period
- Highlights during that period
- Watchlist performance
  - This is important because you can evaluate how close to reality your picks have come based on your strategy and the logic for choosing specific symbols for your list.
- Lessons learned
  - A result of analyzing each of your trades and also what's shown by your strategy analysis journal
- Things that need improvement within your strategy or trading activities
  - Based on your lessons learned, identify what needs to be improved in order for you to become a better trader.
- Your mindset and how the market affects you

These reports should be as long as you deem necessary. Make them as detailed as possible in order to provide you with the greatest analytical benefit.

The suggested time periods for generating your periodic reports are:

- Weekly
- Monthly
- Quarterly
- Yearly

Some traders have been known to include their periodic goals in their monthly and yearly reports in order to gauge how well they've done within their profit expectations.

It's up to you whether you want to set profit goals, just always remember that profit goals should only be used as a tool for gauging performance and not as an absolute requirement to meet when trading, as it can cause forcing trades and generating losses.

Summary

- You can make a journal on about any medium as long as you have the will to do it.
- The Watchlist Journal/Daily Watchlist allows you to establish which stocks you plan on playing and how you will exploit them when the opportunity arises. It is used to identify the potential plays.
- The Trade Journal is used to narrate every single trade you make in order to learn from every trading experience.
- The Strategy Analysis Journal allows you to track the performance of every single strategy you have, based on your trade journal.
- Periodic performance reports allow you to keep track of your trading progress, and provide a bigger picture for your performance as a trader by taking into account all the factors that come into play.

Questions

1. Why do I need a watchlist?

   a.   I don't; I trade my stocks on the spot.

   b.   To keep track of my trades.

   c.   To keep track of potential opportunities to trade.

   d.   To keep track of stocks I shouldn't play.

2. What is the purpose of a trade journal?

   a.   To keep a list of potential opportunities to play.

   b.   To keep track of the trades that I've made and learn from them.

   c.   To keep track of my wins and brag about them.

   d.   To keep track of my losses.

3. What is a strategy analysis journal used for?

   a.   To know what are my strategies at any given time.

   b.   To know how my strategies have performed based on my previous trades.

   c.   To plan for future trades and track opportunities within that strategy.

   d.   To understand the purpose and list the requirements of each of my strategies.

4. How often should periodic performance reports ideally be written?

   a.   Never. It's a waste of time.

   b.   Every day.

   c.   Every week.

   d.   Every month.

   e.   Every quarter.

   f.   Every year.

   g.   As often as I want.

5. Which element should NOT appear in a watchlist entry?

   a.   Potential exit price.

   b.   Potential entry price.

   c.   Position size.

   d.   Stock rating.

   e.   Description of the entry.

   f.   Planned strategy.

   g.   All of the above.

   h.   None of the above.

Homework

- Prepare the trading journals dedicated to your trading activities. You may choose multiple or different media for each type of journal.
- For every trading activity you perform, add an entry to its respective journal
- Start tracking your progress from this point on by completing the various journals and taking note of the lessons you've learned.

- For every trade you make, track your strategy results. (See Section IV and Chapter III.8 for more information on the available strategies).

Chapter I.7 - Brokers and fees

Overview

This chapter will examine how to choose a broker and the associated fees that can be incurred through them. We'll also look at the best brokers for trading penny stocks.

The brokers discussed in this chapter will cover those in the U.S. and Canada. While similar situations may exist in other areas, this is outside the scope of this course.

Goals

The goal of this chapter is for you to understand how brokers work as well as their pricing structure. The objective is to differentiate between brokers who are pennystocking friendly and those who are not.

Brokers and Fees

There are many brokers out there; however, only a subset of these will efficiently allow you to trade penny stocks. Here's what you need to know.

Brokers and Pennystocking

Finding the right broker for trading penny stocks can be challenging. Being a niche field of the investment world, few offer the necessary toolset for you to trade most efficiently.

Many successful traders actually have accounts with multiple brokers in order to maximize their potential opportunities. There are a few cases for which this is practical, including:

- Short selling share availability (found in Chapter III.1)
- Boxing positions (found in Chapter III.5)
- Circumventing the PDT rule (found in Chapter II.3)

However, having multiple trading accounts also requires the necessary capital to keep them open. This may not be suitable to beginner traders, as it also requires some additional management.

Choosing a Broker

This is one of the most important decisions that you'll make as a trader. The broker is the only link that exists between you and the stock market.

Their sole purpose is to provide you with access to the market and to fill your orders in a timely fashion for any trade you want to make.

Consider these things when choosing a broker for penny stock trading:

- Permissibility of trading stocks priced under $1 or $2 per share
- Commission structure and fees
- Data subscription fees (when necessary)
- Short share availability and borrow fees (more on this in Chapter III.1)
- Minimum account value to keep the account open
- Customer support and problem resolution
- Order execution times

When choosing your broker, you must evaluate each of these factors based on your strategy and define which is best for you.

This chapter provides a brief overview of the main suggested brokers for pennystocking. It is, however, strongly advised that you do more in-depth research into these, in order to determine which one is best suited for your specific trading needs and activities.

Interactive Brokers

Interactive Brokers (IB) is one of the most used brokers in the realm of penny stocks. They offer a reliable software platform, data feeds, and pretty much anything you need to get started.

Their platform, Trader Work Station (TWS), is a java application that's compatible with any major operations support system (OSS). So whether you're on Windows, Mac or Linux, you shouldn't have any issues running the software.

Additionally, IB is very flexible in terms of what can be traded: You can trade listed stocks as well as OTC without any issues. Execution times are quick.

IB also offers great availability of shares to short in a lot of cases but they aren't the best to obtain "hard-to-borrow" shares (more on this in Chapter III.1); this is usually achieved through other brokers.

It's worth noting that IB is a big operation, used by thousands of traders. They provide a great interface both on the web, and as a software, plus as a mobile application. That being said, IB has a reputation of offering bad customer service to its clients unless you have a large account.

This broker is one of the most popular among penny stock traders, in general.

Keep in mind that when shorting stocks priced under $1.00 per share, the $2.50 rule is applied (for every share shorted under $1.00, you need to have $2.50 cash in your account).

While very popular in among penny stock traders, IB does not offer a Level 2 data subscription for OTC stocks, and the data/display software needs to be obtained elsewhere.

Also, IB has a Canadian subsidiary and the PDT[3] rule is not applicable to those living in Canada. It's probably the only broker north of the border worth anything.

Requirements

In order to open an account at IB, a trader must make an initial deposit for $10,000. The minimum requirement to keep the account open is $2,000.

For individuals under 26 years old, the initial deposit must be at least $3,000 (a very cool, secret loophole younger traders will appreciate).

Pricing

IB offers various models for pricing, these are all based on a price per share; depending on the chosen plan and the volume of shares traded for any given instrument, the commission per share can go from $0.005 down to $0.0005 (if you're trading more than 100M shares in monthly volume); this commission price is up to a maximum value of 0.5% of the position value.

Full pricing details are available at this address: https://www.interactivebrokers.com/en/index.php?f=commission&p=stocks

Reviews of IB here: http://www.investimonials.com/brokers/reviews-interactive-brokers.aspx

CenterPoint Securities

Timothy Sykes's "special" broker, CenterPoint Securities, is a high net worth broker. While they don't have their own trading platform, they provide very personalized customer service and good fills on orders. They are known for having high prices in terms of commissions.

---

[3] Pattern Day Trader, someone who executes four or more day trades in five business days in a margin account.

CenterPoint offers three trading platforms to place orders and check quotes. These are Sterling Trader Pro, Realtick and Das Trader Pro. Each of these are offered as a pay package and don't include the data, to which customers need to subscribe.

CenterPoint presents itself as a Prime Brokerage firm, offering high-end services and matching their target demographic: wealthy individuals.

Requirements

CenterPoint has an initial deposit requirement of $50,000, making it hardly accessible to beginner traders, although if you follow Timothy Sykes, you may know that a referral from him (with an intro, ask admin@timothysykes.com) may lower that number down to $30,000, but they still require a great deal of active trading to maintain an account with them.

Pricing

CenterPoint offers multiple pricing plans, with prices ranging from $0.004 per share, down to $0.002 per share. They also have a flat fee per trade plan. These prices do not include routing and regulatory fees.

They are known to have very high borrow fees for shortable shares, which makes them prohibitively expensive when shorting for more than a couple of days. These fees are in the same order of magnitude as the commissions per trade on a share cost basis.

If you wish to use the compatible platforms, that will set you back between $150 and $500, which does not include the data feed.

For more information on pricing you can check out their page: http://www.center-pointsecurities.com/pricing/

Thinkorswim

Acquired by TD Ameritrade, Thinkorswim provides very good customer service. It's known for offering good execution times and availability for shortable shares, with decent borrow fees.

There are no monthly fees or maintenance fees associated with a ToS account.

ToS, just like IB, offers its proprietary java-based trading platform to traders at no additional cost. It can be freely downloaded from their website and offers a wide range of features to its users.

It was formerly Timothy Sykes's preferred broker before their borrows for short selling went dramatically downhill after being acquired by TD Ameritrade.

Requirements

ToS has a minimum requirement of a $2,000 initial deposit for trading.

Pricing

ToS has a flat fee of $6.95 per trade using their internet-connected platform, regardless of the number of shares traded. This makes it a rather expensive option for traders starting out and entering positions with a low number of shares.

More information can be found here: https://www.tdameritrade.com/pricing.page

Reviews can be found here: http://www.investimonials.com/brokers/reviews-thinkorswim.aspx

E-Trade

E-Trade is another popular broker for penny stock traders. Much like IB, it offers its proprietary set of platforms to its clients.

Customer service is reportedly fairly acceptable, but not oriented toward highly active traders. That being said, the platform is often used for charting.

Requirements

E-Trade has a $500 initial deposit requirement, which makes it ideal for traders with a small capital.

Pricing

E-Trade has a flat rate of $6.95 per trade, making the commissions quite expensive in the long run when trading small positions. If you make more than 30 trades per quarter, this goes down to $4.95 per trade.

For more information on pricing, go here: https://us.etrade.com/investing-trading/pricing-rates#stocks

For reviews, you can check it out here: http://www.investimonials.com/brokers/reviews-etrade.aspx

Others

Other brokers aren't really worthy of mention, as they considerably limit penny stock traders' ability to perform profitable trades.

Many brokers don't allow trading stocks under $2.00, or they'll give you a hard time executing orders, let alone shorting or finding shares to borrow.

As for prop firms[4], penny stock traders usually avoid them since they are businesses that can blow up from one day to the next, with little chance for the trader to recover the money in the account. Best avoided.

Data Subscriptions

A data subscription is a necessity when trading penny stocks. They provide the information to the broker directly from the market.

Prices for data subscriptions vary from broker to broker, but can be estimated to be around $15-$20 per month for Level 1 quotes and up $250 per month (including L1) for Level 2.

The new data plan on www.stockstotrade.com provides the best option for day traders since there is no other platform tailored for accurate news, charts and data for penny stocks. As I write this, we're finalizing a revolutionary feature that allows our software to integrate with several brokers, all on one screen.

---

[4] Proprietary trading firm: when a trader trades with the firm's own money, as opposed to depositors' money, to make a profit for itself.

Summary

- A broker is the link between the trader and the market.
- Brokers place orders on behalf of their customers and charge a commission on every trade. Fees vary.
- Choose your broker based on your specific needs and do in-depth research prior to opening an account with any of them.
- Most brokers aren't suitable for penny stock trading; only a few will allow you to trade these efficiently.
- Accounts under $25,000 are subjected to the PDT rule with most brokers in the U.S.
- Brokers worth considering for trading penny stocks are:
    - Interactive Brokers
    - CenterPoint
    - Thinkorswim
    - E-Trade
- Account initial deposit varies from broker to broker.

Chapter I.8 - Tools of the Trade

Overview

Here, we look at the various tools available to penny stock traders in order to help them make informed decisions on which stocks to choose and whether to enter a specific position.

Goals

The goal of this chapter is to get you acquainted with the tools available to you, both free and commercial, in order to help you guide your trading decisions and build efficient watchlists, which we'll discuss in Chapter II.9.

Web applications

Web applications and websites for traders come in a wide variety of forms and shapes. Many of them are great tools for penny stock traders.

This is by no means an exhaustive view of all the web applications tools available, but covers the most common ones used when trading penny stocks.

Yahoo Finance

The go-to place for all general information on any given stock, Yahoo provides a wide range of essential features to its users free of charge.

Among these features, you can find the latest news on a stock, SEC filings (more on this in Chapter III.4), fundamental information about the company, as well as a message board.

URL: http://finance.yahoo.com
Price: FREE

Seeking Alpha

Seeking Alpha is touted as a financial platform providing its users with a wide range of articles for stocks. It's populated by around 8,000 contributors and covers all kinds of equities, including penny stocks.

This is a valuable tool for getting information. Keep in mind that free accounts get articles in a delayed manner, and the pro account has very strict requirements, as it's intended for "professional traders."

This application is also known for inducing momentum in stock prices based on the articles that it produces, which is considered by some investors as some sort of manipulation of the price.

URL: http://seekingalpha.com
Price: Free with delayed articles. Pricing available upon request and meeting their requirements

Google Finance

Google Finance shares many similarities with Yahoo Finance, but with a less intuitive platform for users. It's a less popular source, for the most part.

It's free and gives you up-to-date information about stocks, including news and quotes.

Google Finance is mostly suitable for a quick overview of a stock and news.

URL: http://www.google.com/finance
Price: FREE

Stockfetcher

Stockfetcher is probably one of the few must-have tools for penny stock traders. It's a delayed stock scanner offering a variety of features to create efficient filters.

Its core feature is its key concept of creating your own filters based on your trading requirements. Set your filters and it provides a list of all matching stocks based on your criteria, and shows all the specified technical information on a specific instrument, including quick charts.

Stockfetcher also allows you to store the various filters that you created and use them at a later time, to perform intra-day or day-to-day research.

URL: http://www.stockfetcher.com
Price: free with limited features - $24/quarter

Finviz

Finviz is a simpler version of Stockfetcher. It offers a simple delayed stock scanner with lots of criteria to be set. Unlike Stockfetcher, Finviz doesn't offer a programmatic language to create filters suited to your needs.

Of note, Finviz doesn't cover OTC stocks, which means they aren't geared toward stock traders at all.

Finviz is suitable to perform a quick scan of stocks based on simple criteria that doesn't require complex queries in order to find matching stocks.

URL: http://finviz.com/
Price: Free for the scanner. They also offer paid services and provide more in-depth information as well as real-time data for $39.50/month or $299.50/year.

OTC Markets

This is also the official site for OTC stocks. It provides a market scanner with a few features in terms of filtering. Additionally, it provides SEC filings as well as various tools in a similar fashion to Yahoo Finance.

It is suitable for scanning and researching OTC stocks.

URL: http://www.otcmarkets.com/
Price: FREE

BigCharts

BigCharts is a simple charting web application intended to quickly view the basic quote information and chart for any given instrument. It provides a very simple interface to its users as well as the latest news headlines for the selected stock.

URL: https://www.bigcharts.com
Price: FREE

TradingView

TradingView is an advanced charting web application providing users with useful tools for charting stocks and drawing on them.

The free version provides delayed stock information and limited features, while the paid version can include real-time data subscription.

This one is suitable for users wanting a more advanced online-based charting tool that doesn't require the broker's platform to be running. It's also ideal for those who like to save their charts and add indicators to them.

URL: https://www.tradingview.com
Price: Free with limited features. From $9.99/month + subscriptions. Pricing details here: https://www.tradingview.com/gopro/

Investor's Hub and The Lion

Investor's Hub and The Lion are mainly forums and chats for users to share their insight on stocks. They're suitable for finding information based on user input. Interesting tools for side research.

Be advised that forums and chats are full of noise and unnecessary information.

Investor's Hub
URL: http://investorshub.advfn.com/
Price: FREE

The Lion
URL: http://www.thelion.com/
Price: FREE

Twitter

Twitter may seem like an out-of-context tool in this niche, but it's actually one of the most useful social media in trading.

Twitter needs no introduction. For stocks, it offers the possibility to provide quick alerts or relevant information if you're following individuals.

It does take a bit of research to build a follow list and get the relevant information.

URL: http://www.twitter.com
Price: FREE

StockTwits

StockTwits is based on the Twitter backend and is entirely dedicated to stocks. It provides the same features as Twitter with a more refined interface for traders and investors, but they exclude most penny stocks.

URL: http://stocktwits.com/
Price: FREE

Software

StocksToTrade

StocksToTrade is one of the most advanced real-time scanning platforms, and was created by Timothy Sykes (and yours truly) to accommodate the needs of penny stock traders as well as day traders. It offers advanced filtering and preset filters that allow quickly finding potential penny stock plays.

The features offered are very similar to Stockfetcher, but applied to a real-time environment. Additionally, it provides very intuitive charting, stock event tracking and (coming soon) direct trading across brokers, thus removing the need for broker-specific platforms.

This is the must-have trading tool for penny stock and day traders.

We'll discuss this Tool in greater detail in Chapter I.9.

URL: http://www.stockstotrade.com
Price: $179.95-$220 monthly data fee. Contact support@stockstotrade.com and let them know you were referred by this course.

Multicharts

Multicharts is a back-testing software intended to programmatically test strategies with past data and implement algorithmic trading strategies.

It's also a very complete charting tool that can obtain data from various sources and go back in time as far as the data source allows it in different time resolutions.

For those interested in attempting to implement automated trading strategies based on the pennystocking strategies described in this course, this is a great piece of software.

URL: http://www.multicharts.com
Price: FREE with Interactive Brokers (with some limitations). Pricing plans here: http://www.multicharts.com/multicharts/purchase

Spreadsheets (Excel, Google Spreadsheets, etc.)

While spreadsheets aren't specifically designed for trading, the flexibility they offer in terms of calculations is a great tool for performing statistical analysis of trade history, performing quick calculations of positions, risk management, etc.

Spreadsheets are invaluable for traders who want to go deeper into the validation of their data.

There are multiple options available for spreadsheets for traders.

Microsoft Excel
URL: http://products.office.com/en-us/excel
Price: Starting at $139 with Office 2013

Google Spreadsheets
URL: https://docs.google.com/spreadsheets
Price: FREE with a Google account

Libre Office Calc
URL: http://www.libreoffice.org/discover/calc/
Price: FREE

Open Office Calc
URL: https://www.openoffice.org/product/calc.html
Price: FREE

Chapter I.9 - StocksToTrade, the Ultimate Trading Tool

Overview

Everything you need to know about the StocksToTrade real-time trading tool.

Goals

The goal of this chapter is to introduce you to the history and some of the revolutionary features that StocksToTrade has to offer to both novice and advanced traders.

About StocksToTrade

StocksToTrade (STT) is the brainchild of millionaire trader Timothy Sykes. It was originally released as a rebranded version of a different charting software, with the added benefit of having all of Tim's trading strategies and research patterns pre-programmed into it and exclusive to STT customers.

Tim originally envisioned STT as software capable of meeting his every trading need something that no other software would allow him to do at the time. He wanted news, SEC filings and the ability to quickly find stocks matching his strategy criteria.

The trading software industry has always been focused on the big player – analysts and experts, big companies and slow-moving stocks – but none had tackled the market of day traders and penny stocks. Day traders in this niche were left adapting their behaviors to the available tools without the ability to become more efficient.

Version one of STT was made available to its customers for a couple of years, which helped lots of traders improve their trading efficiency by reducing the research time required to build solid watchlists. But this wasn't enough for Tim; he wanted a tool that would be his only stop for anything related to his trading.

Born from those needs, STT version two was fully redesigned from scratch with the purpose of creating the one and only tool day traders would ever require.

After more than a year of development and more than a million dollars invested in creating the software, STT was finally released to the general public on February 15, 2016.

I joined the STT development team in 2015, overseeing the beta and release phases of this revolutionary tool's development cycle.

Lessons from the STT Development Team

Why did I join the StocksToTrade Team?

As you might recall, I have a degree in computer engineering, which has provided me with a high level of expertise related to the software development cycle. You may also know that engineers can be found pretty much anywhere; we like to create stuff.

My motivation for joining the team was rather selfish: I wanted to create something that would dramatically improve my own trading performance. I don't like to do tedious, repeatable tasks by hand. In fact, I find the very idea of doing such a thing insulting if/when it can be achieved by simply automating the process.

I had started working on my own software based on publicly available broker APIs (Application Programming Interface; think: IB, E-Trade) and managed to create fairly nice interfaces that would automate many of the processes described throughout this course. When I joined STT, this gave me the opportunity to not only participate in creating a tool that I would be certain to use to increase my trading profitability, but also something that I could share with fellow novice and advanced traders to make them more efficient at beating the odds.

To me, STT is exactly that: a tool to beat the odds and become a better trader. I want to be the best trader I can be, and for that I needed the best tool for the job. Since there was no such tool, so we created it.

What did I learn from participating in the development process of StocksToTrade?

There's something very few developers in the finance field may understand) and this becomes increasingly evident to novice traders moving ahead in the learning and trading processes): trading is about knowledge and experience.

To create a proper tool, you need to understand the market; not only understand the surface, but also to understand the underlying systems that allow the markets to run.

Working with STT allowed me to familiarize myself with the deep intricacies for trading and all the rules and regulations associated with the markets. Beyond that, it required me to get very intimate with the process of mathematical analysis of data in order to understand and replicate what we naturally do in our heads. Ultimately, a computer has no idea what a stock is – all it sees is ones and zeros.

In order to allow the machine to understand how a trader thinks, the trader has to create the underlying rules, design the thought process of the machine, and how this thought process provides the information.

Knowing the techniques and the strategies is one thing, but what takes you to the next level is breaking down technical analysis into its most basic form: pure math.

A computer doesn't know what a chart is, nor a candle. What it sees is a series of grouped data containing open, close, high, low and time values. Thousands upon thousands of sets.

Understanding how to process all this data in real time has taught me how to improve my analytical skills in the field of trading.

As a trader, I'm absolutely convinced that programming will allow us to achieve greater things – not only from the learning perspective, but from the capabilities that it offers.

Let us get to some of the juicy bits on the subject and cover some of the most interesting facts about StocksToTrade whose website is www.stockstotrade.com.

How Does STT Work?

StocksToTrade (www.stockstotrade.com) is a real-time scanning platform that offers all of Timothy Sykes's stock research strategies. The core idea of STT is to help traders quickly find potential plays intraday or perform nightly research by allowing them to focus only on the relevant stocks that match their criteria.

Basic Features

- Full market L1 and L2 for NASDAQ, NYSE, AMEX, OTCBB and PINK-SHEETS
- Real-time quotes
- Dynamic charts
- Chart indicators and studies
- Real-time price events on chart
- Real-time news events on chart
- One-minute charts up to 60 days
- Daily charts up to 20 years
- Stock SEC filings and news
- Criteria-based news streamer
- Watchlist-filtered news
- Full market real-time scanners
- Linked tabs
- Scanners based on Timothy Sykes's winning strategies
- Custom screener
- Criteria-based stock alerts

- Unlimited watchlists
- Filterable full market end-of-day data for the previous day
- Quick-view sidebar for fast information access

Basics Box

A simple-yet-powerful feature, this stock widget provides the most essential information about a stock. Puzzlingly, it's a feature that has been left out by about every other trading platform. We have it.

Figure I.9.1 - StocksToTrade Basics Box for RPRX

Charting

This feature is critically important to the STT team, as most of our trading decisions rely on carefully watching the chart evolve and eventually match the patterns described in Chapter II.6.

We've put a ton of focus in offering a chart capable of showing the user every important piece of information. Figure I.9.2 shows a chart for RPRX and the price events associated with the stock. These events include:

- Trending up or down
- Crossing Day/5D/10D/26W/52W highs and lows
- Nearing Day/5D/10D/26W/52W highs and lows

The charting environment also offers persistent drawing tools that allow users to add trend lines, arrows and text for better tracking.

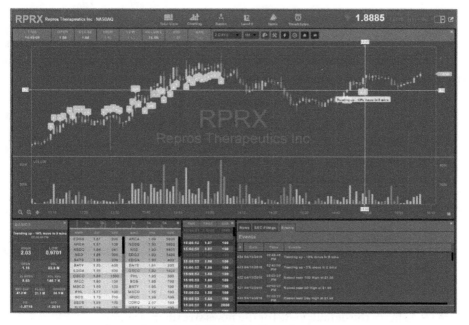

Figure I.9.2 - StocksToTrade Chart showing Events

News indicators can also be shown directly on the chart, allowing you to quickly glance at stock news without having to switch windows or applications. Figure I.9.3 shows this slick feature in action.

Figure I.9.3 - News event on chart for GPRO

News Streamer and Filtering

Along with STT's advanced charting and event detection capabilities, it also has a highly versatile news streamer that displays all news events in real time, with the ability to filter the news based on a variety of different criteria. These criteria include:

- Price
- Volume (total of shares traded on the day) and $ volume
- Day range
- Earnings per share (EPS) and price-earnings (P/E) ratio
- Simple moving average (SMA), average daily volume, average daily range

The streamer also displays news based on other wider criteria such as:

- One or more watchlists
- SEC filings only
- News only
- Headline keywords

Figure I.9.4 shows the default view for the news streamer in action.

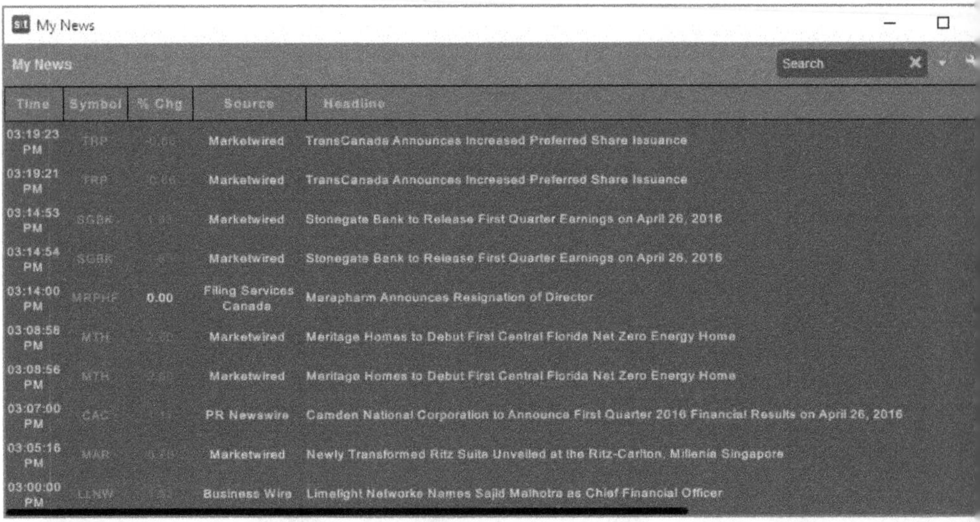

Figure I.9.4 - News Streamer on StocksToTrade

Figure I.9.5 below shows a list filtered for stocks priced between $1 and $15.

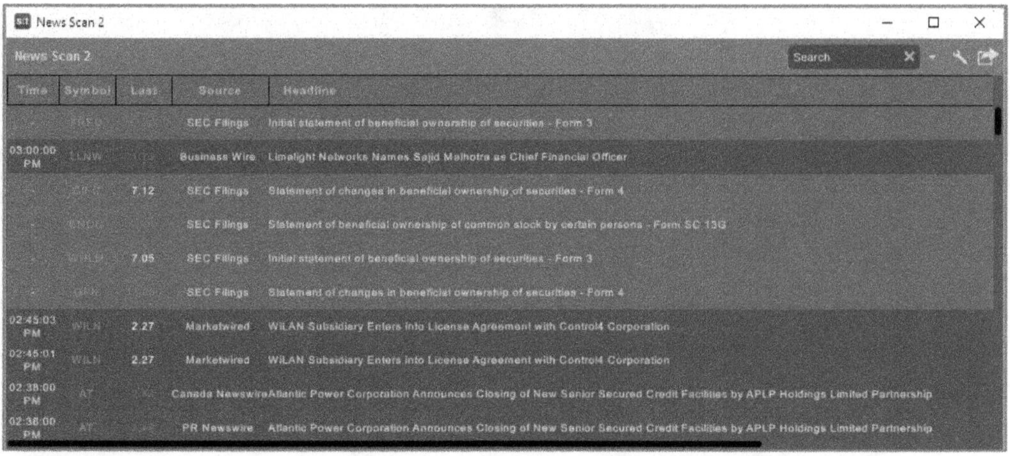

Figure I.9.5 - StocksToTrade filtered news streamer - stocks between $1 and $15

Timothy Sykes Strategy Scanners

One of STT's most important features is the basis of the original premise of the software: the pre-programmed research strategy scans created by Tim Sykes.

These are advanced screeners with very specific criteria that scan all the U.S. markets (NASDAQ, AMEX, NYSE, OTCBB and PINKSHEETS) in real time to provide a specific list of potentially profitable matches.

There are over 40 pre-programmed scans that allow you to quickly find the best plays on the market in real time – especially penny stocks. No other software has ever combined the extensive expertise of successful traders with the advanced scanning capabilities of STT.

Figure I.9.6 shows the results provided by such a scan.

Time	News	Market	Symbol	Bid	Ask	Last	Net Change	% Chg	Volume	Trades
15:43:40	1	NASDAQ	RPRX							
15:43:40	1	PINKSHEETS	FNMA	1.95	1.95				42,659,588	31709
15:38:33	0	PINKSHEETS	FNMAH		3.14	3.14			52,366	132
15:43:38	2	PINKSHEETS	FMCC	1.78	1.79	1.77			14,099,700	4975
15:43:14	0	PINKSHEETS	FNMAS	4.10	4.14	4.14			3,259,870	977
15:43:33	5	NYSE	FELP	1.61	1.62					
15:43:32	0	PINKSHEETS	FMCKJ	4.08	4.14	4.14			1,786,920	545
15:43:36	1	NASDAQ	VYGR	13.14	13.48					
15:43:16	0	PINKSHEETS	NGLOY	4.96	4.99	4.97			215,690	274
15:43:32	1	NASDAQ	UNXL	1.40	1.41	1.40			2,557,240	5449
15:43:39	1	NASDAQ	LSCC	6.46	6.47					
15:43:35	1	NASDAQ	CPST	1.61	1.83	1.83				
15:43:39	2	NASDAQ	EMKR	6.08	6.10					
15:39:36	1	NASDAQ	PYDS	2.05	2.09	2.05			186,702	351
15:43:40	3	NASDAQ	GPRO	13.97	13.98					

Figure I.9.6 - Biggest % Gainers under $20 on StocksToTrade

The Future of STT

STT is a platform designed to constantly evolve with the needs of day traders. It is not managed by a corporation, but by successful traders.

The STT motto is "Created for Traders by Traders." Our team stands and lives by this standard.

One of the most anticipated features at the time of writing of this course is the trading capability (expected release in few months). This feature makes STT a truly game-changing platform, as we'll be the first platform to allow trading from multiple brokers all on one screen. *That's a big deal.*

STT offers several unique features that no other financial industry platforms come close to featuring. We want to be the only trading platform that traders will ever need – one platform to rule them all.

We'll dive back into your course training now. Thanks for reading about STT. As you can tell, I'm incredibly proud of this venture, and look forward to sharing updates with you about STT's future and long-term plans to help give traders a sharp advantage with the most complete trading package on the market.

Summary

- StocksToTrade is a real-time trading platform created by Timothy Sykes, based on his successful research strategies.
- STT offers advanced charting tools, real-time scanners, and news with criteria-based filtering.
- The ultimate tool for both novice and advanced traders.

Chapter I.10 - The Market's Collective Will

Overview

An examination of the general behavior of the market.

Goals

The goal of this chapter is to gain a fundamental understanding of how the market behaves and what causes it to change.

Start with This Understanding...

The stock market is a living creature composed of millions of brain cells represented by each trader present within its brain.

Each trader and investor is just an infinitesimally small part of the overall market, and the raw average of the participation of each trader and investor (while also considering the size of capital investment from a trader or investor) dictates the will of the market.

What Is the "Collective Will of the Market"?

The market is a hive mind, where every stock depends on every trader. Their emotions, their reactions, their hopes and their fears dictate how the price will move. It is the will of the masses that pushes the price up or down based on beliefs that may or may not be rational.

As a penny stock trader, you must understand that trading makes you a part of this collective will, but you also need to understand how the collective will works in order to profit and minimize your losses when they happen.

What Drives this Will?

People are influenced by emotions and therefore, by direct association, the market is influenced by the collective emotions of the group. Even some of the most advanced computer systems that perform algorithmic trading are influenced by this human trait – they have been taught to "feel" based on pre-programmed events.

These emotions are fueled by greed. We all want to make a profit and better our financial situation by playing the stock market. For many, it seems like the "easy" way to make money; that's frequently the case for most novice and inexperienced traders.

What these "green" traders often fail to understand is how the will of the market is determined.

Can It Be Influenced?

Yes, and in a big way. Let's look at the certain factors that can help you predict the price of specific penny stock moves.

Price action and chart patterns are often self-fulfilling prophecies that influence the price of a stock in a certain direction. When these patterns emerge, traders have a tendency to follow and try to chase. Every trader collectively decided that the price should move a certain way, and so it does for no other specific reason.

News is also a big stock price influencer. When the news is good, traders collectively decide that a certain stock is worth having in their portfolio, and the stock price increases as the demand rises. Conversely, when news is not good, traders collectively decide to sell, and as supply overtakes demand, the stock price plunges.

Paid promotions, a.k.a. pump & dumps (covered in detail in Chapter II.8), are mailing promotions sent to novice or unknowledgeable traders who have no experience in dealing with the market. They fall in love with the idea of quick wealth, believing in a new product or company as an incredible long-term investment, only to find out later that what they thought to be so potentially valuable isn't worth much, if anything at all. The collective will of these gullible traders drives the demand and so the stock price rises exponentially for a short period of time, driven by propaganda that creates buying hysteria.

Uncompensated promotions represent another type of promotion intended to generate credibility for the promoters. It's the same principle as paid promotions without the pyramid scheme to drive it.

Analysts and expert reports are probably among the most important factors in influencing the will of the market. They are "professionals" in the finance field; therefore, it can be assumed that they know what they're talking about. Some inexperienced traders and investors rely on this type of insight to make investment decisions. These traders collectively decide that the information is actionable and generates a movement in the stock price.

It is of utmost importance for penny stock traders to understand that the will of the market must be understood rather than attempting to control its movement.

Salmon are big fish that swim against the current. The great majority of traders aren't salmon and can't swim against the current of the river (i.e. the market), and that's perfectly OK.

Penny stock traders must swim with the current and adapt to the changes of the market. They need to comprehend the factors that influence the collective will of the market in order to make profitable decisions.

Understanding the collective will of the market is about reading the signs, understanding the emotions that guide it, and work around the wealth of information that is generally available to all traders. It's about understanding the factors that push the prices, and thinking outside the box to find the right opportunities.

The collective will of the market will be kind to traders who choose to understand its emotions and behavior, and accept that they have no control over what is decided by the hive mind of all traders.

Section II - Trading Penny Stocks

Chapter II.1 - Definitions

Overview

The commonly used terms in the stock market and pennystocking niche.

Goals

The goal of this chapter is to provide you with the basic definitions necessary to understand all the concepts presented throughout this course. You must familiarize yourself with all these terms and feel comfortable understanding their meaning.

Penny Stock Trading Definitions

Throughout this chapter we'll cover the various definitions used in the realm of penny stocks. This is by no means an exhaustive list, but instead some of the most commonly used terms in this domain. For more in-depth definitions, please refer to http://www.investopedia.com, which offers an exhaustive collection of stock market definitions and concepts.

Stock – A stock represents a type of security that implies ownership in a corporation and offers the holder part of the corporation's assets and earnings.

Two main types of stocks exist: preferred and common. Preferred stock does not confer voting rights within the company but offers a higher claim on assets and earning than does the common shares. Common stock confers to the holder the right to attend and vote at shareholder's meetings, and to receive dividends.

Simply put, owning stock is owning a percentage of the company based on the number of shares possessed by the holder relative to the outstanding shares of the company.

Share – See definition for stock.

Equity – See definition for stock.

Instrument – An instrument refers to anything you can trade on the market, which includes securities, commodities, derivatives or index. Simply put, anything that can be traded on the stock market is an instrument.

Symbol – The symbol represents a unique combination of letters assigned to a security for trading purposes. The number of letters for any given security varies from market to market: NASDAQ has 4 or 5 characters; NYSE and AMEX have 3 characters or less.

Symbols are also known as "ticker symbols" or "tickers."

Contract – See definition for symbol.

Penny Stock – Penny stocks, the main subject of this course, officially refers to stocks with a price per share below $1.00. However, the expression is used on stocks priced between $0 and $15-$20 per share.

Penny stocks are often considered as a risky investment due to their volatility and the fact that the general public often misunderstands them.

Small Cap – A small cap is a stock with a small market capitalization. It's generally considered to include companies with a market capitalization between $300M and $2B. Small caps are often the trading instruments of pennystocking because big investors and hedge funds prefer to focus on larger market capitalization companies.

Micro Cap – Like small cap, micro cap regroups companies with a market capitalization between $50M and $300M.

SEC – The U.S. Securities and Exchange Commission, a commission created by Congress to regulate securities and protect investors. Additionally, it also performs corporate takeover monitoring.

SEC Filing – Companies are required to file documents with the SEC on a regular basis in order to comply with federal trading regulations when the corporation in question is publicly traded. (Chapter III.4)

Trading Hours – U.S. markets have a specific time in which trading is allowed. The trading session is between 9:30 a.m. and 4 p.m. Eastern time, from Monday to Friday. Some days the market will close earlier or open later based on holidays. Major holidays are usually a break day for the market.

After Hours Trading – Some exchanges allow trading outside of regular trading hours. This is called after-hours trading and stocks can trade up to 8 p.m. Eastern time.

Pre-Market – Pre-market refers to trading that happens after-hours before the market opens for the day session, usually beginning at 8 a.m. Eastern time, although some orders on truly hot penny stocks have been known to get executed starting at 7 a.m. Eastern time.

After Market – Trading that happens after-hours after the market closes for the day session.

Session – This represents the trading day during trading hours.

Quote – The last price at which a security traded. Simply put, it's the most recent price at which a buyer and seller agreed to make a trade.

Price or Last Price – The monetary value of a security share in the market currency. It's basically the price that you pay for a single share for any given stock.

Bid – The highest value currently on record that a buyer is willing to pay for a single share of a stock.

Ask – The lowest value currently on record that a seller is willing to accept for a single share of a stock.

Bid and Ask Sizes – The number of shares desired respectively for bids and asks.

Spread – The difference in price that exists between the bid price and the ask price.

Open – The initial price at which any given stock is traded during the session. This can also be applied to various time frames, such as minutes, hours, days, etc.

Close – The last price at which any given stock is traded during the session. This can also be applied to various time frames, such as minutes, hours, days, etc.

High of Day – The highest price at which the stock has traded for the current sessions. The HoD does not include after-hours trading values.

Low of Day – The lowest price at which the stock has traded for the current sessions. The LoD does not include after-hours trading values.

52 Week High – Similar to high of day, representing the highest value over a period of 52 Weeks or one year.

52-Week Low – Similar to low of day. Represents the lowest value over a period of 52 Weeks, or one year.

Day Range or Price Range – The difference in price between the high of day value and the low of day value. This represents how much the stock price has moved during the current session.

Volume – The number of shares being traded for any given stock during the trading session.

Liquidity – Liquidity is dependent on the volume. A liquid stock is considered to be a stock that has a high volume, or more specifically, a stock that trades a high number of shares during the session. The concept of liquidity varies, but it's usually considered that liquid stocks have a volume higher than 100,000-200,000 shares.

Volatility – Volatility is directly dependent on the day range or price range. Higher volatility usually indicates riskier stocks, as they have a tendency to have bigger price ranges in a short period of time. They represent high risk, high reward stocks. On the other hand, stocks with a low volatility have a small price range percentage compared to the share price. Volatility varies from one stock to another. Volatile stocks are typically considered to have a ray range above 15-20% of the stock price.

Moving Average – Various averages (price, volume, range, etc.) that can be performed on any given stock. Each point in the moving average represents the average of all values (within its parameters) before that point. Moving averages change as the conditions of any given stock evolve.

Average True Range – A moving average that focuses on the day range over a given period of time. It is often used as a volatility measurement tool. (Chapter II.4)

Buy – The action of trading money for the ownership of a share.

Sell – The action of trading the ownership of share for its monetary value.

Short Sell – Borrowing shares to trade the ownership of those shares for a monetary value. (Chapter III.1)

Buy to Cover – The converse action of short selling. The action of buying back borrowed shares at the indicated price. (Chapter III.1)

Short Squeeze – An event that forces short sellers to cover for various reasons. (Chapter III.1)

Trade – The action of buying, selling, short selling or buying to cover.

Position – The ownership of shares in any given stock.

Open Position – A position is open when the shares are acquired through the process of buying, or owing shares in the case of a short sale.

Closed Position – A position is closed when the shares are liquidated through the process of selling, or returning shares when buying to cover.

Entry or Entry Price – The price at which a position was opened. More specifically, it represents the price paid per share for any given stock causing the position to be opened.

Exit or Exit Price – The price at which a position was closed. More specifically, it represents the price received per share for any given stock causing the position to be closed.

Fill – When an order has been completely executed. In simpler terms, when you place an order for a certain number of shares, if the order goes through for all your shares, the order is filled.

Chart – The visual representation of the price, volume of any given stock over time.

Candlestick – A chart that provides a distinct visual representation of the price changes in stock, clearly indicating the opening price, closing price, high of the bar, low of the bar. (Chapter II.5)

Trend Line – A complement to basic charts that indicate values within which the stock price remains for a certain period of time. It can help determine various potential behaviors of the stock. (Chapter II.5)

Support – A type of trend line above which the price remains for a certain period of time without being crossed. (Chapter II.5)

Resistance – A type of trend line below which the price remains for a certain period of time without being crossed. (Chapter II.5)

Breakout – What occurs when a resistance line is crossed and the price of a stock increases in a very quick manner. (Chapter II.5)

Breakdown – What occurs when a support line is crossed and the price of a stock falls in a very quick manner. (Chapter II.5)

Intraday – Events happening within a given trading session.

Market Maker – A broker-dealer firm that takes the risk of holding a certain number of shares of a given stock or security with the goal of facilitating the trading of that stock. Market makers display buy and sell quotes for a guaranteed number of shares. Upon receiving orders, the market makers sell their own inventory immediately or seek an offsetting order.

Level 2 – A trading service that offers real-time data in terms of quotes and market depth. This allows traders to see which market makers are in queue with bid and ask orders at any given point in time for any given stock. (Chapter III.2)

Pump & Dump – Paid promotions for companies without a real product or any real value for investors. These promotions tend to hike the price before encountering a dramatic drop. (Chapter II.8)

SEC Halt – The temporary suspension of a stock on one or more exchanges. Usually imposed by the SEC when suspicious, unusual or irregular activity is found that needs further verification prior to allowing the stock to continue trading.

Promoter – An individual or corporation that actively promotes a security with the intent of pumping the stock price to a higher point. (Chapter II.8)

Morning Panic – When shareholders mass sell orders to cut their losses following an event that affects the price of the stock negatively and therefore reducing the underlying demand.

Morning Spike – An event market by mass buy orders from interested buyers in order to take profits following an event that affects the price of the stock positively and therefore increasing the underlying demand.

Afternoon Spike/Panic – These are the same as their morning counterparts, but happen in the afternoon.

Fade –When a stock price slowly decreases from its highs. Usually observed after a spike.

Dip – A sudden decrease in price value for a given stock following a spike. Usually followed by a recovery increase of the price that may rise or surpass the previous high in some cases.

Bounce – A sudden increase in price value for a stock following a panic. Usually followed by a decrease of the price that may drop or go below the previous in some cases.

Momentum – Created when a large number of traders behave in the same manner when it comes to trade a stock. Often the cause for major variations in price.

Chasing – Attempting to enter a position after the initial momentum has already spiked the stock price dramatically. It's usually bad practice to chase without a supporting thesis that indicates that the momentum may continue. Chasing a stock frequently results in losses.

Scalping – Quickly entering and exiting positions with small profits of just a few cents per share. Often achieved when chasing momentum in order to capitalize on greater movements. This type of behavior is typically not profitable in penny stocks.

Gap Up/Down – A stock gaps up/down when there is a significant difference in price between the previous day close and the current day open. Illustrated in a candlestick chart by the lack of an overlap between the previous candle's body and the current candle open.

Pattern Day Trader (PDT) Rule – As explained by the SEC:

"FINRA rules define a 'pattern day trader' as any customer who executes four or more 'day trades' within five business days, provided that the number of day trades represents more than six percent of the customer's total trades in the margin account for that same five business day period. This rule represents a minimum requirement, and some broker-dealers use a slightly broader definition in determining whether a customer qualifies as a 'pattern day trader'. Customers should contact their brokerage firms to determine whether their trading activities will cause them to be designated as pattern day traders.

A broker-dealer may also designate a customer as a 'pattern day trader' if it 'knows or has a reasonable basis to believe' that a customer will engage in pattern day trading. For example, if a customer's broker-dealer provided day trading training to such customer before opening the account, the broker-dealer could designate that customer as a 'pattern day trader'.

Under FINRA rules, customers who are deemed 'pattern day traders' must have at least $25,000 in their accounts and can only trade in margin accounts. For more information on pattern day traders and related FINRA margin rules, please read the SEC staff's investor bulletin 'Margin Rules for Day Trading'." (Commission S. a., Pattern Day Trader, n.d.)

Chapter II.2 - Listed Stocks, The Markets

Overview

A look at the various U.S. stock exchanges that allow individuals to perform trades and engage in pennystocking.

Goals

The goal of this chapter is to get familiar with the various exchanges available to traders, and understand the role of penny stocks and trading these instruments within each of these markets.

NASDAQ

The National Association of Securities Dealers Automated Quotations (NASDAQ) is one of the major exchanges in the U.S. It is an electronic marketplace where stocks are traded.

NASDAQ stocks are identified by a unique string of four or five characters that represent their ticker symbols.

As its name states, the NASDAQ is an electronic exchange that completely automates the process of trading within its exchange.

In order to qualify for being listed on the NASDAQ, companies must be registered with the SEC, must have three market makers, and meet the minimum requirements in terms of assets, capital, public shares and shareholders.

The NASDAQ is intended for reputable companies, usually considered to be liquid but non-volatile. The share prices for stocks listed on this exchange vary greatly. There are numerous stocks that trade under $10 with high volatility and good liquidity.

Being a completely automated exchange, the NASDAQ also ensures quick execution times to fill orders, which makes it relatively easy to enter or exit a position at a moment's notice.

Trading stocks in the NASDAQ is most suitable for novice traders, as it offers great stability and reliability in terms of how trades are executed internally. It's also known to be less prone to market maker manipulation since it's heavily regulated by the SEC. Regardless, manipulation exists in all the exchanges.

NYSE & AMEX

The New York Stock Exchange (NYSE) is considered to be the largest exchange for equities in the world. This is based on the total market capitalization of its listed stocks.

The NYSE is also often referred to as the "big board". In the past it heavily relied on floor trading only. Currently, about half of the trades on the NYSE are conducted electronically, although floor trading is still in action for setting prices and dealing with high-volume trading for institutions.

The NYSE has a wide range of stocks that are characterized by a unique three-character symbol. Prices vary greatly for these stocks, and stocks under $10 per share can be found with good liquidity and volatility.

In the world of penny stocks, NASDAQ stocks are usually more common than NYSE stocks, as the latter are usually higher priced. Execution times also vary; however, being a hybrid electronic exchange, it is also a safe bet for novice traders.

In 2008, the NYSE acquired the American Stock Exchange (AMEX), which was promptly renamed as NYSE Amex Equities.

AMEX equities are known to be less reputable than their NYSE or NASDAQ counterpart; however, this exchange remains an electronic exchange and orders are executed in a timely manner.

OTCBB

Over-The-Counter Bulletin Boards (OTCBB) are off-exchange tradable. They include OTC stocks, Pink Sheets and Grey Sheets.

OTCBB stocks aren't suitable for novice traders, as they require a deep understanding of how they are traded in order to be able to become profitable.

We'll look at OTCBB stocks in great detail in Chapter III.3.

Summary

- There are three major exchanges in the United States:
  - NASDAQ
  - NYSE
  - AMEX
- NASDAQ stocks are the most suitable for novice penny stock traders
- All three major exchanges process orders electronically in a quick and reliable manner
- OTCBB stocks aren't suitable for novice traders

Chapter II.3 - Stock Information, Placing Orders and Making Trades

Overview

How to read stock information and charts, and how to put an order with any given broker.

Note: Though some of the screenshots taken for this course have been obtained from the Interactive Brokers TWS platform, the concepts are still applicable with most platforms.

Goals

The goal of this chapter is for you to become intimately familiar with the action of placing orders through your broker, and understand the information of a given security and the requirements for quickly placing orders for any given play.

Requirements for Ideal Penny Stock Plays

Before we get into the meat of the trading process, there's an important factor to take into consideration when engaging in the trade of penny stocks...

Trading penny stocks has important requirements that must be respected in order to increase the odds of your trades becoming profitable. While not applicable to every single case, and while there are a few exceptions to these baseline rules, it is accepted as the general basis for trading this type of security.

Penny stocks have two basic requirements:

- Volatility
- Liquidity

Volatility is necessary to ensure that the price of the stock will move in a quick manner. Penny stocks are not long-term investments; they are quick trades. What volatility ultimately implies is that the price of a stock can move significantly, increasing both potential profits and the associated risk. It's one of the key elements in how profitable traders make money. Non-volatile stocks simply don't move enough to offer much profit opportunity for traders.

Liquidity is the second basic factor that ensures the profitability of any given penny stock. Liquidity implies that there is a high enough volume to allow traders to quickly enter and exit their positions at a moment's notice. Non-liquid stocks, or illiquid stocks, simply don't trade enough shares to offer much profit opportunity for traders.

We'll take these factors into consideration in Chapter II.9 when you learn how to research penny stocks.

Obtaining and Understanding Stock Information

Before a stock can be successfully traded, a trader must know what is to be traded and obtain all the necessary information to perform a given trade.

Obtaining the stock information is one of the most basic concepts when it comes to trading. You must properly understand this information in order to be able to make informed decisions.

The Quote

This is the basic information regarding the stock price. It will usually include information such as:

- Last price
- Open and close
- Volume
- Day and 52-week highs and lows
- Bid and ask prices and sizes
- Percentage and net change since open

Quotes are used to presently determine the current state of any stock. It is the factual, actionable information that allows you to make an immediate decision.

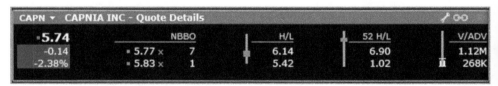

Figure II.3.1 - Interactive Brokers TWS Quote window

Figure II.3.1 is an example of what a simple quote window looks like on a platform. Quotes can be obtained from a variety of different sources, but ideally this should be taken from your primary trading platform.

If you use multiple brokers, you may use a single platform to obtain your quotes and each individual broker platform to perform your trades.

The Volume

Volume indicates the number of shares being traded at any given time. This is used as the main metric for establishing liquidity of the stock and its suitability for being treated as a penny stock.

The average daily volume provides additional information in regards to the average of volume over a certain number of days. This is usually calculated in a period of one year or 52 weeks and indicates the normal liquidity of the stock. A daily volume higher than the ADV (average daily volume) usually indicates some type of event or momentum.

The Tape, Time and Sales

The time and sales window, also known as "The Tape", represents the list of trades over time. Each actual exchange of shares is listed on this window. The time and sales offers a view into the movement of the stock during the day.

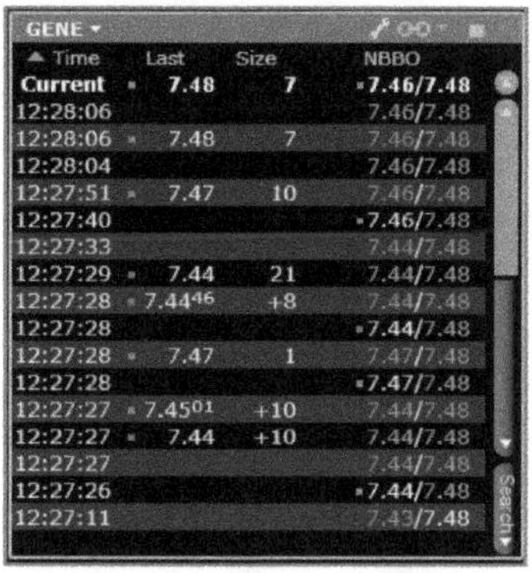

Figure II.3.2 - Interactive Brokers TWS Time and Sales

Figure II.3.2 Shows the time and sales window. This usually contains the following information: time of trade; price traded; number of shares traded; bid and ask at the time of the trade.

The time and sales can often be used to identify momentum or potential behavior of the stock in real time. It's important to get familiar with this screen in order to better understand how the stock price moves and how it could potentially move based on the previous actions of buyers and sellers.

Reading the chart

Knowing how to read the stock chart is an important requirement when dealing with penny stocks.

The chart is simply the visual representation of the time and sales values. There are multiple ways to display the time and sales values on a chart. This course focuses mainly on candlesticks, which provide the most useful information when trading penny stocks.

Candlestick Chart

Figure II.3.3 – StocksToTrade Candlestick Chart - 1 Day candles

Figure II.3.3 shows a typical candlestick chart. This type of chart provides the following information:

- Candle duration (can go from seconds to months per candle)
- The period open and close prices; denoted within the colored part of the candle
- The period highs and lows; indicated by the lines sticking out of the colored part
- Whether the close is higher than open for that period (increase in value, represented in green) or vice versa, the open is higher than the close (decrease in value, represented in red)

The candlestick is a real-time tool that gets updated at the same rate as time and sales.

Having multiple charts open at once with different time periods per candle allows you to get an overview of the long-term past behavior (with day candles you'd get the "big picture") as well as the immediate past behavior that can help identifying momentum (by using one- or five-minute candles).

Candlestick charts can also be used to establish trend lines that may help you determine the potential future behavior of the stock.

Additionally, charts may include indicators like volume, average true range, and a multitude of studies. The availability of these indicators varies from platform to platform, but volume is always included.

Figure II.3.4 - StocksToTrade Candlestick chart with volume

As seen in Figure II.3.4, the chart can be accompanied with volume as an additional indicator. Volume will also be updated in real time based on the calculations of the time and sales for that candle period.

Types of orders

Trading stocks ultimately comes down to two basic operations: buying and selling. These operations can be made in a variety of ways, depending on the results you wish to achieve.

This section focuses mainly on examining the various main types of orders you can make.

Order Parameters

Before getting to the types of orders, let's look at some of the most-used parameters when dealing with penny stocks.

Duration
An order may be set to last for the session, until cancelled, or other types:

- A DAY order is only valid during trading hours in the current session. If not filled by end of session the order is cancelled.
- A GTC, "good 'til cancelled", order is active until the trader actively cancels it. GTC orders will work after hours. A GTC order usually expires within 30 to 90 days.
- A FOK, "fill or kill", order ensures that order isn't partially executed. If the broker cannot fully obtain the position at a given price, the order is cancelled. This type is not often used in penny stock trading.

There are multiple other order duration parameters that may be set, but for our pennystocking purposes, we're not so interested in them. You can find more information here: http://www.investopedia.com/tags/order_types/definition/

Masking Size
Many traders choose to hide the size of their position when making a trade; this is especially true with bigger position sizes.

The idea behind hiding a position stems from traders having access to Level 2 and being influenced by the position sizes on the bid or ask.

This will be discussed in more detail in Chapter III.2.

Market Order

The market (MKT) order is the most basic type of order. When you place a market order, your order is filled at the current market price.

While it's good to know about its existence, due to the volatility and liquidity of penny stocks, it's usually bad practice to use these types of orders.

Additionally, placing market orders puts you at the mercy of market makers and potential manipulation of the price, which could cause you to get filled at a bad price.

Avoid market orders at all costs when trading penny stocks. They're strictly to be used in desperate situations when no other option is available.

Limit Order

The limit (LMT) order is the most used type of order when dealing with penny stocks. It allows you to set the price at which you want your order to be executed.

The limit order instructs the broker to fill your order at your limit price or better. A limit order won't get executed if the stock price never reaches your limit price. You may cancel a limit order at any time before it is filled, allowing you to control whether you want to continue waiting for a specific price to be reached.

A limit order may not get executed, but ensures that the trader won't trade a security at a less beneficial price that was originally intended.

Limit orders are also known to incur higher commissions, as they require additional work from the broker to be executed; this also adds a small delay to an order.

Example: A buy limit order for a share at $10 means the buyer doesn't want to pay more than $10/share for that specific stock. Conversely, a $10 sell order stipulates that the seller doesn't want to receive less than $10/share for his/her shares.

Stop Order

The stop order (STP), also known as a "stop loss" order, allows the trader to automatically exit a position at a pre-established price point to limit the potential losses.

A stop loss is set by the trader at the price point at which he/she wants to exit in order to limit losses or lock profits. Once this price point is crossed, the broker is instructed to automatically execute this order at the specified price of the stop loss.

A stop order doesn't necessarily guarantee the price: In case of fast-moving stock, a gap up or gap down, the fill price of the stop loss will be significantly higher or lower than originally expected, resulting in great potential losses.

Most successful traders like Timothy Sykes use what is referred to as, a "mental stop loss". This implies that they mentally prepare their LMT orders beforehand and visually confirm that their tolerance threshold has been crossed before sending the order.

This is done mentally because market makers have been known to manipulate the price in order to force exit actual stop-loss orders to execute at a given price point before pushing the price back to its original state. This is a very questionable practice that isn't uncommon in the penny stock marketplace.

It's usually not advised to use STP orders. It's often preferable to use LMT orders while keeping an eye on the price movement, and then perform the exit manually.

Trailing Stop

A trailing stop order (TRL) is a programmatic type of order offered by some platforms. This kind of order provides the possibility of having a moving virtual stop that adapts with the change of the price.

More specifically, trailing stops allows traders to lock in profits while limiting the downside of their trades.

A trailing stop has a parameter that can either be a percentage amount or a dollar amount that is considered as the trail that will follow the moving price. When the price reaches the trailing value, the broker is instructed to exit the position.

This represents a safer option than the STP order type, as market makers don't have access to the trailing stop information. This type of order is stored on the broker's platform and triggers a LMT order at the trailing price when this price is reached.

Example: You entered a long position with a buy order at $1.00. You set your trailing stop at 0.05 below the current price for your SELL order as your trailing stop. The price goes up to $1.55. Once the price falls to $1.50, your trailing stop triggers the LMT SELL and your position is exited.

Placing an order

All brokers provide you with some type of interface to perform orders on their platforms.

Keep in mind that orders can be submitted in a wide variety of ways ranging from scanner screens, order windows, charts, etc. Here, we'll cover the basic concept of placing an order and its related common elements. For further information, refer to your broker's platform user guide on placing orders.

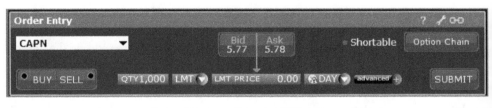

Figure II.3.5 - IB TWS Order Entry

Figure II.3.5 illustrates the order entry window that allows you to create and submit an order. It is set to a LMT DAY order.

A few elements are always required:

- The ticker symbol – the instrument that you're trading.
- The type of transaction: buy or sell. Some brokers offer separate buttons for "short sell" and "buy to cover"; keep this in mind and refer to your manual.
- Position size for the order – the number of shares you want to trade
- The type of order you wish to perform: MKT, LMT, STP, TRL, etc.
- For LMT orders, you'll be required to enter a limit price – the price limit at which your order will be executed. Other order types may require additional parameters.
- Duration of the order: DAY, GTC, etc.
- The "submit" or "transmit" button used to complete the order

Unless actively disabled, most brokers will pop up a confirmation window indicating your order details, estimated commission, and position value that you need to confirm prior to getting the order officially submitted.

Once your order is transmitted, the broker will take care of performing the trade for you and credit or debit your account immediately and virtually. All trades take about three days to settle in terms of transferring shares and funds.

The role of the broker from this point on is to quickly find the best match for your order and associate it with a market maker that will perform the actual transaction of buying/selling.

Profit and Loss

As soon as an order is placed, you're immediately in a situation where you either profit or lose.

Once your entry in a stock has been completed, you're entitled to unrealized profits; these are the profits or losses that you would actually incur if you were to exit your position at the last traded price.

Unrealized profits will usually give you a general idea of your gains or losses, but once you exit your position, the final result may be different.

Once you have exited your position at a given price point, your unrealized profits become realized. This means that the profits have become a tangible financial gain or loss based on how the stock moved.

Bear in mind that the realized profit will often add commissions and – when applicable – borrow fees, plus possible other regulatory fees depending on your broker.

Dealing with the Pattern Day Trader Rule

One important limitation for traders with accounts under $25,000 in the U.S. is the pattern day trading rule (see Chapter II.1 for the definition).

This rule essentially limits the number of trades that an individual may make during a five-day period of time. Basically, a trader that falls under this rule is limited to making a maximum of three day trades per five-day period.

Remember, the SEC states that:

> *"FINRA rules define a 'pattern day trader' as any customer who executes four or more 'day trades' within five business days, provided that the number of day trades represents more than six percent of the customer's total trades in the margin account for that same five business day period."* *(Commission S. a., Pattern Day Trader, n.d.)*

A **day trade (DT)** is the action of following one or more buy orders with a single sell order, or conversely one or more short sell orders followed by a single buy to cover order.

Here is a quick example:

- Buy 1,000 shares of MSFT
- Buy 500 shares of MSFT
- Buy 1,500 shares of MSFT
- Sell 1,000 shares of MSFT

The action shown in the example constitutes a day trade. Pay attention to the fact that the sell order doesn't necessarily need to "close" the position that was opened by the buy orders.

In this example, emphasis is put on the opening a position by buying multiple times followed by a converse partial sell order. Once this converse order is executed, a DT is accounted. The sell order may be partial or full (you could sell 1,000 or 3,000 shares); the action is considered a DT regardless.

A day trader may perform a maximum of three DT over a five-day period. This basically means that under the PDT:

- If the first DT is made on a Wednesday and
- The third allowed DT is performed on a Thursday

- Then the trader will have to wait until the following Wednesday before being allowed to make another DT.

More specifically, the trader has to wait five days (business/trading session days, Monday through Friday) after the initial DT was made. On the sixth day, the trader is allowed to trade again.

Important note: As long as an open position on the same security does not have a converse order (i.e. a set of buy orders followed by a sell order) on the same day, it won't be considered as a DT. This is very practical for performing what is known as "overnight" positions, which implies opening a position before market close, and exiting that position at or near the market open the next day (or really anytime the next day). Holding overnight allows traders to escape the PDT rule, but there are risks holding overnight, such as breaking news and big up or down moves from which stop losses won't protect you.

Here's an example:

- Execute buy order for 100 shares of GOOG at 3:50 p.m. Eastern time.
- Market closes at 4 p.m. Eastern.
- Market opens on next trading day.
- Execute sell order of 100 shares of GOOG at 9:30 a.m. Eastern the next day.

The example above isn't considered as a DT, based on the fact that the two converse orders on the same security happen on different trading sessions.

It's also worth noting that, as shown in our first example, a DT may be accounted even if a position is not closed, which could leave the trader stranded with an open position if the last DT has been used.

Traders who perform four day trades or more while under the PDT rule may have their accounts frozen for a 90-day period, but most brokers have trade restriction systems that prevents traders under the PDT from performing the fourth trade and breaking the rule.

As a way of circumventing the PDT rule, traders with equity under $25,000 can open multiple accounts with various brokers. This would, in turn, provide them with three trades with each of their brokers, increasing the number of possible trades per five-day period by the number of accounts being held (so three accounts would give nine day trades). The same limitation of the third day trade still applies.

Summary

- Quotes are used to obtain the current state of a given stock.
- Time and sales offer insight into a stock's behavior.
- Charts give a visual representation of a stock's price and volume movement.

- There are two types of actions when trading: buying and selling.
- There are multiple types of orders available. Penny stock traders should focus exclusively on placing LMT orders.
- Stop losses can be dangerous if not properly managed. The alternative is using "mental stop losses."
- Trailing stops can also be used as an alternative to STP orders that allow traders to lock profits and exit when the desired trail is reached.
- Position sizes can be masked to show a lower number of shares on the bid/ask board (Level 2).
- DAY or GTC parameters are the most common orders when trading penny stocks. Others may be suitable depending on the situation.
- U.S. traders with accounts under $25,000 need to know and understand the PDT rule.

Questions

1. What information does NOT appear on a basic stock quote?

   a.   Last price
   b.   Volume
   c.   Bid and ask prices
   d.   Average true range

2. What is the time and sales screen?

   a.   A display that shows all orders waiting to be processed
   b.   The chart of the stock
   c.   The screen showing the executed sales their sizes and the time of execution
   d.   The screen where your orders are processed

3. What does each bar of a candlestick chart show?

   a.   Open price for the period
   b.   Close price for the period
   c.   Volume for the period
   d.   High of the period
   e.   Average true range for the period

4. What is a limit order?

   a.   An order that gets executed when the price is equal or worse than the specified amount
   b.   An order that gets executed when the price is equal or better than the specified amount
   c.   An order that follows the price and executes when the price drops below the specified amount
   d.   An order that gets executed at the current available price

5. Which order duration is valid for 30 to 90 days from the date of transmission?

   a.   DAY
   b.   FOK
   c.   GTC
   d.   GTD

6. How many trades can be made under the PDT?

   a.   5 day trades in a 3-day period
   b.   No limit in the number of trades
   c.   3 day trades in a 5-day period
   d.   5 day trades every week

Homework

- Make trades
  - Take a small long position into a trade ($50-$100 total position value).
    - Example: Buy 100 shares of a stock priced around $1.
  - Profit or lose $10 (or close the position if the stock price doesn't show enough movement) and exit the position immediately.
    - Example: Sell the position when the price reaches $1.10 or $0.90.
  - Stick to listed stocks (NASDAQ, AMEX, NYSE).
  - Experiment with:
    - LMT GTC orders when buying

- LMT GTC when selling
- STP GTC when selling
- MKT orders for buying and selling
- TRAIL order for selling

o Stick to stocks that have good liquidity but low volatility and show small price variations.

- 26-week high should be close enough to the 26-week low

o Take notes:

- On your experience and describe your actions, emotions and state of mind.
- On the action and the expected result.
- On the actual result compared to your expectations.

Chapter II.4 - Risk Management Strategies

Overview

Here, you'll learn risk management strategies that will help you to maximize your profits and minimize your losses.

Goals

The goal of this chapter is to help you find the right risk management strategy suited to your needs. At the end of the chapter you'll be able to assess how much you're willing to lose on a single trade and when exactly you should exit a position from the moment you enter it.

Choosing a Risk Management Strategy

Quite possibly the most important part of trading penny stocks is knowing how much you're willing to lose and when you should get out of a bad trade. This concept is known as risk management.

Choosing the proper **risk management strategy** (RMS) is crucial to your success or possible demise. Having a risk management strategy is only one part of the equation; respecting and sticking to your chosen RMS is the key to being successful.

Throughout this course, we've learned the importance of discipline. The RMS is truly where the trait of self-discipline must especially be applied.

This chapter focuses on presenting two risk management strategies. One is based on the concept of the **risk/reward ratio**. The other is more technical, based on the Turtle Trader's strategy adapted to penny stocks.

What Is the Purpose of a RMS?

A RMS is intended to establish your exit point when you're subjected to a losing trade. It defines your rules of engagement for dealing with an undesirable situation and allows you to know exactly how you will deal with such a situation.

More importantly, the RMS is your contingency plan – a thoroughly established set of actions intended to protect you from harm's way.

Managing your risk on any given trade will ensure that your profits are sound and that your losses are minimal. Managing your losses is as important as making profits.

"Know what you are going to do when the market does what it is going to do." – Michael W. Covel, The Complete Turtle Trader (Covel, 2009)

Simple Risk and Reward Ratio – The R³ RMS

The simple risk and reward ratio (R³) strategy is based upon determining the risk to your capital and potential winning trade reward.

Ask the following questions:

- What is the potential downside or loss to entering this trade (measured in a dollar amount)?
- What is the potential upside or profit to entering this trade (measured in a dollar amount)?

Once you have established the values for both the potential downside and the potential upside, factor them to a common denominator, bringing the downside amount to 1 and adjusting the upside amount accordingly.

This will give you a risk/reward ratio in the following form: 1:U

U being the value obtained for the upside.

What this means, is that for every dollar that you risk, you have a potential gain of "U" dollars.

A trade is usually considered acceptable when the risk reward ratio is at least 1:2. This, however, will vary from one individual to the next, as some may wish to have better odds than "for every $1 dollar lost I can win $2".

The upside can be calculated as follows: $U = \frac{potential\ \$\ profit}{potential\ \$\ loss}$

The value obtained for U should be rounded to the nearest natural number below that value.

Example of the R³ strategy:

GENE (Genetic Tech LTD.) is a stock that has been at trading a price of $9.69 for no specific reason over the last couple of days. Your hypothesis indicates that the stock will probably fall back to its previous high point soon.

You consider short selling this stock (short selling will be discussed in Chapter III.1). Your downside is $10.08, the previous unbroken high, meaning $0.39/share loss when entering a short position.

Based on your research, you expect the price to fall down to $7.20. The upside is then $2.49.

You have the following equations system:

$0.39 = 1$
$2.49 = U$

We can infer the following:

$$U = \frac{1 \times 2.49}{0.39} = \frac{2.49}{0.39} = 6.38$$

We can round U to the nearest natural number below that value, which would give us:

$R^3 \Rightarrow 1:6$

In this case the R³ RMS indicates that entering GENE could potentially be a profitable trade with the possibility of getting a six-fold return on every dollar risked (not on investment).

The downside of the R³ RMS is that while it provides a good indicator for the potential reward based on the amount risked, it does not offer a proper way to evaluate how big your position should be or how much money you should invest in that position.

This RMS often leaves the details of determining the position size to the discretion of the trader.

Managing Risk Like a Turtle–The Ninja Turtle (NT) RMS

When I learned the intricacies of the world of penny stocks, I came upon a dilemma shared by many novice traders in the chat rooms.

The questions usually read like: "How big should my position be?" "How much should I invest?"

The answer provided by more experienced traders and gurus repeatedly expressed that every trader should decide for him/herself, as we all have different tolerances in terms of what can be lost.

While I was in agreement with the fact that tolerance is relative to each individual, I found the "gauge it yourself" approach difficult to accept, especially as a beginner.

This is around the time that I stumbled upon a book written by Michael W. Covel. His trading strategy, commonly known as trend following, differs greatly from penny stocks, as it deals with longer-term positions and much bigger accounts. In Covel's book, "The Complete Turtle Trader" (Covel, 2009), he shares Dennis Richards' 1980s social trading experiment, in which Richards claimed that he could teach anyone to trade with his strategy and become highly successful.

Chapter five of the book covers the whole trend following trading strategy as developed by Richards, upon which the Ninja Turtle RMS was based and adapted to penny stocks.

The NT RMS offers an alternative way to establish not only the risk, but also a way to determine exactly what the ideal position size should be to enter a trade, and an absolute exit price. The NT RMS takes into consideration the current available capital of the trader as well as the state of the traded instrument.

Average True Range – The N

As defined in Chapter II.1, the average true range is a moving average. The purpose of the ATR is to determine the average difference of price over a given period of time – in our case, 15 days.

The **ATR**, to which we'll refer as **N** from this point on, will serve two main purposes in the NT RMS.

Its first role is to help determine the price point of the absolute stop – the price at which the trader should exit a position, should the price of the traded instrument cross that line.

The second role of N is to help determine the position size, or number of shares that will be traded for that specific instrument.

The ATR or N can easily be obtained by enabling it in most platforms. It does not need to be calculated manually and the range of calculation parameter (i.e. 15 days) can be set in the settings.

Taking the previous example, GENE would have an **N=$1.676**.

Establishing a Risk Unit – The U

The next step in the NT RMS is to establish the risk unit. Put simply, how much financial risk you are willing to take?

The **risk unit**, or **U**, is established as a percentage of the available trading capital. This allows the trader to adapt the potential gains to the current financial availability dedicated to trading.

The idea behind labeling the risked capital a risk unit has multiple reasons. First and foremost, it helps "demonetize" the position you're trading, which helps in dealing with trade anxiety.

Labeling this the risk unit also serves the purpose of being able to quickly add to your position in terms of risk units rather than in number of shares. This will be discussed in Chapter III.6.

The risk unit is based on your current trading capital, or trading equity; we will call this E. The calculation is made by picking a suitable percentage value (labeled p) that will be at risk, or more specifically, how much you're willing to lose on any given trade.

Your risk unit is then calculated as follows:

$U = E \times p$

Example:

Your total trading account is $15,000 and you wish you only want to risk 2% of that equity on every trade.

We then have:

$E = \$15,000$
$p = 2\% = 0.02$
$U = E \times p = \$15,000 \times 0.02 = \$300$

Your risk unit is U. Here, **U is $300**, how much you're ready to lose on any given trade, based on your personal requirements.

The base unit percentage may vary from one individual to another, although it's usually advised for novice traders to keep a 1%-2% percentage unit. This gives the trader a fair amount of trades before blowing the account, if all trades failed to generate a profit.

Upgrading and Downgrading the U – Risk Adjustment

There are times when the risk unit percentage needs to be adjusted based on various situations.

The first situation that is covered by the NT RMS aims to limit losses. For every 10% down in the account (your equity is down 10%), the risk unit percentage is reduced by 20% until the gains have been recovered for that tier.

Example:

Before your last three trades you had an **equity of $10,000** with a **risk unit percentage of 2%**. After these trades, your equity has been reduced to $9,000.

For all the coming trades, your **risk unit percentage is reduced to 1.6%** (20% reduction of the risk from the original value).

Your risk unit **U will be $144 instead of $180**.

This allows you to limit the potential losses while giving you time to grow your account back.

A few trades later, your account is down to $8,000. You **adjust your risk unit percentage to 1.2%**; your risk unit U becomes $96.

A few profitable trades come by and your account raises to $11,000, your **risk unit percentage is restored to its original 2%**, giving you a U of $220.

Upgrading the risk unit percentage can also be done in certain cases and will be left at the discretion of the trader; these cases include a higher level of conviction on how the stock price will move, a higher level of confidence in the trades, etc.

It is advised to increase the percentage of the risk unit by 1% increments until comfortable with the potential losses associated with the new value.

Setting a Stop Multiplier and Establishing the Absolute Stop

The absolute stop is the indicator by which you will decide to exit your current position once the price is crossed.

This can be achieved through the use of stop losses (not recommended), trailing stops, and mental stop losses.

The absolute stop is established by N and a multiplier, "x". The "x" multiplier allows the trader to set the threshold within which he/she is comfortable taking a loss.

Stop = entry price $\pm$ *x* $\times$ *N* (+ or − depends on whether you are entering a long or a short position)

Example:

GENE has a price $6.3254 per share.

N is $1.55

Your absolute stop is set to be at x=1, giving you a 1N Stop.

If you were to buy GENE at $6.3254 your absolute stop exit price would be set at:

$$Stop = \$6.3254 - 1 \times \$1.55 = \$4.7754$$

A higher multiplier would give you more flexibility in terms of the price movement tolerance, but would also conversely reduce the size of your position, as we'll see in the next section.

Defining Your Risk and Position

The final piece is establishing your position size (defined as P) based on your Equity (E), The Average True Range (N), Stop Multiplier (x) and the defined risk unit (U).

The position size is calculated as follows:

$$P = floor\left(\frac{U}{x \times N}\right)$$

This means that the Position size will be rounded to the lowest nearest natural number. Depending on the type of stock, this is rounded to the 10, the 100 or the 1,000 below.

Example:

- If the obtained position size is 45.69, this would be rounded to 45
- If the obtained position size is 323.22, this would be rounded to 320
- If the obtained position size is 1,435.57, this would be rounded to 1,400
- If the obtained position size is 54,325.15, this would be rounded to 54,000

Rounding in this manner allows you to match the minimum order requirements for trading a given security.

Example:

You have defined the following:

$$U = 125.23$$
$$N = 0.45$$
$$x = 2$$
$$P = floor^5\left(\frac{U}{x \times N}\right) = floor\left(\frac{125.23}{2 \times 0.45}\right) = floor(139.14) = 130$$

Your position size in this situation would be 130 shares of the security in question.

---

[5] Floor is a mathematical function that rounds a decimal point value to the closest integer less than or equal to the given number. It is equivalent to truncating the decimals from the number.

Putting It All Together

Now that we have all the elements to establish the NT RMS, we'll go over an example that combines all the concepts described above in order to provide you with a position size based on your equity and risk tolerance.

For the purpose of this study case, we'll again use GENE as our basis.

Here are the basic parameters:

$E = \$16387.23$
$p = 2\%$
$x = 1$
$N = \$1.55$

$GENE\ price = \$6.16/share$

Establishing the risk unit:

$U = E \times p = \$16{,}387.23 \times 0.02 = \$327.74$

Establishing your stop loss exit price:

$Stop = GENE\ price - x \times N = \$6.16 - 1 \times \$1.55 = \$4.61$

Establishing your position size:

$$P = floor\left(\frac{U}{x \times N}\right) = floor\left(\frac{327.74}{1 \times \$1.55}\right) = floor(211.44) = 210$$

Your position would be 210 shares of GENE at $6.16. Your position value would then be:

$\$P = P \times GENE\ price = 210 \times \$6.16 = \$1{,}293.6$

Simply put, you're making an investment of 7.8% of your total capital and risking at most $327.74 by sticking to the stop loss exit price of $4.61.

The ninja turtle risk management strategy offers the trade the flexibility to define how much money is put at risk during any given trade, but also provides a robust framework that helps quickly define position sizes and exit stop loss prices.

In this manner, a trader can know exactly how to enter and exit a position at any given point in time without wondering how many shares should be traded or how big of an investment should be made.

Summary

- Risk management represents the most important aspect of trading.
- Risk management ensures that losses are controlled at all times while maximizing profits when the opportunity arises.
- Risk management provides a way to determine when a position is worth considering as a potential play or abandon altogether.
- Choosing the proper risk management strategy (RMS) is crucial to minimizing losses and maximizing profits.
- An acceptable R^3 RMS must be at least 1:2 in order to consider the position playable.
- The NT RMS gives the trader proper position sizing guidelines based on the risk assessment and available trading capital.
- The average true range can be used as a measure of volatility.
- The NT RMS provides you with a guideline on when you should exit a position.
- You might not always know when you enter a position, but you should always know when you must exit. That is the purpose of having a RMS.

Questions

1. What is the purpose of a risk management strategy?
   a. Establish when to enter a position
   b. Establish when to exit a position
   c. To get a general idea of how to enter and exit
   d. To cut losses quickly

2. What should you always know before entering a position?
   a. How much money I have
   b. When I should enter
   c. When I should exit
   d. The potential upside
   e. The potential downside

3. What does the upside represent?
   a. The highest price the stock is expected to reach
   b. The potential amount in gain that the stock is expected to provide
   c. The peak of the price

4. What is the purpose of an absolute stop?
   a. A guideline indicating when I should exit a position
   b. The price that indicates when I have reached my profit goal and exit
   c. The price where I must exit in order to limit my losses to my tolerance
   d. The price indicating when I should increase my position

5. What percentage of the cash account should a novice trader invest in each play?
   a. 100%
   b. 50%
   c. 30%
   d. 10%
   e. 2%
   f. 1%

Exercises

1. A stock has been determined to possess a potential upside of $0.75 and a down side of $0.23. Please establish the following:
   a. The risk-reward ratio by using the R^3 method.
   b. Whether the stock is worth considering as a potential play. Explain why.

2. As a trader you have a cash equity of $27,593.46. You have added a stock to your watchlist with a potential entry price at $2.63. This stock has an average true range of $0.25 and a risk multiplier of 1. As a novice trader, you have established your risk unit to be 1.5%. Please determine the following:
   a. The total dollar value risk to your equity
   b. Your estimated position size
   c. Your absolute stop
   d. The market value of the position at the entry price

Homework

- First, find popular stocks other people are watching (gurus, experts, etc.) and talking about.
- For each of these stocks, determine the following information based on your personal parameters for trading (i.e. 1% risk unit, take into account your existing equity):
  - Risk-Reward Ratio by attempting to determine the up- and downsides based on the available information.
  - The estimated position size you would be taking into that stock
  - The total market value of the position

Chapter II.5 - Technical Analysis and Price Action

Overview

Here, you'll grow comfortable with the concept of technical analysis and understanding the various elements that come into play in real-time when the trading session is active.

Goals

Among your top goals for this course is to become intimately familiar with the various elements of technical analysis commonly used in penny stock trading. At the end of this chapter, you'll know how to identify established support and resistance trend lines, spot potential breakouts/breakdowns, understand the possible consequences of sideway action and identify behavior based on reversal.

What is Technical Analysis?

Technical analysis is the concept of basing trade decisions solely on numerical factors by considering the various characteristics of the stock being analyzed. This takes into consideration a wide array of various elements. Typically, the main technical factors we follow with penny stocks are price and volume.

Technical analysis is often considered as a self-fulfilling prophecy when it comes to predicting price action on any given stock. Why? Because people look for technical patterns and expect these patterns to behave in a certain way, which gives way to collective actions by the will of the market.

Volatility and Liquidity

Penny stocks and the viability of a play is based on two main factors: volatility and liquidity.

Volatility implies that the stock is able to quickly perform price chances within a short period of time. This is considered necessary, as quick price action within a wide range means big potential profits when predicted properly. On the other hand, a volatile stock can mean rapid significant losses when you aren't prepared and don't have a proper risk management strategy in place (See Chapter II.4).

Liquidity means that the stock has a significant volume throughout the session, hence allowing the trader to quickly enter and exit a position. This is a consequential necessity from the volatility of penny stocks. As the price moves quickly, you need to be able to enter an exit a position as quickly as possible in order to maximize your profits and limit your losses to remain within your RMS.

When choosing penny stocks to trade, these are the first two factors that must be considered; this will be covered in greater detail in Chapter II.9.

Trend Lines

When it comes to technical analysis, penny stock trading strategies require a KISS (Keep It Simple, Stupid) approach. You'll only rely on a few technical indicators to make trading decisions.

A trend line is a graphic indicator on a chart that indicates a certain type of linearity for a given stock. Trend lines usually allow the trader to establish levels where the price remains, or price points considered to be significant for that stock.

You can build trend lines based on the information available on any period of time, being day charts, hourly, 5-minute, minute or a combination of these.

Pennystocking strategies rely on two main types of trend lines: support and resistance.

Support

A support trend line, simply called "support," represents a line drawn on the chart that seems to be sustaining the price above a certain level. This level indicates that within the chosen period of time the price has been unable to cross that line. A support line will show multiple failed attempts of crossing below that price.

Support allows you to identify multiple potential behaviors and possibly predict price action based on previous price data and some fundamental support.

Some of these behaviors will be discussed later in this chapter.

Figure II.5.1 - StocksToTrade - Support lines on VALE

Figure II.5.2 - StocksToTrade - Support on PTCT

Figures II.5.1 and II.5.2 show examples of intraday support lines for VALE and PTCT. As can be seen in the figures above, the price fails to fall below certain points that represent the support prices.

Along with basic support, a 'stronger' type of support line can be established. Often referred to as "key support", it's based on the price analysis over multiple days and the identification of price points below which the price has been unable to fall. Key support often indicates that a stock retains that value as a minimum and can usually be established over a period of multiple days, months and even years, depending on the instrument.

Figure II.5.3 - StocksToTrade - Key Supports, 1 year chart for SAAS

Figure II.5.3 provides a good example of key support on a one-year chart. As you'll see in the image, the price fails to fall below $7.50 for about nine months. An additional key support line can be identified just below $8.50 based on two months of price action.

Resistance

On the flip side, resistance lines represent the price above which any given stock fails to raise. Resistance helps establish the maximum price point that the stock has been unable to cross on multiple occasions.

Much like support, a resistance line may be used to predict various types of potential future behavior of any given instrument, as you'll learn later in the course.

Basic intraday resistance can be seen in Figures II.5.4 and II.5.5. Resistance levels are established intraday. Shown are one-minute intraday charts on which we identified resistance points respectively around $7.75 and $7.85 for VALE and around $8.88 for MTG.

Figure II.5.4 - StocksToTrade - Resistance on VALE Intraday

Figure II.5.5 - StocksToTrade - MTG Intraday resistance

Much like key support, key resistance is a strong resistance point that has lasted over a certain period of time, and during which the price has been unable to increase past the resistance level.

Shown below on Figure II.5.6 is a representation of key resistance for SAAS at around $10.17. You'll see that the price fails to go over that price for about seven months.

You'll also notice that once the resistance point is crossed, there's a quick surge in price over the next day. We'll examine this in the following section.

Figure II.5.6 - StocksToTrade - Key Resistance for SAAS

Key resistance is an important indicator in determining how the price could move in the foreseeable future.

Momentum

The momentum refers to price action that is directly caused by a surge in trades, commonly identified by a sudden increase in trading volume and a quick price movement in either direction.

Momentum can be caused by purely technical factors as well as fundamental elements that may affect the response to the instrument in question. Usually the fundamental elements are backed by technical elements like resistance and support.

When trading penny stocks, we use two main types of momentum: breakouts and breakdowns.

Breakout

A breakout typically refers to an instrument for which a major increase in volume and price can be identified. Breakouts are often characterized by three factors:

- Price increase

- Strong volume
- Price above a resistance or key resistance line

A breakout is often a predictable event when you consider the main technical factors, but also consider the fundamental context that surrounds the instrument in question.

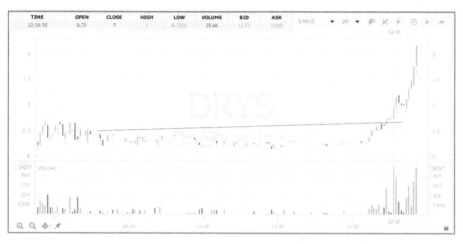

Figure II.5.7 - StocksToTrade - DRYS breakout

Figure II.5.7 shows an intraday resistance line at $6.69. Once the price crosses that line, a strong increase in volume can be observed and a parabolic movement of the price, rising from $6.69 to $8.17.

Morning spikes and afternoon spikes are also usually the result of a breakout situation.

Breakdown

Conversely to the breakout, a breakdown will result in the price of the stock crashing down. This can usually be associated to the same factors as the breakout:

- Price decrease
- Increased trading volume
- Price below a support or key support line

Similarly, a breakdown can be catalyzed by the presence of a fundamental element that causes the will of the market to move the price; however, it usually relies on the support indicator that traders set to happen.

Figure II.5.8 - StocksToTrade - FSM breakdown below support levels

Figure II.5.8 shows two breakdowns on FSM based on support lines being crossed and failure of the price to increase.

Sideways Price Action

Another important technical indicator when dealing with penny stocks is the presence of sideway price action. Sideway price action represents small variations in stock price without displaying a major change in the current state of the instrument. In simpler terms, the price remains at the same price for a prolonged period of time. This type of event can last from a couple of hours to a couple days before observing any significant change in price.

Sideway price action is usually characterized not only by small variations in price, but also by a small trading volume (although not always) during the concerned period of time.

Sideway price action may also be an indication of a major move in the stock price ahead, as it offers time to potential investors to assess their position or desired position in the given instrument and make some further research into the fundamentals of the company.

Because of this, sideway price action is usually followed by a breakout or a breakdown depending on the context of the stock.

Reversal

Reversal is often used as an indicator for establishing trend lines. When a stock experiences reversal, it marks a general change of direction for the price based on the candle period being analyzed.

There are two types of reversal: "red to green" and "green to red".

Red to Green

Red to green (R2G) indicates that the price changes from negative open-close difference for the previous bar to a positive value. While the change in itself isn't significant, it is worth considering when the reversal follows multiple red bars as a possible indicator of a bounce or recovery.

Figure II.5.9 – StocksToTrade – Intraday chart, Red to Green on PCTC

Figure II.5.9 shows some of the chart R2G changes with arrows.

Red-to-green are often considered the underlying basis for support when they follow important down moves. When using daily bars for the candlestick chart, a R2G change following multiple red days marks key support for that stock.

Figure II.5.10 - StocksToTrade - Red-to-Green Key support on SAAS daily chart

Figure II.5.10 shows key support based on R2G changes on SAAS. This is established over multiple days in a period lasting multiple months, which creates a strong support for the stock.

Green to Red

Conversely to the R2G, green-to-red (G2R) indicates the opposite reversal: the price changes from an uptrend to a downtrend, and is often used as the basis for establishing resistance and key resistance levels.

Just like for R2G, G2R isn't necessarily worth considering unless it follows multiple green bars, as it marks a clear reversal of stock price and is indicative of the potential start of the drop or dip.

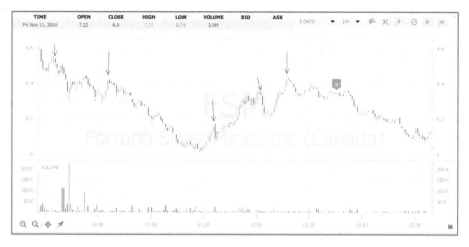

Figure II.5.11 - StocksToTrade - Green to Red on FSM intraday 1min chart

Figure II.5.11 shows the G2R changes with blue arrows for FSM on an intraday one-minute chart.

G2R can also be used on multi-day charts to establish key resistance in a similar manner as R2G.

Figure II.5.12 - StocksToTrade - Key resistance on ZAGG multi-day chart based on G2R

Figure II.5.12 shows key resistance being established based on G2R price reversals on ZAGG on a multiday chart over a period of multiple months.

Dips and Bounces

Major reversals are often the prelude to dips and bounces. These types of events are often the result of overextended stocks with significant price movements.

When such major moves occur, they're often followed by a reversal, indicating that traders are attempting to clear their positions in order to take profits. This drives the price in the opposite direction, giving the chance to a new set of traders to pick up the stock at a better price and profit from the movement.

Dips and bounces often use resistance and support lines, although in the case of stocks breaking new highs or new lows, such trend lines do not exist, and traders must rely on intraday sideway price action to determine such potential events.

Figure II.5.13 - StocksToTrade - DGLY daily chart - dips and bounces

Summary

- Technical analysis is used as a set of numerical indicators in order to predict possible stock price movement.
- A purely numerical approach, technical analysis strongly relies on some fundamental factors when applied to penny stocks, in order to predict price movement.
  - Timothy Sykes uses a combination of both technical and fundamental.
  - Tim Grittani focuses mainly technical analysis and price action.
- Trend lines help identify important price points that indicate a possible change in behavior for the stock price.
- Penny stocks rely on volatility and liquidity for being considered as tradable instruments.
- A support line defines the price point below which the price has failed to go under.
- A support line is a good indicator for the lowest possible price for that stock during that period.
- A support line may be used to predict a rebound or a breakdown based on some fundamental factors and price/volume momentum.
- A resistance line defines the price point above which the price has failed to go over.
- A resistance line is a good indicator for the highest possible price for that stock during that period.
- A resistance line may be used to predict a dip or a breakout based on some fundamental factors and price/volume momentum.
- Reversal following a same-direction trend is used to establish support and resistance lines.
- Multi-day reversals can be used to establish key support and resistance when following a same-direction trend.
- Dips and bounces are good indicators of potential breakouts and breakdowns.

Questions

1. What is resistance?

a. A type of trend line that indicates that the stock price is unable to go higher.

b. A type of trend line that indicates that the stock price is unable to go lower.

c. It indicates a sudden increase in price and volume.

d. It indicates a sudden decrease in price.

2. What is a breakdown?

a. It indicates a sudden increase of price typically crossing above resistance.

b. It indicates a price point below which the price fails to drop.

c. It indicates the change from a positive change to a negative change.

d. It indicates a sudden decrease in price typically crossing below support.

3. What is a bounce?

a. It represents a hyperbolic move in price action.

b. It represents a drop following a hyperbolic move in price action.

c. It represents a spike following a dip.

d. It represents a sudden increase in price and volume.

4. What is red to green?

a. It indicates a change in the direction or the price action from negative to positive.

b. It indicates a change in the direction of the price action from positive to negative.

c. It indicates a sudden decrease in price typically crossing below a resistance line.

d. It indicates a flat price action over a period of time.

Exercises

For the charts below, establish:

- Support and resistance
- Breakouts and breakdowns
- Major reversals

Homework

- Find popular stocks other people are watching (gurus, experts, etc.) and talking about. For each of these stocks, visually determine the following information by using charting tools (broker platform, Multicharts, Tradingview, etc.):
    - Resistance
    - Support
    - Key resistance, if available
    - Key support, if available
    - Breakouts, if available
    - Breakdowns, if available
    - Major price reversals (R2G, G2R) following a trend
    - Increases in volume with price action
- Make sure you look at various periods including one-year daily charts as well as intraday one-minute, five-minute, 15-minute, and 30-minute bars.
- Take note of the volatility (wide price range) and liquidity (trading volume) of each of these stocks.

Chapter II.6 - Learning the Chart Patterns

Overview

These are the main profitable pennystocking patterns originally developed by Timothy Sykes. We'll also cover the chart patterns to avoid when trading penny stocks.

Goals

The goal of this chapter is to teach you the main pennystocking charts that will allow you to become a profitable trader. At the end of this chapter, you'll know the chart patterns that are relevant when choosing stocks to trade. You must get intimately familiar with these patterns.

What is a Chart Pattern?

History is often representative of future behavior. This is often the case with penny stocks.

Penny stocks follow a repeatable behavior over time that is directly translated into price action and represented on the chart.

Chart patterns take past behaviors of penny stocks and provide guidelines for choosing and establishing which instruments might yield a profit by predicting how they're likely to move, based on what other stocks have done before in similar manners.

Pennystocking Chart patterns

As introduced by Timothy Sykes in his original "PennyStocking" DVD (Sykes, PennyStocking, 2010) and manual, there are five main patterns to look for when establishing a list of potentially tradable picks.

Though you don't necessarily need to memorize each of these patterns, knowing the general guidelines offered by each of them is critical to performing successful and profitable trades in the realm of penny stocks.

Patterns are usually observed over a period of multiple days, months and even years in order to identify the past and be able to somewhat predict future behavior based on price action.

These patterns also serve as the main basis for intraday chart analysis, and help you make informed decision before entering or exiting trades.

The Irregular "Messy" Patterns

Irregular or "messy" patterns refer to stocks that don't have a clear identifiable price action. The price moves in an erratic manner with no particular way to predict how it will move in the short term.

When trading penny stocks, it's usually best to avoid messy, as they represent more gambling than trading with a calculated risk, which could cause you to incur significant losses.

Below are a few examples of irregular patterns to <u>avoid</u> when looking for potential plays.

These examples are illustrated in Figures II.6.1 to II.6.10.

Figure II.6.1 – StocksToTrade - Irregular Pattern AMMJ, daily chart

Figure II.6.2 - StocksToTrade - Irregular Pattern PRTS, daily chart

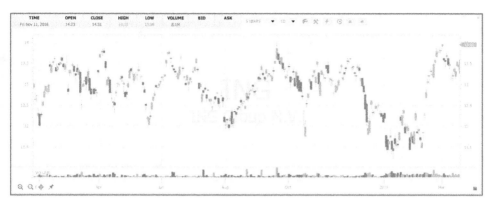

Figure II.6.3 - StocksToTrade - Irregular Pattern ING, daily chart

Figure II.6.4 - StocksToTrade - Irregular Pattern REED, daily chart

Figure II.6.5 - StocksToTrade - Irregular Pattern SSRI, daily chart

Figure II.6.6 - StocksToTrade - Irregular Pattern POEFF, daily chart

Figure II.6.7 – StocksToTrade - Irregular Pattern EPXY, daily chart

Figure II.6.8 - StocksToTrade - Irregular Pattern KOS, daily chart

Figure II.6.9 - StocksToTrade - Irregular Pattern EGO, daily chart

Figure II.6.10 - StocksToTrade - Irregular Pattern DGAZ, daily chart

The "Clean" Patterns

Clean patterns are the most basic technical analysis patterns that follow some logic when it comes to price movement. These patterns are widely recognized by traders in different areas (not only penny stocks), and represent coherent motion of the price of an instrument.

Clean patterns allow penny stock traders to make informed decisions and make calculated risks about any given stock.

The Supernova

The supernova pattern is one of the most coveted patterns in pennystocking. It is represented by a quick rise in price that could be due to a pump & dump (Chapter II.8), a catalyst (Chapter II.7), or sometimes for no valid reason.

Supernovas are attractive patterns, as they indicate a positive overextension in the price action, which ultimately – regardless of the worth of the company – results in a significant drop in price. This type of pattern can be exploited both on the long and short sides.

Figures II.6.11 through II.6.20 illustrate the supernova pattern.

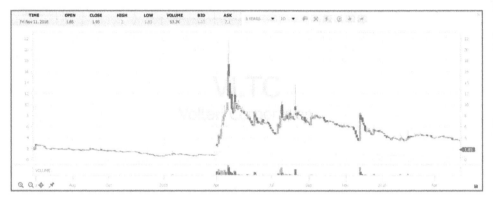

Figure II.6.11 – StocksToTrade – VLTC

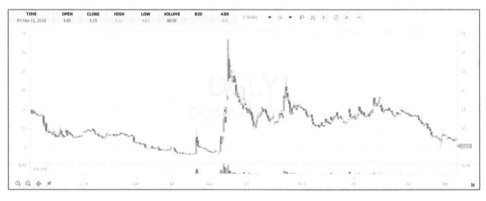

Figure II.6.12 - StocksToTrade – DGLY

Figure II.6.13 - StocksToTrade – CUBA

Figure II.6.14 - StocksToTrade – GENE

Figure II.6.15 - StocksToTrade – LEI

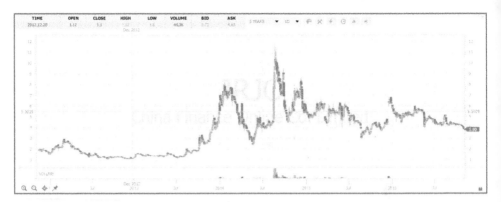

Figure II.6.16 - StocksToTrade – JRJC

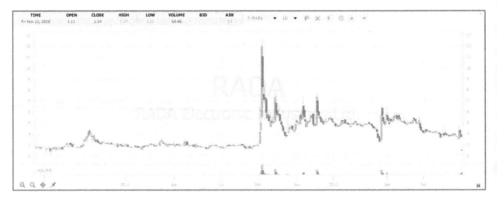

Figure II.6.17 - StocksToTrade – RADA

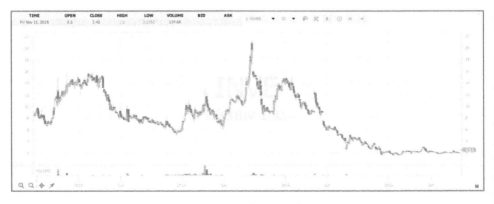

Figure II.6.18 - StocksToTrade – INVE

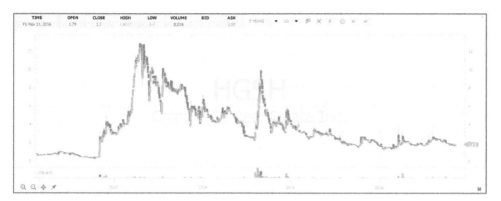

Figure II.6.19 - StocksToTrade – HGSH

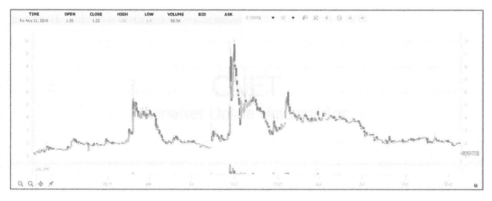

Figure II.6.20 - StocksToTrade - CNET

The Stair-Stepper

The stair-stepper is a pattern characterized by a progressive rise in the price similar to stair steps. The stock price raises, drops, then encounters sideway price action. This usually indicates a rising trend in the stock.

A stair-stepper is the slow-motion version of a supernova, as it rises progressively. Traders seek gains by buying on the step up and shorting on the drops. This pattern can quickly reverse if the price is overextended for prolonged periods of time with no proper catalyst.

This pattern is illustrated in Figures II.6.21 to II.6.30.

Figure II.6.21 - StocksToTrade – ADXS

Figure II.6.22 - StocksToTrade – IFON

Figure II.6.23 - StocksToTrade – ACN

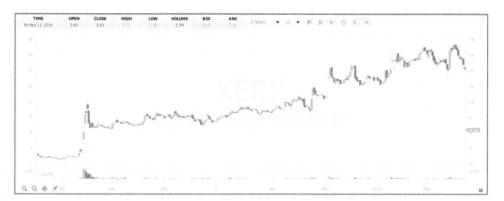

Figure II.6.24 - StocksToTrade – KERX

Figure II.6.25 - StocksToTrade – CPRX

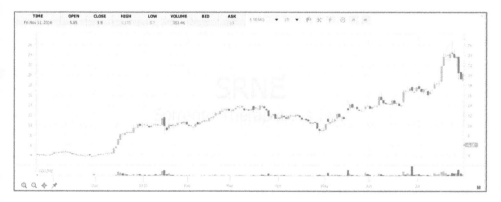

Figure II.6.26 - StocksToTrade – SRNE

Figure II.6.27 - StocksToTrade – ZAGG

Figure II.6.28 - StocksToTrade – RESN

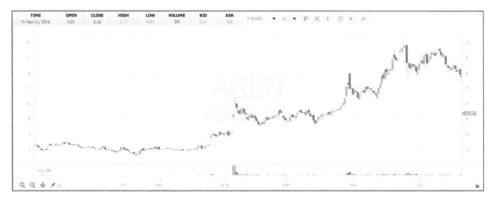

Figure II.6.29 - StocksToTrade – AGEN

Figure II.6.30 - StocksToTrade - CJJD

The Snore

The snore pattern is usually best avoided when trading penny stocks, as it doesn't offer proper play opportunities. Moreover, the pattern itself doesn't offer distinguishable features that would make a stock a potential position.

When met with catalysts, these types of stocks usually show little to no change in their price action. Snore stocks are characterized by an erratic behavior that is impossible to predict in terms of assessing odds and taking calculated risks.

Figures II.6.31 to II.6.38 illustrate the Snore pattern.

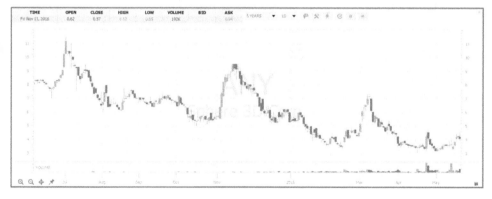

Figure II.6.31 - StocksToTrade – ANY

Figure II.6.32 - StocksToTrade – ENZN

Figure II.6.33 - StocksToTrade – KDUS

Figure II.6.34 - StocksToTrade – OREX

Figure II.6.35 - StocksToTrade – SMSI

Figure II.6.36 - StocksToTrade – CAMP

Figure II.6.37 - StocksToTrade – NVDQ

Figure II.6.38 - StocksToTrade - NERV

The Crow

Our final pattern is the Crow, which is characterized by a continuously downtrending price action. Crow patterns are ideal for short positions and are prone to encounter bounces before continuing to gradually drop.

Long positions on these types of plays should never be engaged, since the probability of a bounce at the proper time is unlikely, unless supported by a catalyst that would lead the stock price into another pattern behavior.

The Crow pattern is illustrated in Figures II.6.39 to II.6.49.

Figure II.6.39 - StocksToTrade - GORO

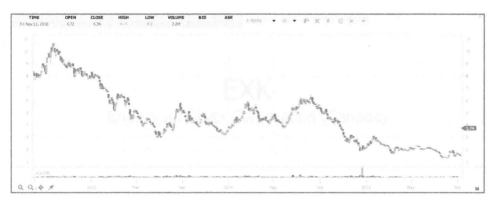

Figure II.6.40 - StocksToTrade - EXK

Figure II.6.41 - StocksToTrade - ONVO

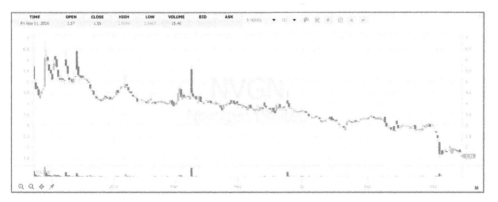

Figure II.6.42 - StocksToTrade - NVGN

Figure II.6.43 - StocksToTrade - XGTI

Figure II.6.44 - StocksToTrade - TZOO

Figure II.6.45 - StocksToTrade - ZAZA

Figure II.6.46 - StocksToTrade - XNET

Figure II.6.47 - StocksToTrade - FRO

Figure II.6.48 - StocksToTrade - HMNY

Figure II.6.49 - StocksToTrade - ANGI

Summary

- Knowing the chart patterns and how to play each pattern is crucial to trading penny stocks.
- Avoid messy patterns at all costs, as they represent more of a gamble than a proper calculated risk.
- Stick to clean, playable patterns.
- A supernova pattern can be played on both long and short sides.
- A stair-stepper pattern can be played on both long and short sides.
- Snore patterns are best avoided since they offer no discernable characteristics to enter a position.
- A crow pattern is best played on the short side and should never be attempted as a long position.

Questions

1. **What is a chart pattern?**
   a. A pattern trend lines that indicate when to buy or sell
   b. A pattern of candle bars that indicate a type of price action in the stock
   c. A pattern of colors on each candle that indicate potential future behavior
   d. A pattern of prices that show how the price will move

2. **What is a supernova pattern?**
   a. A pattern that shows an overextension in price in a short period of time
   b. A pattern that progressively goes up, displaying sideway action
   c. A pattern that progressively goes down with time
   d. A pattern that shows no clear indication in future movement

3. **What is a stair-stepper pattern?**
   a. A pattern that progressively goes down with time
   b. A pattern that progressively goes up, displaying sideway action
   c. A pattern that shows no clear indication in future movement
   d. A pattern that shows an overextension in price in a short period of time

4. **What is the typical action for a super-nova pattern?**
   a. Buying when the price is up
   b. Buying when momentum starts
   c. Shorting when close to the peak
   d. Shorting at the bottom after the peak

5. **How to deal with a snore pattern?**
   a. Buy early
   b. Avoid trading
   c. Short at the peak
   d. Buy at the bounce

6 – **What does a crow pattern indicate?**
   a. A progressive increase in price with sideway price action between increases
   b. A quick spike in price breaking new highs
   c. A progressive decrease in price over time
   d. An irregular price action with no discernable pattern

Homework

- Find popular stocks other people are watching (gurus, experts, etc.) and talking about. For each of these stocks, determine the following information:
    o Chart patterns for each stock
    o Explain the chart features
    o Attempt to predict future movement based on the chart pattern
    o Apply the pattern recognition to one-day, one-minute, five-minute, 15-minute, and 30-minute charts

Chapter II.7 - Understanding Catalysts

Overview

Here, we examine stock catalysts, how they affect price action, and how you can use them in your trading.

Goals

The goal of this chapter is for you to become familiar with the concept of catalysts and to understand the effect that each type of catalyst has on the price action of any given stock.

At the end of this chapter, you'll understand what each catalyst does and how you can exploit them to help generate profits on trades.

What is a Catalyst?

Just like in chemistry, a catalyst is something that accelerates a reaction on a certain type of solution. When it comes to penny stocks, catalysts are events that affect the price action and create momentum.

There are different types of catalysts that create a movement in the price of a stock. Each has its own particularities and intricacies when it comes to moving an instrument either positively or negatively.

Earnings Winner

The SEC requires public companies in the U.S. to file earnings reports every quarter (three months). These provide the shareholders with all the necessary information regarding the financial health of the company, along with detailed revenue and profit numbers.

The exact dates for earning reports vary from company to company.

An earnings winner is a company that has a positive reaction to earnings and is able to generate enough hype to force the stock price to rise in a very quick manner. This is especially true with penny stocks.

Penny stock earnings winners can run up for multiple days and even weeks, as news takes longer to be priced in in this niche. Successful ones are often subjected to morning spikes and gap-ups.

Earnings winners are often an indicator of a potential long position, by identifying key resistance, key support and watching for breakouts past the resistance line or dips at the key support.

Figure II.7.1 - StocksToTrade - TZOO Quarterly Earnings Report

It's important to consider that the earnings numbers alone aren't as important as reaction to the earnings. This means that while positive earnings may mean a hike in price, it may do just the opposite depending on context.

If a company reports strong earnings numbers for the most recent quarter but warns of slowness in the future, the stock price will likely react poorly, as future concerns outweigh past performance.

The reaction to the earnings is what drives the stock price, so pay close attention just after earnings are reported and how people react. Conversely, bad past or present earnings still may result in a stock price spike if management hypes up future products or future earnings.

Earnings must be matched with price action, not guessed ahead of time – too many traders attempt to do this, with very low odds of success.

It's dangerous to short sell or bet against earnings winners, as the downside can be minimal, and conversely the upside can last longer than expected.

Contract Winner

More random in nature, and depending on the day-to-day actions of the company, a contract usually means a positive cash flow into the company by means of an agreement between the company and a third party acquiring their products or services.

Similar to earnings winners, contract winners are often an indicator of positive price action with the chance of potential morning spikes and gap-ups. Contract winners are usually potential long positions and can run over multiple days.

When the contract is won from the government or a major brand, the effect on price action is even more pronounced. This usually provides additional credibility to the event and creates more interest among traders, thus driving the price action up.

Much like earnings winners, contract winners can be exploited in the same manner on the upside, by establishing key resistance and support, and observing how the price action moves around those levels.

It's also dangerous to short contract winners, for much the same reasons as earnings winners.

Figure II.7.2 - StocksToTrade - SYRX contract win with NASA on Apr 7th 2015

The News

Media information can affect the company directly or indirectly.

News can take many forms for traders: news networks, blogs, articles from reputable sources, social media, PRs, etc. When it comes to price action, they can either affect a stock positively or negatively depending on the information being advanced to the reader/watcher.

Stocks are real companies (for the most part) and their business models revolve around the state of the world. So news affecting the given stock's industry, main operational field or competitors may have a direct impact on its price action.

This is where understanding the fundamental factors is critical in predicting how the stock price may move.

Take for example the August 2014 news frenzy over police violence in Ferguson, Missouri. Issues with police behavior raised awareness for the necessity of some type of oversight or control over the actions taken by each officer. This became more prominent as the situation escalated over the following weeks. Emotions ran extremely high.

Figure II.7.3 - StocksToTrade - DGLY daily chart, news mid-August 2014

This led to police departments acquiring wearable cameras to help control and oversee the actions of their officers post-event. One of the main companies in this industry, Digital Ally Inc., designs and manufactures these types of devices for law enforcement. Traders know this company as DGLY, a stock that jumped from around $3.00/share to $34.00/share within two weeks. Check it out in Figure II.7.1.

In this case, the news influenced the company and created a viable business opportunity that resulted in winning contracts with various law enforcement agencies. Companies in the same industry also encountered the same type of behavior in their price, what can be called a "sympathy play," with traders expecting the price to do just as the big winner did. Figure II.7.4 shows such a stock.

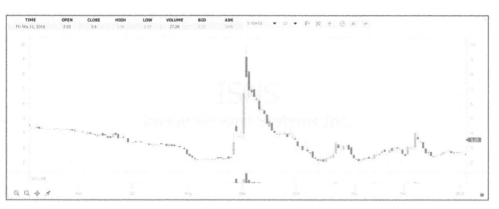

Figure II.7.4 - StocksToTrade - ISNS daily chart - DGLY sympathy play mid-August 2014

Stock price action driven by news can be played both long and short depending on the context and the events being reported.

Hype, Speculation and Anticipation

Hype, Speculation and Anticipation are all within a subset of news. Stocks that move based on these factors are hard to play unless there are very strong factors that drive the price.

Hype is a social behavior where a company or a product might seem to be a bigger deal than it actually is. It defies the laws of sense and is entirely based on the emotional response to a brand, product, or the feeling that these bring to the hype "leaders". The rest of the sheep then follow and the end result is a snowball movement in price action that will drive the stock up.

Hype is usually associated with a positive reaction; however, hype does die down and as it decreases, so does the price.

Hype plays allow a trader to trade both the long and short sides of the price action, as the price in these types of plays tends to overextend before retracing all its gains within a matter of hours.

The danger in hype plays is that a stock may continue to rise and draw attention to the company, thus creating a situation where additional news may arise, and with it the price. Though uncommon, it's possible. Conversely, it may seem like the price may keep on rising, only to encounter a cliff and nosedive into the rocky shore.

Trade hype plays with caution, since they tend to be unpredictable in their price action behavior.

Figure II.7.5 - StocksToTrade - CUBA Daily chart, Obama announcement of improving relations with Cuba Dec 2014

Similarly, speculation and anticipation are usually pushed by so-called analysts who provide a great deal of "insight" into the reasons behind the potential imminent success of a given company. Often these analysts have a conflict-of-interest type of situation where it becomes beneficial for them to write these types of articles. This applies to a great percentage of analysts. Sad, but true.

Speculation and anticipation will often drive the price of a stock one way or the other depending on what is being presented by the speculator or analyst. It's often hard to trade these plays without having some good fundamental understanding of the traded instrument.

Figure II.7.6 shows speculation on the rise of price of CURM, a stock expected to announce a big upcoming service. The CEO was slated for an interview on Fox News. The company was supported by major industry players. CURM's price spike followed a February 3 conference call and 8-K (more on SEC Filings in Chapter III.4) filing on the Feb 5, indicating an agreement with a major record label. Speculation was rampant. However, Fox News did not feature the interview, and the stock's price immediately crashed the next day.

Figure II.7.6 - StocksToTrade - CURM daily chart - speculative price action and drop on news

Billionaire Plays

This trend has been in full effect since 2015. Stocks like VLTC, EARS, and XRX, among many others, have been very profitable for day traders when properly identifying the underlying catalyst.

The name of this type of catalyst says it all: "billionaire plays" bank on the concept of following the investment ideas of billionaire investors in small cap stocks and banking on the parabolic move that follows the announcement of such an investment.

The core idea is that when billionaires buy a stake in a small business, it boosts public credibility and traders are enticed to buy in a sheep-like mentality. "If the rich guys do it, it must be worth something!"

While billionaire plays result in parabolic moves, over time they have a strong resemblance to the behavior of a pump & dump (Chapter II.8) and must be traded with caution when entering a position late.

Profiting from billionaire plays relies on the trader identifying the investment or acquisition of a stake by a billionaire investor, and entering a buying position early in the process. Some stocks show gains over 100% in the course of a few days. Look at the example in Figure II.7.7 below.

Figure II.7.7- Billionaire Play - VLTC with 52% stake owned by Carl Icahn

Biotechs

Last but not least, the biotechs. While not a catalyst per se, they deserve a fair mention in this section. Biotech refers to biotechnology, a.k.a. more widely known pharmaceutical companies. They specialize in creating medicine and drugs with the intent to patent and license.

Biotechs follow a very specific set of rules, which makes it a very intricate niche for penny stocks. These rules are set by the development cycle that is involved in the creation of a drug. With each phase, you'll often see different type of price actions that are solely based on speculation, since these companies spend most of the development phase asking for money and not generating any type of income whatsoever.

The type of plays offered by biotechnology stocks are usually long-term positions focused on intimately knowing the traded instruments, their filing schedules, understanding their PRs and following the developments associated with their FDA statuses.

Biotechs are widely considered hard-to-play stocks due to their price-action unpredictability and the complexity of the process that leads the prices up and down. They are, however, profitable when properly understood. This, however, would be a course of its own, and isn't covered in this general course.

Summary

- Catalysts are a type of information that can create price-action in a stock.
- There are multiple types of catalysts.
- Earnings winners are good long and dip positions.
    - Don't short earnings winners.
- Contract winners are good long and dip positions.
    - Don't short contract winners.
- News can drive the price of the stock based on content.
    - They may be directly or indirectly related to the stock.
    - They may target the industry of a set of stocks; the most prominent in those sectors will be the most affected by the news.
    - The context will lead the price action either up or down, making it possible to play both long and short positions.
- Hype is a social type of behavior that drives price action based on emotional perception of a brand or product.
    - It can be difficult to play, as the price action is unpredictable based on fundamental factors.
    - It can be dangerous due to the risk of quick reversal of the price action and retrace of the previous movement.
- Speculation behaves similarly to hype based on expert opinions that may or may not reflect the reality of the company.
- Biotechs are a complex type of penny stocks with a very specific type of catalysts and rules that affect its price action.
    - Should be avoided by novice traders.

Questions

1. What is a catalyst?
a. A biotech term to indicate a potential increase in price
b. Negative news about a stock
c. Positive news about a stock
d. An event that may induce price action on a stock

**2. What action should be taken with earn-
ings winners?**
a. Short these stocks
b. Wait for momentum & price action and buy early
c. Buy pre-market and take profits on
the morning spike
d. Buy on dips at support

3. What are biotechs?
a. Stocks that focus on biological and
technological companies
b. Stocks in the pharmaceutical industry
c. Stocks that conform with FDA
rules
d. None of the above

4. How to deal with hype and speculation
a. Watch for price action and momentum and take a position if the
opportunity arises
b. Buy when news come out
c. Assume that the price will go up
and it is a good buy opportunity
d. Sell before the news are released

5. Which of these should never be shorted?
a. Contract winner with momentum
b. Earnings winner with momentum
c. Positive news with momentum
d. All of the above

Homework

- Find popular stocks other people are watching (gurus, experts, etc.) and talking about and. For each of these stocks, determine the following information:
  - What type of catalyst, if any, is at play?
  - What is the reaction to the catalyst (price and volume)?
  - What is the social media coverage of the catalyst?
- Take notes on the current behavior of the stock and try to determine how it will move based on the catalyst and resulting reaction.

Chapter II.8 - Understanding Pump & Dumps

Overview

Here, we examine the infamous "Pump & Dump" concept, and how to profit from its predictable price action.

Goals

The goal of this chapter is to provide you with a deep understanding on how a Pump & Dump works, how you can profit from it, and the dangers associated with trading these types of stocks.

At the end of this chapter, you'll be able to recognize the very characteristic chart of a Pump & Dump, and know what to look for when searching for potential plays. You'll know how to find promoters, and how to potentially profit from playing a Pump & Dump type of trade.

What is a Pump & Dump?

A pump and dump (P&D) is a stock that represents an often-worthless company that is being promoted as being worth a lot more than its real value.

P&Ds are often paid or uncompensated promotions mandated (in some cases) by a third party wishing to unload their shares for a profit in spite of other gullible traders who aren't experienced with these types of events.

The price action of a successful P&D is usually a gradual-but-strong rise in price for the duration of the promotion (the pump) until the promotion ends and there is a very quick drop in the price (the dump), bringing it back to its original state.

These promotions are crafted to entice the "make-money-fast" crowd, who are usually the most easily manipulated into gambling on the stock market for a quick – but unreal – profit.

Paid Promotions

Again, paid promotions are in most cases mandated by an unknown third party in possession of a large number of shares for a worthless company, obtained at a discounted price. In a pyramid scheme type of setup, the third party hires promoters to advertise the stock and drive its price up for a certain duration of time.

These types of promotions are characterized by a long bottom-line disclaimer stating the amount received to promote the stock in question. This is required by the SEC in order to remain in compliance with the rules and avoid having the trading halted for the stock. Promotions of this type often come as newsletters, blogs and paper mail promotions.

Uncompensated Promotions

The other type of P&D is uncompensated. This promotion is usually pushed by those building lists of paid followers of their subscription and access services.

In order to gain credibility, these types of promoters attempt to push the stock price up, offering their followers certain profits, before dropping the ball.

Uncompensated promotions are often less successful than paid promotions, due to the lack of "organized-crime" type structure that exists within the inner circles of paid promoters.

The Physiology of a Pump & Dump

The P&D is one of the most predictable patterns in penny stocks. Unlike other types of plays, the outcome is almost always the same.

A promotion often starts with a teaser mentioning an upcoming stock that will make a lot of money. This is often announced weeks in advance before the main course of the promotion starts, just to get people enticed.

Less successful promoters often skip that step and move directly to the promotion part of the P&D: the mailer promotion. This phase focuses on mass mailing subscribers with the promoter's pick of a stock with the sole purpose of pumping the price sometimes by up to 400% during the course of a couple of weeks, up to a month.

Figure II.8.1 - Multicharts - AMLH Pump & Dump Daily Chart

The main characteristic of this phase is the successive green days for a stock that has no real worth as a company or doesn't have any real product. Novice traders and the get-rich-quick crowd get caught in the hype, driving the price even higher.

The final phase of the P&D is the dump. Once the promoter's target price or maximum price achievable for the promotion has been reached, the promoter stops sending emails and people soon realize the scam. This phase is characterized by a very quick drop in price, often losing up to 75% of its value over a couple of days and going back to its pre-pump level within weeks.

Figure II.8.2 - Multicharts - AMLH daily chart, 95% drop

As for the promoters, they liquidate their free-floating shares as the promotion advances, and not the whole inventory at once. Let's take a closer look at this...

Promoters

The very basis of a P&D lies upon the promoters' capacity to successfully reach their target demographic and achieve a massive rise in price on a given stock. The world of promoters is quite complex, and follows a pyramid-like structure when it comes to who mandates and who promotes.

For a compelling, detailed description and in-depth workings of the world of promoters check out a presentation by "The Dean," a C-list penny stock promoter, at the Third Annual Pennystocking Conference in Las Vegas. It's available on a DVD called The New Rules of Pennystocking (Sykes & et al., The New Rules of Pennystocking, 2011), available on profit.ly, or Timothy Sykes's store.

Now let's do a quick overview of the various players in pennystocking promotion, with the aim of quickly understanding the role of each of these players when it comes to running a promotion.

Figure II.8.3 below shows the basic pyramid setup that exists in the realm of promoters and P&Ds.

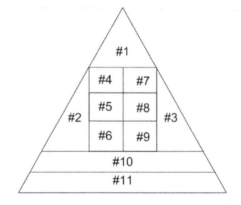

Figure II.8.3 - Stock promoter pyramid as presented by The Dean

#1 – The Smartest Man in the Room

At the top of the pyramid, we find "the smartest man in the room." This entity has obtained a large number of shares for a given company at a highly discounted price and is usually responsible for bringing the company public through a reverse merger or S-1 registration. This entity provides the base capital for the promotion and its identity is concealed by multiple corporations. Usually has no interest in the company or the product.

#2 – The Quarterback

The QB promoter has the responsibility of building a "team" of promoters and paying them in cash to perform the promotion. They are directly paid by the Smartest Man in the Room in either cash or free-trading stock. By knowing which promoters are successful, they make some easy money. They are also legally liable, as they are the "companies" that appear as compensating the promotion in the legal disclaimers.

#3 – Private Placement Subscribers

They purchase free-trading stock at a discount in order to trade during the public opening. Private placement subscribers usually know about the promotion in advance through a "verbal agreement" with the Smartest Man in the Room.

#4 – The A-Lister

These so-called "grave diggers" get paid the most to ensure that their subscribers hold the stock for the long term, as an investment. Their promotions usually start later than all other promoters. A-List promoters continually reinvest a percentage of their gains to reel in more subscribers, and they're usually the ones at the top of paid ads in search engines. They're the most in demand and are usually booked a month in advance.

#5 – The B-Lister

B-Listers may offer their subscribers a better chance to do well while trading this stock. Like the A-Listers, they must continually reinvest part of their gains to gather more subscribers, though to a lesser extent. They usually start covering the promotion before the A-Listers promote.

#6 – The C-Lister

C-List promoters are the smallest promoters in the group. They receive modest cash compensation per promotion. C-Listers often start the promotion in conjunction with other C-List promoters as a group, and usually don't have the resources or know-how required to build more efficient lists. C-Listers often fly under the radar and have less respect for SEC laws. They must usually scavenge for deals with the QB promoters, but can make up to $25,000 a month.

#7 – Promotion Insiders

This is an entity with first-hand knowledge of how and when the promotion will take place. It might include individuals or companies that know about the promotion deal. They are often the ones to jump the gun and start buying shares before the start of the promo, in anticipation of the move. Promotion insiders are usually the ones selling on the day that the promotion begins. They're often responsible for 'killing' promotions by engaging in this type of behavior.

#8 – Pre-Promo Buyers

Pre-promo buyers are speculators on upcoming promotions who buy shares of the company preemptively in order to benefit early from the price spike. They base themselves on recent trading volume and price swings to determine which stocks are worth playing, but take a lot of speculative risks.

#9 – Traders with Sheep-like Followers

These traders may play a stock before, during or after the promotion takes place. They have profitable track records that novice or inexperienced traders follow blindly by simply following their trades. This provides the traders with background support from their followers performing the same trades. They usually have an advantage over other traders because of their following base.

#10 – Newsletter Suckers Who Trade the Promoted Stock (NSWTPS)

NSWTPS buy a promotion based on the recommendation of a promoted stock. This is usually the category in which penny stock traders with knowledge of a P&D fall into as well as traders who don't necessarily realize that it's a promotion. NSWTPS will stay in the trade for a very short period of time, and exit their positions within 48 to 72 hours.

#11 – Newsletter Suckers Who Trade the Promoted Stock & Believe Long Term

These types of traders are at the bottom of the pyramid and buy the stock based on the recommendation of a newsletter, usually put forth by A-List promoters. They believe all the hype and half-truths advanced by the promotion and believe in the possibility of a viable long-term investment without realizing that it's a worthless company. They are the ones who lose the most money.

Mailing Lists

Subscriber-based mailing lists are the foundation of promotions. As you've learned, promoters invest a great deal of money into building subscriber lists they can send their promotions to.

Finding Promoter Mailing Lists

This is usually as simple as searching for terms like "hot stock tips," "stock tips," or similar wording/synonyms and looking for the top paid and unpaid results provided by search engines.

There are tons of promoters, and very few are successful. Finding the right ones means doing some research and finding how well the promotion for a given promoter has done.

"Pump tracking" tools may offer some insight as to which stocks are currently being promoted, as well as the amount of compensation received. These websites often come and go, but can provide useful insight about a promotion.

Subscribing

Many promoters send promotions through e-mail subscription lists. To be successful in tracking these promotions usually means subscribing to a fair amount of mailing lists. This also means going to each of the promoters' sites and signing up with your email address.

It's good practice to use a separate email account to receive mailing list promotions, in order to separate these types of messages from all your other relevant emails.

When it comes to which promoters to follow, the list changes constantly. Some become more successful; others disappear. The game changes quickly. The absolute best place to find the latest pumps is Timothy Sykes's chatroom (sign up at http://timothy-sykes.com/plans). There are usually over 1,000 traders in the chatroom looking for signs of pumping... a thousand pairs of eyes are better than one.

Price Action, Volume and Patterns

P&D follow a very specific pattern that often repeats over time. It's easily recognized when taking a look at the chart.

A promotion usually focuses on a stock that normally has very little to no trading volume over the past few months. Keep in mind that promotions aren't usually run twice for the same stock in the short term.

Figure II.8.4 - Multicharts - ECRY daily chart - Pump and Dump

In the weeks before the promotion starts, there's usually an increase in volume but price action remains flat. This is known as the pre-pump stage and is what pump speculators (#8 in our promoter pyramid) look for. It's also where all the upper pyramid blocks have their hands.

The second phase of the promotion is when the promotion finally starts and the emails start to go out. Successful promotions are marked by a massive increase in volume and a spike in price over the next few days or weeks (depending on how long the promotion lasts).

Promoters are usually hired for an unspecified period of time that varies from promotion to promotion.

The final stage of the promotion is the dump, when everyone (except for long-term bag-holders) realizes that the company is really worthless, and the price drops back to its original price point within a matter of days.

This, in essence, is how a P&D works...

> *"From many shares in the hands of few, to few shares in the hands of many"* – The Dean (Sykes & et al., The New Rules of Pennystocking, 2011)

How to Profit from Pump & Dumps

Now that we understand how P&Ds work, how can we make money from it?

P&Ds are highly predictable patterns that repeat over time. While the exact price action always varies from stock to stock, the daily charts are often very similar, sometimes to the point of a carbon copy from one P&D to the next.

Being predictable patterns, and knowing that the companies represented by the P&D aren't worth much (if anything at all), it's easy to plan for all possibilities in those cases. The hardest aspect of trading these types of stocks is timing, as you'll learn in Chapter II.10.

P&Ds can be profitable opportunities on both long and short sides if you've prepared by studying past setups and being ready for future setups.

Profiting Long

Making profits on the long side of a P&D is an art and can be risky. It takes practice and experience to achieve profitable results in buying a pump & dump, knowing the stock price will eventually collapse.

The key to taking a long position in these types of promoted stocks is to know about the promotion early, and getting in on the very first day when the price is near its multi-month average.

I must repeat: Taking a long position late in the pump is risky. Let's go into more detail about this.

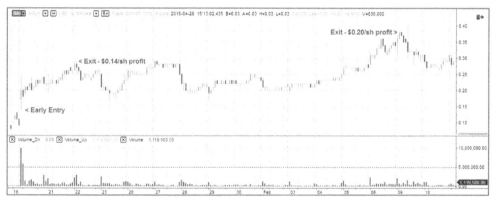

Figure II.8.5 - Multicharts - AMLH 30 minute chart, profiting long

Profiting Short

This is where most penny stock traders who follow this strategy make their money. Unlike taking a long position, a short position (covered in Chapter III.1) on a P&D is an assured gain, provided you obtain shares to short and have enough patience to hold through the dumping process.

While you might not know at which point the stock will encounter a reversal on the long side, the short side is practically guaranteed to be a success, considering the company itself truly isn't worth anything at all. The trick is finding shares to short, which can be a difficult process.

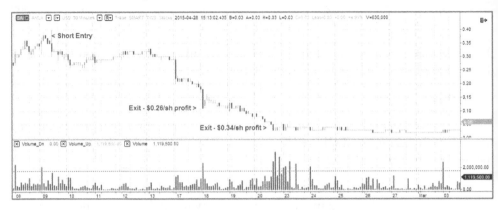

Figure II.8.6 - Multicharts - AMLH 30 minute chart - profiting short

However, shorting P&Ds does require good training, experience and an excellent understanding of how to trade these types of securities, which sometimes involves boxing a position (covered in detail in Chapter III.5).

Beware

P&Ds are very predictable patterns and can lead to very profitable trades, but only by understanding how they work – and more importantly, the risks associated with it.

Companies that are candidates for promotions are usually listed as OTC stocks since they don't meet the requirements to be listed under the major exchanges. OTC stocks are bound by a specific set of unspoken trading rules that make them difficult to trade without prior experience. I'll explain this in greater detail in Chapter III.3. Entering OTC stocks without understanding these rules can lead to major losses.

I must also repeat that the availability of shares to short for a P&D is often limited, making it difficult to short a stock right before the dump. This often necessitates the use of a technique called **boxing**, which you'll learn in Chapter III.5.

It's important to understand that trading P&D implies trading shady, worthless companies that have no real product or service to offer. You must also understand that these promotions do not always follow the rules, and companies can be subjected to SEC halts, which suspends trading until the company provides the necessary information to continue the trading. This is very dangerous for long positions, as post-halt price action can mean a 50-75% drop.

Bottom line. Don't trade P&Ds until you have completely familiarized yourself with Chapters III.1 (Short Selling), III.3 (Over-the-Counter Bulletin Boards) and Chapter III.5 (Position Boxing).

Summary

- Pump and dumps (P&Ds) are the result of paid promotions for shady, worthless companies.
- P&Ds rely on promoters' subscribers to pump the stock.
- P&Ds offer very predictable, repeatable patterns.
- Taking a long position in a P&D must be done early in the pump. Otherwise, it's very risky and can lead to potential losses.
- Taking a short position can be profitable, but timing is important.
- Beware of P&Ds, as they are often OTCBB stocks and exist within a different set of rules that must be understood.
- Complete Chapters III.1, III.2, III.3 and III.5 before attempting to trade P&Ds.
- The promoter structure is quite complex and there are multiple levels of penny stock promoters.
- Not all promotions are successful; some fail from the start.
- Most promoters do not lead successful P&Ds.
- Search for "hot stocks" or "hot stock picks" on your search engine and sign up to newsletters using a dedicated email account for pumps.

Questions

1. What is a pump & dump?
- a. A stock that spikes on news and keeps increasing over time
- b. A stock that drops in price following negative news
- c. A stock being artificially promoted in order to raise the price
- d. A stock with little to no value that is encountering a sudden increase in price action and momentum

2. What chart pattern does a pump & dump usually follow?
- a. Stair-stepper
- b. Snore
- c. Supernova
- d. Crow

3. Who are the promoters?
- a. Individuals on Twitter talking about the stock
- b. Companies paid to promote the stock
- c. Individuals who promote the stock to their followers in order to increase their reputation
- d. News networks and media

4. What is the purpose of a promoter list?
- a. To provide general news about the stock market to subscribers
- b. To tell subscribers about upcoming picks
- c. To tell subscribers about the best current pick
- d. To get traders to buy a security

5. Who mainly benefits from pump & dumps
- a. The Smartest Man in the Room
- b. The promoters
- c. Traders
- d. List subscribers

6. What type of stocks are usually the main focus of pump & dumps?
- a. NASDAQ securities
- b. AMEX securities
- c. NYSE securities
- d. OTCBB securities

Homework

- Open a dedicated email account for pump & dump promotions.
- Go on your favorite search engine and look for promoters. Sign up for their newsletters.
- Research each promoter. Establish their credibility by determining their last promotion and how well they've done in the past.
- Look for current promotions happening in the market and observe their behavior. Take notes on the price action behavior on a day-to-day intraday movement.

Chapter II.9 - Building a Watchlist and Doing Research

Overview

Here, you'll learn how research potential plays and establish a robust daily watchlist.

Goals

The goal of this chapter is to get you proficient at performing stock research and establishing a daily watchlist of stocks that will be potential plays for the next trading session.

At the end of this chapter, you'll be able to:

- Look for stocks and recognize the patterns and catalysts discussed in Chapters II.6 and II.7,
- Perform in-depth stock research and understand basic fundamental information
- Document your choices about why a stock should or shouldn't be on your list
- Rate your picks in terms of potential profitability
- Create your daily watchlist based on the information collected in the previous steps

Getting started

"Amat victoria curam" (victory loves preparation) – Latin proverb

The daily watchlist is among the most important tasks when it comes to trading penny stocks. It's one of the most crucial elements of learning Timothy Sykes' strategy, which is why he sends his subscribers a watchlist every night before the stock market opens the next day – to prepare students for the potential best setups. It represents your plan for the day. It establishes what you should be looking at, why you should be looking at it, and what you should expect from what you're watching.

Your daily watchlist allows you to have a proper strategy on how to play any given stock that you're watching, and to weed out the plays that are potentially profitable and separate them from the stocks that present no opportunity.

Building a watchlist is the last thing you do on your previous trading day and the first thing you do for the coming session. More importantly, this task represents the most work-intensive part of your trading process. Without it, trading is nothing more than an uninformed gamble with little information to make a decision.

At the end of the watchlist building process, you should end up with a list of no more than 10-12 potential picks. While the list could easily become longer, it's hard to concentrate on so many potential plays, as it often leads to missed opportunities within your own list. Ideally, you should focus on 5-6 top picks.

Not spending a good amount of time building a watchlist only leads to mediocre performance and/or losses. Don't risk it.

Finding Stocks

The first step in building a watchlist is finding potential stocks that represent profitable opportunities for the next trading session. Being able to identify these stocks takes knowledge and experience.

In order to do this step, you must be intimately familiar with Chapter II.6 in order to quickly identify profitable patterns, and Chapter II.7 to understand which stocks are being driven by events, and Chapter II.8 to know which are pump & dumps.

Here are some ways to start building a list of potential stocks, and filter the good ones from the less interesting plays.

The examples below will show you how to use some of the tools described in Chapter I.8 when it comes to actually performing stock research for potential plays. While this isn't an exhaustive description of all the ways to find your stocks, you'll learn the foundation of how to do so. Look around and find your favorite tools.

Google Spreadsheets

While not a finding tool in itself, Google spreadsheets allow you to quickly list your initial picks before doing in-depth research.

Below is a Google spreadsheet that I used to prepare my lists and input my initial picks, then cleaned up to only reflect my main plays.

Symbol	Action	RU %	N	Res.	Sup.	Up.	Down.	$ Goal	Rating	Info	Notes	Concerns
Capital	$12,120.77								★			
OREX		1.00%	$0.5114	$9.38, $9.10	7.40	1.5	1.64	0.5-1.00	3	P230 - N0.5114	This biotech stock is a $3+ winner yesterday and finally encountered some resistance at $6.10 before dropping down to the 6.70s on multiple occasions. $9.10 was retested 3 times before a major drop in price back to around $7.64 at close. Potential short if it spikes some more during the day.	The price may spike some more, possibly back to its resistance level at the $9.10 level before it is worth shorting. Lots of sqeezes on this play yesterday.
GENE		1.00%	$1.6386	$5.48	$5.34	1.5	0.35	0.4-0.5	2	P70 - N1.6385	This biotech stock has been on the watchlist for multiple days. Price has been overexetended for a while but price action has not been kind to traders. Potential short every day.	Very irregular stack, lots of traders getting burned both on the long and short sides. Trade with caution.
EYES		1.00%	$1.5957	$14.79	$14.59	2.5	1	0.3-0.5	2	P70 - N1.5957	Eyes is on its second red day after a $2 spike a couple of days ago, currently in the high $14s, may possibly revert to the $12 or $10 price point.	Shortable shares are hard to borrow on IB, lots of competition to enter this play as a short.
BIOC		1.00%	$0.7450	$3.48	$3.26	0.8	0.16	0.3-0.5	2	P160 - N0.745	This is another overextended biotech stock as has been the trend lately, lots of these plays going around. This is a potential short on a daily basis.	Shares are hard to find and the stock has also presented irregular price action.
ONCY		1.00%	$0.1450	$1.22, $1.40	$1.12	0.32	0.2	0.2-0.3	2	P830 - N0.145	potential short similar to GENE, BIOC and EYES	May attempt to spike, share availability
TSRI		1.00%	$0.1671	5.50	4.75	1.3	0.3	0.3-0.5		P720 - N0.1671	potential short similar to OREX	May spike some more before dropping down, too high priced
RESN		1.00%	$1.8421	$11.00	$10.40	2	0.5	0.4-0.75	2	P60 - N1.8421	This stock is a potential buy on price action. It had a favorable Seeking Aiona article that yielded no immediate results in price action, keeping it a relatively boring play; it later reached $10.94 from it's $10.45 level.	Yesterday was marked by a big drop followed by a recovery by the time it reached close; this stock might be boring today if price action and volume are not there to move it
TIVO		1.00%	$0.2971	$11.54	$11.17, $11.12	0.5	0.12	0.3-0.4	2	P400 - N0.2971	earnings winners, potential buy or dip buy	Price action may fail on 2nd day
EFUT		1.00%	$0.0829	$4.25	$3.73	1.3	0.5	0.3	2	P1460 - N0.0828	earnings winners, potential buy or dip buy	Price action may fail on 2nd day
IFON		1.00%	$0.1129						2	P1070 - N0.1128	ID - earnings winner	

Figure II.9.1 - Google Spreadsheets watchlist and pick details

As you see in Figure II.9.1, that's my personal way of gathering stock information and organizing my data prior to posting my watchlist on my blog. It's your job to create a system that suits your needs in terms of how you collect and sort your information.

Timothy Sykes does this with Microsoft Word. Some users use the built-in Profit.ly (http://profit.ly) watchlist sharing utility. You'll establish your own stock acquisition method. Everyone is unique.

Finviz

As seen in Chapter I.8, Finviz is a delayed data stock screener for listed stocks. It provides a neat way to quickly find stocks based on user-determined filters.

What you should look for:

- Stocks under $5 or $10, ideally under $5 per share
- Average volume above 50K, 100K or 200K
- Price change up 5%-10% or more

This type of filter allows you to find stocks that are up 5%-10% within the pennystocking range.

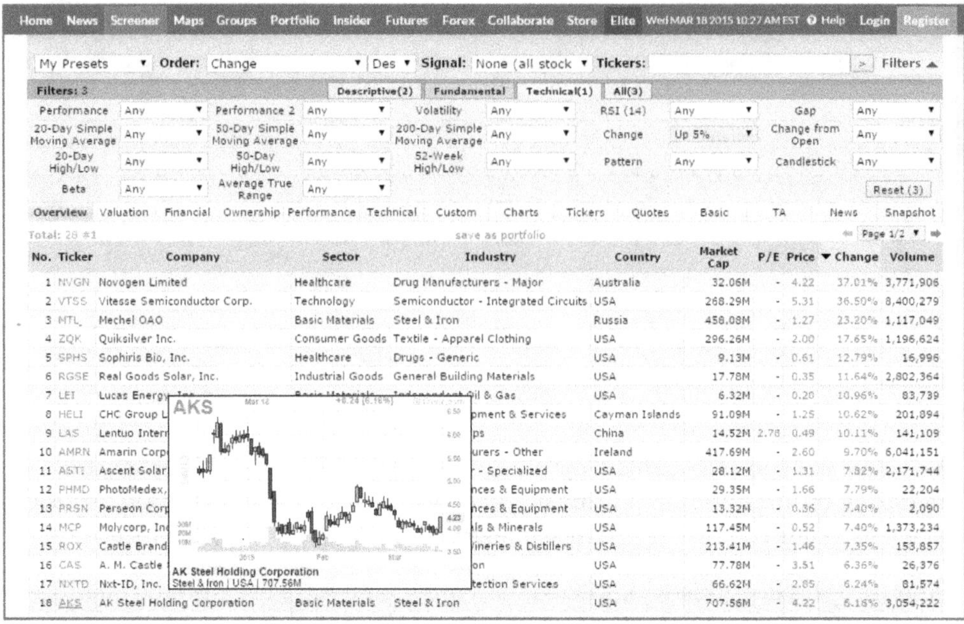

Figure II.9.2 - Finviz screener

Figure II.9.2 shows the results of the Finviz screen with filters applied and results returned. Finviz lets you to quickly look at charts by hovering the mouse over the stock ticker, so you can recognize chart patterns and add them to your temporary list for further analysis.

Stockfetcher

Stockfetcher is a paid alternative to Finviz with a great range of features to help you perform much more precise in-depth filtering of all available stocks based on your defined filters. What sets it apart is the ability to program your own filters using their scripting language.

Providing a list of filters to find potential plays is outside of the scope of this course because the possibilities for creating filters is limited only by users imaginations and their capacity to understand how the scripting language works. Stockfetcher offers a good primer to help you achieve this task.

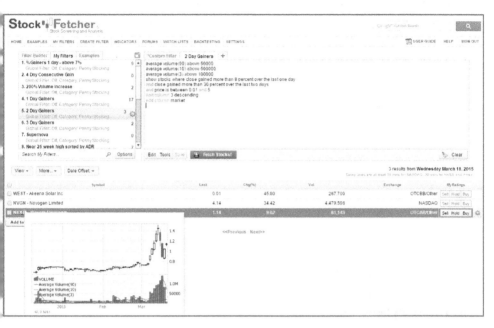

Figure II.9.3 - Stockfetcher filter

Much like Finviz, Stockfetcher lets you to hover the stock ticker and quickly view the stock chart so you can recognize chart patterns and add them to your temporary picks.

However, unlike Finviz, Stockfetcher also covers OTCBB stocks.

StocksToTrade

StocksToTrade (STT) is an advanced programmable scanner that lets you quickly find potential plays based on a wide availability of real-time quotes.

Among the main features of STT is the real-time scanner of stocks that have earnings, news and filings. It filters these in terms of price range and volume range, among many other criteria.

This is a real-time version of StockFetcher, making it ideal to quickly identify potential plays intraday.

Biggest % Gainers $10 and under

Time	Symbol	Market	Bid	Ask	Last	Net Change	% Chg	Volume	Trades
11:16:05	TRXC	AMEX	2.69	2.70	2.71	0.63	+30.29 %	6,100,541	13214
11:16:06	ICA	NYSE	1.16	1.17	1.15	0.2333	+25.45 %	372,542	513
11:16:01	MNKD	NASDAQ	1.12	1.13	1.11	0.1881	+20.53 %	10,671,531	19958
11:15:50	CAPN	NASDAQ	1.53	1.55	1.54	0.26	+19.33 %	1,924,309	3465
11:15:53	KTCC	NASDAQ	7.51	7.53	7.50	0.94	+14.33 %	95,409	388
11:14:42	ALQA	NASDAQ	1.78	1.78	1.7772	0.1972	+12.46 %	50,238	175
11:09:27	BBEPP	NASDAQ	6.22	6.38	6.23	0.66	+12.25 %	93,695	245
11:15:59	EARS	NASDAQ	4.83	4.86	4.88	0.49	+11.16 %	403,380	1205
11:16:06	SUNE	NYSE	3.38	3.39	3.36	0.31	+10.82 %	20,341,496	34868
11:16:02	BCEI	NYSE	2.74	2.75	2.77	0.27	+10.80 %	1,426,871	7203
11:13:44	TOLWF	PINKSHEETS	1.04	1.07	1.0551	0.101	+10.59 %	53,727	121
11:15:48	CJES	NYSE	2.08	2.09	2.09	0.20	+10.58 %	631,322	1459
11:15:01	JPEP	NYSE	4.16	4.28	4.18	0.39	+10.29 %	57,419	186
11:15:22	ZHNE	NASDAQ	1.60	1.62	1.5173	0.1373	+9.95 %	75,373	142
11:15:52	AMDA	NASDAQ	1.49	1.51	1.4927	0.1237	+9.04 %	616,811	1226
11:16:00	CIG	NYSE	1.20	1.21	1.21	0.10	+9.01 %	1,378,656	1275
11:13:26	EBR	NYSE	1.23	1.24	1.24	0.10	+8.77 %	83,746	120

Figure II.9.4 - StocksToTrade Biggest % gainers for stocks under $10

STT has many research features, and centralizes all the necessary information in relation to the stock being examined.

Much like StockFetcher, it's hard to cover all the possible ways of finding plays, but focusing on the biggest gainers screens, percent gainers with earnings, and percent gainers with news is typically key to finding potential plays intraday. Screen examples are shown in Figures II.9.4 and II.9.5.

STT's main advantage it's fantastic real-time scanner, plus its ability to help you efficiently and quickly find potential picks for your list.

Earnings in past 24 hours up 5% intraday 24h

Time	Symbol	Market	Bid	Ask	Last	Net Change	% Chg	Volume	Trades
11:16:17	KTCC	NASDAQ	7.50	7.55	7.50	0.94	+14.33 %	95,409	388
11:16:41	HA	NASDAQ	36.61	36.74	26.74	4.39	+13.57 %	3,080,659	18284
11:16:17	FFIC	NASDAQ	21.74	21.84	21.80	2.06	+10.44 %	53,435	543
11:16:44	TEX	NYSE	22.42	22.45	22.45	1.95	+9.51 %	5,257,071	21101
11:16:40	EVER	NYSE	14.21	14.22	14.21	1.16	+9.06 %	431,383	3132
10:04:13	RILY	NASDAQ	9.05	9.80	9.80	0.75	+8.29 %	335	6
11:16:43	ELP	NYSE	4.98	4.99	4.99	0.36	+7.76 %	253,735	1091
11:16:13	DQ	NYSE	14.48	14.89	14.74	1.06	+7.75 %	61,321	405
11:15:24	HMST	NASDAQ	20.65	20.70	20.64	1.33	+6.88 %	188,796	1435
11:16:44	MTG	NYSE	6.40	6.41	6.40	0.41	+6.84 %	6,197,680	10626
11:16:42	OAS	NYSE	5.50	5.51	5.51	0.35	+6.78 %	4,852,094	19631
11:16:43	BIIB	NASDAQ	276.97	277.38	277.21	17.34	+6.67 %	1,889,580	18368
09:59:16	VALU	NASDAQ	14.25	15.20	15.20	0.88	+6.07 %	146	3
11:16:34	GIB	NYSE	42.05	42.12	42.0501	2.0001	+6.50 %	235,389	1261
11:16:06	BELFA	NASDAQ	12.73	13.47	13.84	0.84	+6.45 %	5	2
10:47:07	CCM	NYSE	4.72	4.78	4.7385	0.2885	+6.01 %	19,787	93
11:16:45	FCB	NYSE	33.04	33.12	33.04	1.87	+6.00 %	201,016	946

Figure II.9.5 - STT Scan showing Stocks up 5%+ with Earnings over the last 24h

STT also offers pre-programmed filters with a fast overview of the relevant stocks at play. These filters are based on Timothy Sykes's winning strategies, providing quick access to stocks that match the play criteria used in penny stock trading. You'll see some of the available filters in Figure II.9.6.

Timothy Sykes uses STT as his top tool to find his potential plays, establish his daily watchlists, and execute intraday picks. The figure below shows a screenshot of the various filter categories offered by STT.

Figure II.9.6 - StocksToTrade - List of pre-programmed filters

Another STT benefit is that it's designed as a trading platform from the ground up, providing advanced charts, time and sales, Level 2, and stock behavioral events. Figure II.9-7 shows the basic interface.

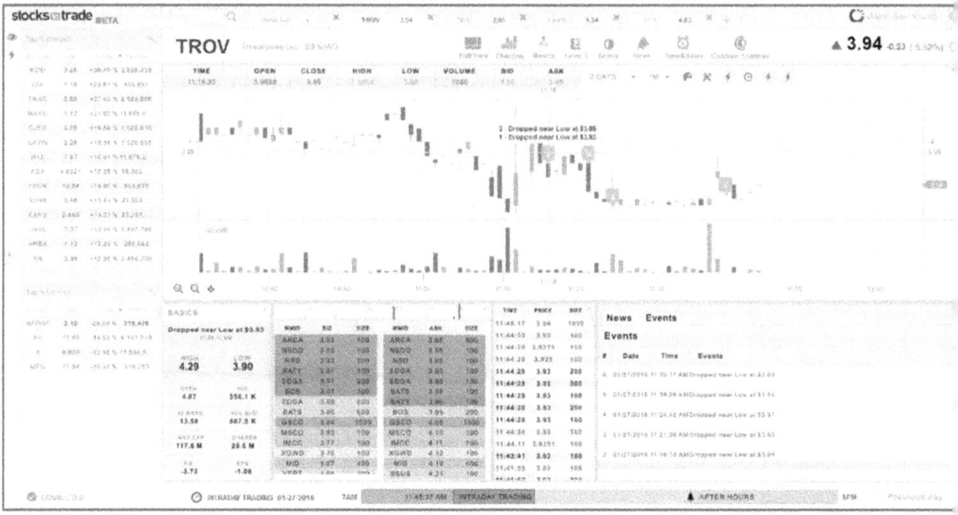

Figure II.9.7 - StocksToTrade - Trading Platform

STT has also features trading capabilities from within its software, making this application the ultimate tool for penny stock day traders – a pennystocking one-stop-shop.

Yahoo Finance

This is an excellent free resource for both finding potential plays and performing in-depth research on stocks, which we'll cover later on.

In order to find potential plays, Yahoo Finance offers a practical tool called "Market Movers", which basically displays the most active stocks, the 10 highest percent gainers and the 10 highest percent losers.

Yahoo Finance recently implemented a real-time display for their market movers which applies to the biggest markets and updates every about second on their main screen.

Market movers can be found at the following link: http://finance.yahoo.com/stock center/#mkt-movers.

The not-so-great part: Recently, Yahoo Finance drastically changed its visual interface making it more difficult for day traders to quickly find the information they need.

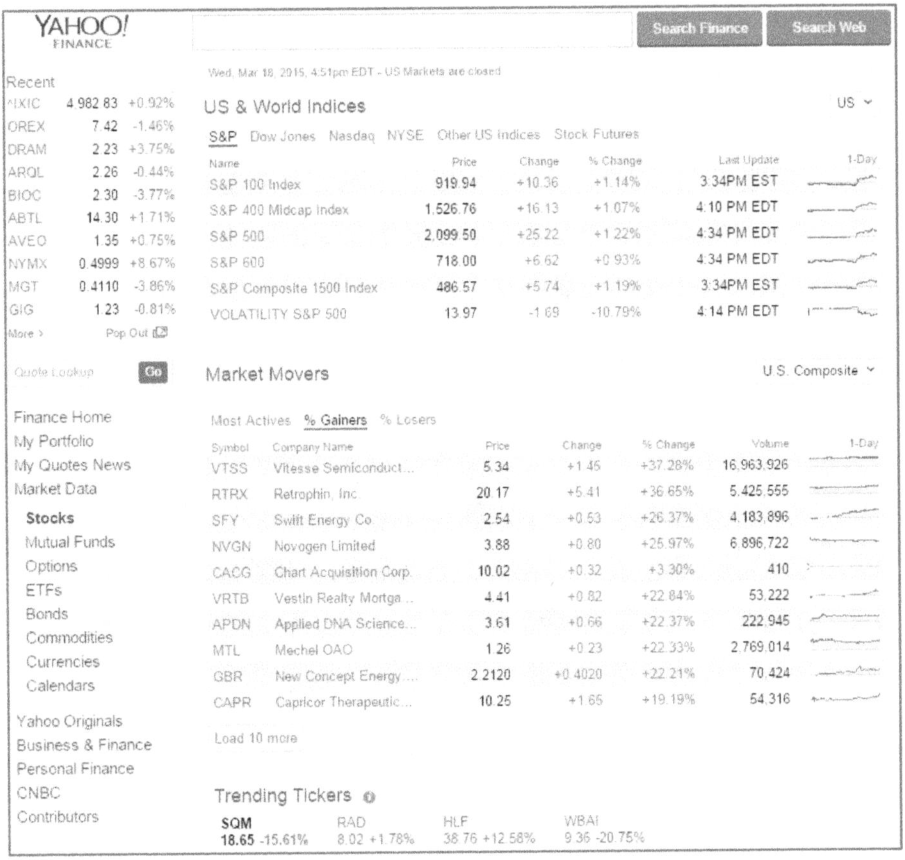

Figure II.9.8 - Yahoo Finance Market Movers

While the Market Movers display isn't customizable, it often displays plays that could be of interest as potential trade opportunities. The Market Movers screen appears in Figure II.9.7.

Seeking Alpha

Seeking Alpha (SA) focuses on providing expert articles and news for stocks. Moreover, traders have a tendency to rely on SA to make trade decisions, which sometimes has a pump-like effect when a new stock feature article is published.

In terms of picking potential plays, it's worth looking at their top and latest news in order to identify potential earnings and contract plays that might pop up.

Their news link is: http://seekingalpha.com/news/all

Twitter

This tool can be a source of great confusion as well as very select trade opportunities.

Knowing whom to follow is key to using Twitter to establishing potential watchlists. Your job is to identify and follow successful traders, and follow the people they follow. I recommend Michael Goode, Tim Grittani, Michael Croock, Timothy Sykes, Superman (Paul Scolardi) and LX21. Follow them, and follow those they follow.

The hard part in choosing potential stocks from Twitter is cutting down the noise and being able to recognize potential plays based on who provided the information and the context surrounding the mention of the stock.

Doing In-depth Research

At the end of the "finding" process, you should have a fair amount of stocks that are potential opportunities based simply on chart pattern and current price action. This preliminary list may have any number of tickers, based entirely on your findings.

Once that part is done, it's time to weed out plays of little to no interest. You do this via in-depth research into the stock fundamentals and taking a more demanding look at the patterns found versus the ideal trading patterns for your strategy.

Cutting Out the Weeds

You have your list and you're happy with it, but your job is far from done. Now you need to look at the different factors that can affect a stock and how it relates to your intended play.

First, identify how you want to play your stock. This is directly related to the type of strategy that you plan to use. How you ultimately word or establish your strategies is entirely up to you. Section IV provides a detailed look at the strategies developed by Timothy Sykes.

Once you've established the type of play that you want to follow for a stock, you focus on its fundamental aspect and take a second look at the chart.

To help weed out stocks in your list, ask yourself these questions:

- Is there a catalyst for this stock?
    - What is it?
- Is the price point near resistance/support?
- How has the stock done in the past?
- Why is the stock price up/down?

- Is it being promoted somewhere?
  - o   Is it a pump & dump?
- Is the company healthy or untrustworthy?
- How is the stock sector doing?

Chapter III.4 covers SEC filings, which involves a higher level of in-depth research when it comes to understanding the financials of a company, their financial health and knowing whether a company is or isn't providing a real product or service.

Keeping the Best Plays

While the aforementioned questions help you weed out the potential plays, you should always go one step further to keep the best plays at your reach...

Ensure that stocks that have proper catalysts matching the right chart pattern.

At the end of this process, you should end up with 5-6 top picks and a few other potential plays.

Rating and Categorizing Your Picks

Now that you have your picks and have a good idea why you should keep those on your list, you should rate and categorize your plays.

Rating Your Ricks

This concept is based on how LX21 trades. In one of his presentations (during the 2011 Annual Pennystocking conference, available on Timothy Sykes's Pennystocking Framework DVD), LX21 shared how he rates his picks from 1 to 4 based on tradability.

- 1 – Tradable
- 2 – Good
- 3 – Great
- 4 – The best

He also has a 5 rating that is the "11" on the volume knob. It's the cherry on top, the best of the best. They come rarely but offer the greatest potential for profitability. Unsurprisingly, these are often among his most profitable opportunities.

This will help you identify the picks you should truly keep an eye on and those that are less important to watch during trading hours.

Categorizing Your Picks

Categorizing in this context means connecting each of the picks with one of your trading strategies. This is particularly important when tracking strategy performance in the future and knowing exactly how you should behave with a given stock.

Knowing which strategy a stock belongs to tells you how to act when the right conditions present themselves, or it can tell you when not to act at all.

Documenting Your Choices

Now that you have your picks chosen, rated and categorized, it's time to document your choices of potential plays.

Documenting your choices not only helps you establish your hypothesis in writing, but it also helps reaffirm your initial ideas regarding the stock and the potential dangers.

Your Reasons for Choosing a Stock

The first part of documenting your picks is about clearly establishing the hypothesis behind the choice of any given stock by describing the reasons, patterns, price action, supports and resistances. You must also consider the past behavior of the stock in order to provide the big picture, rather than focusing on the tick-by-tick action.

Understanding past behavior is key to making informed decisions and taking calculated risks in a stock.

Your description should also state how a stock falls into a given strategy and why it does so.

Your Concerns with a Pick

The basic hypothesis covers why you chose a given stock, why you decided to add it to your watchlist, and what to expect from it. The other side of the coin focuses on any concerns that you may have with a stock, and what could go wrong once you decide to enter a position.

Clearly establishing concerns about potential plays adds another layer of preparation to your trading techniques. By making you aware of the possible negative outcomes that you could encounter, you'll be able to establish the necessary countermeasures beforehand.

Creating a Daily Watchlist

The final step consists of putting all of the collected information together in a manner that is easily readable and easy to use as a quick reference while the trading session is open.

This is usually located in your journal, blog, or whatever means you decide to use to document your day-to-day picks.

Creating a daily watchlist is not only crucial in giving you a quick reference during the trading session, but also provides you with a historical account of your picks over time, and how your choices rate as you gain experience.

The figure below shows how I present my own daily watchlists on my blog.

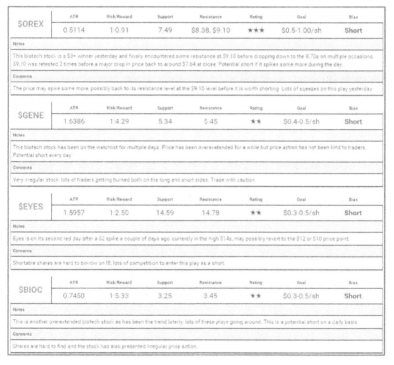

Figure II.9.9 - Red and Green Ninja blog, Daily Watchlist excerpt

What your watchlist truly represents is your trading plan for each potential opportunity that the market has to offer. The more dedication and attention to detail you put into developing a plan, the greater your chances of obtaining an acceptable outcome, regardless of how the opportunity turns out in reality.

Summary

- Creating watchlists is one of the most important steps when trading penny stocks.
    - o It represents your trading plan.
- Finding stocks requires the use of the tools, knowing the chart patterns, and what catalysts mean for each match.
    - o Choose based on known chart patterns.
    - o Choose based on your price, volume criteria.
- Doing in-depth research allows you to weed out potential plays from plays that have a low probability of yielding a profit.
    - o Find support and resistance lines.
    - o Multi-day, month highs and lows.
    - o Average true ranges.
    - o Price action and intraday movement.
    - o Past behavior.
    - o Find what trading strategy a stock fits into.
- Keeping the best potential plays is crucial to keeping your list to a reasonable size.
- Rating your picks will allow you to keep the focus on the most interesting plays in your list.
- Categorizing your picks by specifying the trading strategies they belong to will allow you to keep track of your performance and have a plan on how you should enter or exit a stock.
- Documenting your picks helps reaffirm your hypothesis and clearly state the reasons why a given stock is a potential play.
    - o Describe your hypothesis.
    - o Describe your concerns with the play.
- Publish your watchlist.

Questions

1. **What is the purpose of a watchlist?**
   a. To watch stocks that have done well in the past
   b. To watch potential trading opportunities and describe the potential behavior of the stock
   c. To follow individuals on various social media platforms and use their picks as potential opportunities
   d. To watch stocks that have done poorly in the past

2. **What tool does not represent a research tool per se?**
   a. Google Spreadsheets
   b. Yahoo Finance
   c. Stock Fetcher
   d. StocksToTrade

3. **What information should be included in your watchlist for each item?**
   a. Symbol
   b. Potential down side
   c. Hypothesis
   d. Risk reward ratio
   e. All of the above

4. **What should you look for when searching for potential plays to add to your watchlist?**
   a. Biggest gainers over the past few days
   b. Catalyst stocks
   c. Stocks with low volume and low volatility
   d. Past performers

5. **Which tools are ideal for creating a watchlist?**
   a. A notepad
   b. WordPress
   c. Profit.ly
   d. All of the above

6. **Why should you document your watchlist choices?**
   a. To know the mistakes that have been made in the past
   b. To keep track of the signals to look for during trading hours
   c. To establish the reasons why a stock may or may not encounter momentum
   d. You shouldn't document your choices

Homework

- Build a watchlist every day.
  - Find potential stocks using the tools at your disposal that match potentially profitable chart patterns.
  - If you subscribe to a guru watchlist, avoid looking at their picks until you have established your own list.
    - Compare for similarities and try to explain why your lists differ.
  - Do in-depth research to separate potential plays from boring ones.
  - Rate your picks and build your watchlist.
  - Document and publish your watchlist publicly.
    - Post it on Profit.ly.
    - Post it on your blog.

- Post it on Twitter.

Chapter II.10 - Entries and Exits

Overview

Here, you'll learn how to enter and exit a position based on various criteria that is established based on the information collected, as covered in the previous chapters.

Goals

The goal of this chapter is for you to become familiar with the concepts of entries and exits in regards to any stock that you wish to trade.

At the end of this chapter, you'll know:

- When to enter a position based on various criteria.
- How to time your entry based on price action and fundamental information about the stock.
- When to exit a stock.
- How to cut losses quickly when the price action affects your profits negatively.
- How to stick to your exit rules.
- How to lock profits and keep half positions open.

Introduction

Entries and exits are the final step in completing your basic understanding on how to trade penny stocks. Entering and exiting a stock is the result of the all the preparation that you've done throughout the previous chapters.

Entries and exits rely not only on all your preparation, but also on timing.

Much like in martial arts, during a sparring match, timing is essential in attacking or countering an opponent. If you strike too soon, you open yourself to be struck and not land your attack; doing so too late results in the same outcome.

In order to control the outcome of your trade, you must be able to understand the role of timing in both entries and exits.

Preparing Your Orders Before Trading

First, let's cover an important element for pre-trade preparation: improving your trade efficiency by preparing your order before your trade.

While entries and exits are the main concept of actionable trading, preparing orders is as important in saving time and being ready when a suitable event happens.

Creating an order takes time and usually involves performing the following actions:

- Choosing your trading instrument
- Entering an order type (MKT, LMT, STP, etc.)
- Setting the desired trade price and auxiliary values when needed
- Setting the desired position size

This process is time-consuming and can take more time than you'd like when a stock starts showing signs of interesting behavior.

Not preparing your orders usually means having to do this whole process while the price action is favorable, and can potentially lead to missing profitable opportunities. This is especially true in the world of penny stocks, where volatility and liquidity usually go hand in hand.

This can also be a limiting factor when trading OTC stocks, as we'll cover in Chapter III.3.

Preparing your orders in advance and only having to submit saves considerable time and increases your chances of properly timing your entry or exit without having to fiddle with setting your trade information in a rush.

It also allows you to quickly adjust your values as the stock price evolves and adapt to the situation.

Entry Strategies

Entry is the first phase of taking a position in a stock. Before entry, you're not subjected to any profit or loss due to the fluctuation of the stock price. When you enter a position you go from having a cash account to becoming a shareholder in that company, and automatically the value of your shares either goes up or down based on the price fluctuations.

When you enter a position, the position is considered to be "open"; this essentially means that you own shares (or owe shares if you're shorting, covered in Chapter III.1) of a stock at the price value per share of that stock for a total market value equal to:

$$\$\,Mkt\ Value = Position \times \$\,Stock\ average\ fill\ price$$

As mentioned previously, entering a stock heavily relies on timing. It's also necessary to understand technical analysis and the fundamental elements that drive the price.

Now let's cover some things to consider and ways to enter a stock with proper timing.

The Catalyst Entry

A catalyst entry relies on determining the impact of a given catalyst on a given stock. The various types of catalysts are covered in detail in Chapter II.7.

A catalyst usually results in a dramatic raise of trader's interest in a specific stock. In some cases, for the most potentially profitable picks, the direct consequence is a massive increase in trading volume and a gain in momentum either up or down, depending on the catalyst content and the context surrounding the stock.

Timing a catalyst entry usually means being early and spotting the stock right when the event happens – or in some cases before – by obtaining some insight through various sources and in-depth research.

Positive catalysts usually result in a spike, with a gain of momentum and a dramatic increase in price, that can range anywhere between $0.15 to $2+ depending on the stock, the catalyst and its popularity.

Conversely, negative catalysts may have the same effect on the way down.

A catalyst entry relies on the trader knowing the following information:

- Key resistance
- Key support
- Past behavior of a stock when subjected to a catalyst of the same type (news, contracts, earnings, etc.)
- Other traders' perception on the catalyst
- The catalyst source, popularity and credibility (the more popular the source, the higher chances of a spike or panic; think: Seeking Alpha articles)

Knowing the key resistance and support lines allows the trader to understand at which levels the stock price is likely to remain. It also provides the trader with a baseline to predict when a breakout or breakdown can occur.

Your catalyst entry point is determined by the established trading strategy for tha
stock, your hypothesis on the potential price action, and how it fares to the actual price
action when it happens.

Example:

Figure II.10.1 - Multicharts - DGLY 30 minute chart - catalyst entries

The Dip Entry

A dip entry is usually associated with a positive catalyst. Dips are often the results o
price spikes, where traders convert their profitable share into hard cash profits.

This type of event is reflected by a significant drop in price, in spite of the contextua
support offered by the catalyst.

A dip entry always involves a long position by expecting the stock price to bounce back
from a support level.

A dip entry relies on the trader knowing the following information:

- Intraday support and resistance
- Key support and resistance
- Stock past behavior on dips
- Quality of the catalyst

In order to enter a dip position, it's crucial to know both intraday and key support lines
This allows the trader to establish a baseline below which the price is not expected to
drop.

A dip buy typically involves having the trader taking a long position once the price ha
reached the support line without becoming a breakdown or fade situation.

This means that the traders will buy shares of the stock once the lowest possible support price has been reached and not crossed, with the expectation of a bounce back.

Stocks with a positive popular catalyst will often bounce from their support line and increase in price, sometimes breaking out past previous resistance levels as interest for a given instrument grows with the interest in the catalyst.

Example:

Figure II.10.2 - Multicharts - DGLY 30 minute chart - Dip entry

The Bounce Entry

Conversely to the dip entry, a bounce entry represents shorting (which we'll discuss in Chapter III.1) a stock with a negative catalyst that has bounced and reached a support line.

The hypothesis behind a bounce entry is that the stock price is going down due to a negative catalyst. This often causes the price to drop significantly. However, numerous traders often see this type of price action as an opportunity to "buy low and sell high". This collective mentality, in essence, causes a bounce in the stock price that will reach a resistance line before crashing again.

A bounce entry relies on the trader knowing the following information:

- Intraday support and resistance
- Key support and resistance
- Stock past behavior on dips
- Quality of the catalyst

Much like the dip entry, the bounce entry relies on knowing key and intraday resistance lines in order to determine what the maximum expected price is that the stock should reach during the bounce phase.

A bounce entry implies taking a short position at the resistance level once it's been determined that the stock won't breakout and remains at or below the resistance line.

Stocks with a negative popular catalyst will often dip from their resistance line and decrease in price, sometimes breaking down below previous support levels as panic for a given instrument increases with the interest in the catalyst.

Example:

Figure II.10.3 - Multicharts - SAAS 30 minute chart - Bounce Entry

Do Not Chase

Among the biggest mistakes that entry-focused traders can make: chasing stocks that have already gone up. Don't do this.

"Chasing" is when you feel like you missed an opportunity and attempt to profit from an already profitable stock that may have reached its peak for the current event.

It's always difficult to determine whether a stock will continue its momentum, but it's important to try and figure it out. This can be determined by performing in-depth fundamental analysis and taking a look at the stock's past behavior.

Chasing a stock without a good reason can lead to dangerous outcomes and significant potential losses. Just don't.

Example:

Figure II.10.4 - Multicharts - OREX 30-minute chart - chasing the price action

Exiting Strategies

Exiting a position is the converse action to entering. It's also known as "closing" a position and is usually marked by selling a long position or buying to cover a short position, as you'll learn in Chapter III.1.

While timing is very important when it comes to entries, and entries are the first step of actually taking a position in a stock, the role of exits is far more important, as it is the final and absolute determining factor on whether a stock becomes very profitable, profitable, a simple loss, or a cripplingly negative loss for your account.

> *"The turtles where taught not to fixate on when they entered a market. They were taught to worry about when they will exit." – Michael W. Covel (Covel, 2009)*

Knowing when you will exit your position is far more important than the entry because it establishes whether your trade will be profitable or losing.

Goals: To Set or Not to Set?

One question often asked by novice traders is whether a profit goal should be set in order to exit at a pre-determined profit.

Setting a profit goal implies establishing pre-trade how much profit one should take before exiting a trade. This is usually presented in the dollar amount per share or a total dollar amount profit for the trade.

On the upside, setting goals creates an expectation of how high the trader believes the price can potentially go. It also allows the trader to lock profits if the stock price is subjected to a price action reversal and the price suddenly drops.

On the downside, setting goals may prevent the trader from fully profiting from a trade opportunity – in some cases exiting long before the price has reached its peak. As Sykes says, it can be considered as "leaving money on the table".

Setting profit goals is left to the discretion of the traders. In some cases, setting goals can be beneficial, while in others it's a limiting element to potential profits. It all comes down to understanding the stock at play, the catalysts, and the context surrounding that instrument.

Cut Losses Quickly

Timothy Sykes's first and most important trading rule: **Cut losses quickly.**

It's simple as it gets. When a stock doesn't go your way and your losses reach your threshold, exit your position at once. Take your losses and move on. Don't wait for 5% 8% or 10% losses like many traders do, because penny stock trading is so inherently risky traders must reduce that risk by being extremely disciplined in not letting small mistakes turn into big disasters.

Cutting losses quickly is where the discipline section of Chapter I.5 really comes into effect.

Cutting losses quickly requires discipline. It requires a trader to completely separate from the illusory attachment to the money and make a logical, purely mathematical and statistical decision to exit a position at a loss – just like a computer or a robot with fixed programming would.

Not respecting this crucial rule is where the true danger of trading penny stocks lies. This is where 90% of traders lose money on the market.

In order to cut losses quickly, you must know what your exit strategy is. We examined this in Chapter II.4, when you learned risk management concepts and how to establish your absolute stops.

Cutting losses quickly means exiting a position at your absolute stop as soon as it is possible. Once you have reached your maximum loss threshold, **you must exit**.

Even when your absolute stop hasn't been reached, if the stock price doesn't behave as you expected in your hypothesis, **you must exit**.

In some cases, cutting losses quickly could prevent making potential profits, but more importantly, this golden rule protects traders from themselves by limiting the potential downside and setting clear limits about how much money should be lost at a very maximum on a given trade.

As you've learned in this course, Sykes and many other successful traders rely on mental stops in order to exit their positions once the price action no longer meets their criteria. This type of behavior requires a great deal of self-discipline and respect for the established rules.

Some traders prefer to set hard stops, which allows them to let the system decide when a position should be exited without having to deal with the emotional ramifications of making the decisions and expecting/hoping the price to "return" to a profitable point.

Successful traders distinguish themselves from losing traders with this penny stock trading golden rule: **ALWAYS CUT LOSSES QUICKLY**.

Stick to Your Rules

Another big rule you must follow is to stick to your strategy rules. This allows you to consistently perform similarly on resembling trades following the same set of behavior.

Each of your strategies will have their own set of rules pertaining to entries and – more importantly – to exits. Understanding and respecting these rules is mandatory to become a successful trader and maximize potential profits.

Sticking to your rules requires discipline and conviction, so ensure that you hone these personal traits in order to obtain repeatable results from one trade to the next.

Locking Your Profits and Half Positions

When it comes to exit actions, locking profits and keeping half positions is a way to ensure that, regardless of how the stock does in the future, you recover some cash whenever you have a successful trade that might continue to be profitable. It's often wise to take partial profits and let the rest of your shares play out.

Locking profits is often achieved by using your established profit goal as an indicator to partially exit a position.

Exiting a partial position implies that your unrealized profits for the shares you exit become realized and you end up with real, hard cash for half your play – while the rest keeps riding the stock wave.

From this point on, you can choose to continue letting the shares follow the stock price momentum and keep generating profits or, if the stock encounters a reversal, you may exit your position without being subjected to losses.

Example:

Figure II.10.5 - Multicharts - OREX 30 minute Chart - locking profits & taking half positions

Conclusion

Entries and exits are the last and final phase into understanding the basic concepts of trading penny stocks. All the chapters leading this point have provided you with all the necessary information required to start trading and evolve into a self-sufficient trader.

But if you think you're done with your training, think again. You must keep studying and practicing in a big way. Trading penny stocks requires an intimate knowledge of these concepts, rules, strategies and patterns. As long as you trade without possessing a reflex-like knowledge of these ideas, you're trading with gambling-like behavior. Please don't risk it.

Summary

- Prepare your orders pre-trade to be ready to simply submit when the timing is right.
- Time your entries based on catalysts and the desired play strategy.
    - Catalyst entry, price action, support and resistance.
    - Dip buy, catalyst, price action, support and resistance.
    - Bounce short, catalyst, price action, support and resistance.
- Always remember to **CUT LOSSES QUICKLY.**
- Exit based on your absolute stops and respect your risk management rules.
- Exit based on your strategy.
- Exit when you no longer feel confident about the behavior of a trade or when faced with uncertainty.
- When necessary, lock your profits for half your position and let the other half keep riding the stock momentum, or exit based on your strategy and risk management rules.

Questions

1. Which stocks should you prepare orders for?
a.   All the stocks that I can find.
b.   All the stocks on my watchlist.
c.   The stocks most likely to display price action and momentum.
d.   You should not prepare your orders until the stock shows price action.

2. When should you exit a losing position?
a.   As soon as the stock doesn't do what was expected of it.
b.   As soon as the stock reaches the stop threshold.
c.   As soon as the investment for that position starts moving back up.
d.   As soon as the stock price action reverts and provides profits.

3. What does cut losses quickly mean?
a.   You should exit a position when the position in the stock is no longer satisfactory.
b.   You should always be quick about recovering losses right after they happen.
c.   You should wait for the price to go back up and cut your losses when you get some gains.
d.   You should never cut your losses and wait for the stock to spike.

4. Why should you stick to your rules?
a.   To minimize losses and maximize profit over time.
b.   Because it is necessary to become a successful trader.
c.   You should only use rules as general guidelines.
d.   Because I've been told to do so.

5. What does locking profits and half positions mean?
a.   You should always trade half the number of shares you normally would and profit from them.
b.   When a stock behaves as expected and surpasses your goals, you should exit half your position and let the rest play.
c.   You should add half the number of shares you originally had to the current position in order to increase the potential gains.
d.   None of the above.

Homework

- Based on your daily watchlists (Homework Chapter II.9), establish the following information:
  - Support and resistance (including key levels).
  - Establish a potential entry point.
  - Using the RMS set your absolute stop based on your expected entry point.
  - Document how the stock moves at your potential entry point.

- o Document how the stock has moved at your exit point determined by your trading parameters (profit goal, absolute stop).
- Follow the stock real time and observe its behavior.
  - o Prepare your orders on your platform and be ready to enter a position without relying on direct external factors to influence your decision (i.e. People stating their entries in chats, alerts, Twitter, etc.)
  - o Enter a trade on a stock you're watching with a very small position ($50-$100 position market value) at your expected entry point (based on your hypothesis and stock research).
    - Let the stock play.
    - Exit the position when your hypothesis is no longer confirmed.
    - Exit the position when your absolute stop is reached.
    - Set a profit goal of $0.15-$0.30 per share depending on the opportunity.
    - Stick to listed stocks (NASDAQ, NYSE, AMEX).
  - o Repeat this process as long as necessary to increase your experience. Attempt to make 100% cumulative profit on investments of the same size before moving onto the next level.
    - In essence, repeat trading with $100 position value until you have grown your account by $100.
    - Gain experience with entering and exiting positions in order to increase your ordering comfort level and reduce trade anxiety to a manageable level.
- Using the knowledge acquired throughout Chapters I.1 through II.10, start trading by using a 0.5-1% risk unit.
  - o Remember to always **cut losses quickly**.
  - o Stick to your rules.
  - o Focus on one or two strategies at a time and stick to the rules (see Section IV for sample strategies).
    - Trade with one or two strategies for a period (weeks, months) of time and document your results before switching.
    - Suggested strategies starting out:
      - BECW (Chapter IV.1).
      - BD (Chapter IV.2).
  - o Do not increase your risk unit until you have gained enough experience to trader properly.
    - Generate 500% in risk unit profits before increasing your risk unit.

- For every $1 risked, try to make $5 in cumulative profits.
- In essence, for a risk unit of $150, make $750 with all your trades before increasing your risk unit.

o When increasing your risk unit, avoid going over 2%-4% of risked equity (10%-20% of total equity being played in the position).

o Adjust your risk according to necessity once you become proficient.

Chapter II.11 - Sykes Sliding Scale - SSS

Overview

Here, you'll learn the Sykes Sliding Scale (a.k.a. SSS or S3) to provide an efficient way to determine whether a given stock can potentially show adequate momentum to generate profit.

Goals

The goal of this chapter is learning the essentials of S3 and the components that define this method in order establish the potential profitability of a security based on technical and fundamental factors.

Introduction

Recently unveiled by Timothy Sykes in his DVD, "Trader Checklist" (http://trader-checklist.com/), the S3 method provides a step-by-step metric to determining whether a stock has the potential of becoming a profitable play during market hours or whether it should be left alone altogether.

This method was born out of necessity for having a proper rating system to help novice and experienced traders get reliable metrics about their plays, based on multiple factors established by the P.R.E.P.A.R.E. acronym, which you'll learn in a moment.

For this course, the S3 method requires manual calculations, but we're currently integrating this method into StocksToTrade, so soon all traders can have digital access this valuable tool. That's great news.

Now, it's time for you to learn this great approach to narrowing down a crowded watchlist and focusing on stocks that have the best potential for profit based on the trader criteria for performing the method. Let's dive in.

P.R.E.P.A.R.E. and the sliding scale

In order to become a successful trader, you must **P.R.E.P.A.R.E.** You must prepare ahead of time, BEFORE you risk your hard-earned money on any trade. The key to success in trading is preparation and planning. As boring as that sounds, a good, well thought-out plan increases your odds of success dramatically.

This is the premise behind the S3 method. Each letter focuses on a factor that needs to be taken into consideration as obtain the resulting S3 rating. **P.R.E.P.A.R.E.** is the basis for the Sliding Scale and can help traders find the most interesting stocks based on the technical, fundamental and personal environments for each given security.

P.R.E.P.A.R.E. is presented as a set of questions/factors to be evaluated about the stock and the environment surrounding the play. Each of the elements will be presented below.

P – Pattern and Price

The first indicator of the S3 is the pattern and price, which essentially requires you to evaluate how well the stock being analyzed matches the criteria for a tradable long or short pattern.

Ask yourself the following question: How well does the price level and pattern match the criteria for a profitable long/short play?

The price and pattern indicator is evaluated to a maximum of 20 points.

The goal of the price and pattern indicator is to help you identify stocks that have the potential to follow through with price action based on the long- and short-term trading patterns and price levels.

R – Risk/Reward

The risk/reward indicator of the S3 focuses on establishing the risk profile for this stock. Chapter II.4 goes over this approach in great detail.

The goal of this indicator is to provide a grade on how beneficial or detrimental a given stock play can be. Based on the risk/reward ratio and your personal tolerance

The Risk/Reward indicator is evaluated to a maximum of 20 points.

E – Ease of Entry and Exit

The ease of entry describes essentially a metric that describes the overall general volume of the stock currently being watched. This criterion allows determining whether entry and exit in and out of a given security can be performed with ease or whether it will take some time for an order to be executed.

The more liquid the stock, the easier the entry and exit.

The Ease of Entry and Exit indicator is evaluated to a maximum of 10 points.

P – Past Performance and History of Spiking

The Past Performance and History of Spiking takes a look at the historical data of the stock and establishes whether a given security has performed well in the past, and has displayed identifiable behavior or patterns in the past, such as a supernova, or general spiking following specific events.

If a stock provides a repeatable past pattern that can be identified against its current behavior, then it would score higher in this metric, as it provides good odds of repeating that behavior under the right circumstances.

The Past Performance and History of Spiking indicator is evaluated to a maximum of 10 points.

A – At What Time Does this Happen and Personal Schedule

The Personal Schedule indicator is entirely relative to the trader and relies heavily on identifying availability for trading a specific security. In essence, it provides a way to evaluate the time that can be dedicated to a given security.

In order to assign a value to this indicator, it's important to consider all the external factors that would affect the ability of the trader to focus on a given security; in other words, personal appointments, grocery shopping, commute times, etc., all contribute to establishing this metric.

The At What Time Does This Happen and Personal Schedule indicators are evaluated to a maximum of 20 points.

R – Reason or Catalyst

The Reason or Catalyst indicator focuses on what can potentially make a stock move. You'll learn a lot about catalysts in Chapter II.7.

In order to properly evaluate this metric, consider the following things:

- Is there a catalyst that would make the stock move?
- Is there a reaction to said catalyst?
- How pronounced is the reaction to the catalyst?

Based on this information, a trader can establish the value for this metric.

The reason or catalyst indicator is evaluated to a maximum of 10 points.

E – Environment of the Market

The final indicator is the Environment of the Market, which focuses on the behavior of the general market for the type of stocks being looked at. Simply put, this takes a look at the current behavior of the market regarding:

- Sector/industry
- Bear/bull
- General reactions to catalysts during this period
- Trader general sentiment

The environment of the market indicator is evaluated to a maximum of 10 points.

The Sliding Scale

The S3 method is based on a 100 point scale total, broken down into each of the components of **P.R.E.P.A.R.E.** Every component is given a rating and the sum of all question values provides the total S3 rating based on the points collected for the stock being taken into consideration.

The score obtained for each stock will determine the potential profitability of the security being rated.

The table below shows the stock grading based on the S3 result obtained for a given stock.

Score	Rating
100-95	Excellent
90-95	Very good
80-90	Good
75-80	Playable
65-75	Watch
0-65	Poor

Putting It All Together

Putting S3 into practice only requires very simple tools in addition to your stock data. For instance, StocksToTrade can be used to scan for potential plays of interest based on your criteria, as described in Chapter I.9, and establish your initial watchlist.

The next step involves simply creating a spreadsheet and setting the information with the scale names on one column and the assigned values on the following columns.

The first column focuses on establishing the base criteria for P.R.E.P.A.R.E.; their maximum values may also be added for point assignment reference.

The only thing that remains is to have a single column added for each stock being observed and establishing the values for each of those stocks.

If you're using Excel or Google spreadsheets, simply use the `SUM(...)` function and add all the values of the P.R.E.P.A.R.E. components.

This will provide you with the final values for each stock. If you are a bit versed in scripting, it's pretty easy to add a matching filter to let you know, based on the scoring table, whether the stock has potential profitability, either by assigning a color to the column (conditional matching) or however you find ideal to describe the results.

Note: The approach depends whether you're looking at the S3 based on a long or short bias, as the evaluation will change dramatically depending on how you want to trade the security.

Practical Approach

Now let's take a look at a couple of examples that describe the use of the Sykes Sliding Scale in a practical environment.

Check out DRYS:

Figure II.11.1 - DRYS current 1day-1min chart on StocksToTrade

A bit of context: DryShips Inc is a shipping company whose stock has been pushed up following the legalization of recreation marijuana in various states. DRYS, which has strictly no affiliation to marijuana stocks, has been directly affected by this external catalyst without news about the company itself.

Let's go over the various steps of the S3 for a long position on DRYS. We'll assume that we were looking at the chart during pre-market time.

It's important that there was really little activity pre-market; however, we can take a look at the minute chart of the previous day in Figure II.11.2.

Figure II.11.2 - DRYS Previous day 1day-1min chart on StocksToTrade

This stock has gone from around $4.66 to the high $15's over the course of the previous day.

Also note how this stock has continuously dropped over the course of the last few years. Figure II.11.3 shows a basic view of the last year:

Figure II.11.3 - DRYS 1day chart on StocksToTrade

In order to evaluate the market environment, be sure to look at how other stocks in the same industry and related stocks are performing. Figure II.11.4 shows screener results matching similar stocks to DRYS:

Time	Symbol	Company Name	% Chg	Net Change	Bid	Ask	Last
10:47:46	DRYS	DryShips Inc.	+30.91 %	3.6661	15.46	15.70	15.5661
10:47:46	SINO	Sino-Global Shipping America Ltd.	-27.00 %	0.3201	1.48	1.49	1.48
10:47:21	NM	Navios Maritime Holdings Inc.	+13.11 %	0.16	1.38	1.39	1.38
10:47:44	EGLE	Eagle Bulk Shipping Inc.	+11.57 %	0.5054	5.63	5.65	5.6454
10:47:45	SHIP	Seanergy Maritime Holdings Corp	+7.14 %	0.15	2.25	2.30	2.25
10:47:32	TOPS	TOP Ships Inc.	+6.48 %	0.19	3.07	3.15	3.12
10:46:55	SALT	Scorpio Bulkers Inc.	+3.61 %	0.15	4.25	4.30	4.30
10:47:39	AXU	Alexco Resource Corp (Canada)	+2.23 %	0.0361	1.85	1.86	1.8561
10:47:49	BLDP	Ballard Power Systems Inc.	+1.82 %	0.03%	1.93	1.94	1.955

Figure II.11.4 - StocksToTrade Screener Industrial Sector Result

- **P**attern/Price
  - This stock fits into the high end of what we would normally tolerate as a penny stock.
  - This would likely get an **11/20**.
- **R**isk/Reward

- o Over the course of the previous day, this stock has gone up about 200% (over $10 net gain), which may qualify it as an over extended stock.
  - o Risk Reward ratio can be evaluated to be around between 2:1 and 3:1.
  - o This could be given a score of **12/20**.
- Ease of Entry and Exit,
  - o Following the news on the previous day, volume on this stock has been relatively liquid, which makes entry and exit actions are not likely to be delayed in any way.
  - o A minor concern is the volatility of the stock, which may present some very dramatic price changes over the course of a short period of time.
  - o This could be given a score of **7/10**.
- Past performance and history of spiking,
  - o Figure II.11.3 shows that the stock has constantly been dropping over the course of the last year, and the trend has been ongoing since early 2014.
  - o There is no indicator of spiking but the stock has been known to be high priced in the past.
  - o This could be given a score of **5/10**.
- At What Time Does This Happen and Personal Schedule
  - o This is very subjective and depends on personal availability.
  - o Right now, I would personally be available all day to trade this security.
  - o This would be given a score of **15/20**.
- Reason/Catalyst,
  - o This stock has spiked massively on speculation only based on the unrelated performance of a completely unrelated stock.
  - o There's no news or catalysts that would prompt such behavior on this stock.
  - o This would be given a score of **3/10**.
- Environment of the Market
  - o Based on Figure II.11.4, we can see that other stocks in the shipping sector have also seen an increase in their price and seem to be doing well,
  - o This could be given a score of **7/10**.

Now that we've established all the criteria for this stock, we come up with the following result:

- 11+12+7+5+15+3+7 = 60

While this stock has been performing well, given the diverse information and assessments that we've been able to establish around it, this stock would fall into the **POOR** grade, which would make it unsuitable for trading at this time.

Though it probably goes without saying, due to the subjective nature of the Sykes Sliding Scale, use this method as a guideline to make better trading decisions, rather than an absolute factor maker for deciding on taking a position.

Summary

This chapter taught you basics of the Sykes Sliding Scale. Here are your highlights:

The S3 is a general approach to evaluating the "playability" of a given security based not only on the current stock parameters, but also on the personal environment

- Remember the P.R.E.P.A.R.E. Acronym,
    o Pattern/Price - scored from 0 to 20
    o Risk/Reward - scored from 0 to 20
    o Ease of Entry and Exit - scored from 0 to 10
    o Past Performance and History of Spiking - scored from 0 to 10
    o At What Time Does This Happen and Personal Schedule - scored from 0 to 20
    o Reason/Catalyst - scored from 0 to 10
    o Environment of the Market - scored from 0 to 10
- The Sykes Sliding Scale is graded on a scale of 100
- Potentially profitable stocks have scores of 75 and above.

Questions

1. **What should you look at when considering the first P of P.R.E.P.A.R.E.?**
   a. The past performance of the stock.
   b. The last price of the stock.
   c. The pattern being followed by the stock.
   d. The Price action of the stock.

2. **When you look at past performance, what should you take into consideration?**
   a. The volume of the stock.
   b. The average price of the stock.
   c. The 52-week high of the stock.
   d. The price reaction of the stock.

3. **What is the score required to consider a stock as a potential play?**
   a. 50
   b. 65
   c. 75
   d. 85

4. **How do you determine the ease of entry of the stock?**
   a. By looking at price action.
   b. By looking at the average daily volume.
   c. By looking at the range.
   d. By looking at the liquidity.

5. **What factors should you taking into consideration when establishing the schedule score?**
   a. The market hours.
   b. Personal availability.
   c. Earnings calendar.
   d. Market open and close.

6. **What is the maximum score a stock can ever receive with the S3?**
   a. 120
   b. 85
   c. 100
   d. 150

Homework

- Create a spreadsheet with the criteria column:
  - For every stock in your watchlist, evaluate the S3 and establish the score.
  - See if the S3 score matches your expectations at the end of the trading day.
  - Take notes about what you find out.
- For every stock in your watchlist, re-evaluate the S3 multiple times over the course of the day.
  - Take note of the value changes and how it affects your trading decisions.

Section III - Advanced Concepts

This section is dedicated to covering the advanced concepts of penny stock trading These concepts didn't appear in Section II because they reflect a riskier and more complex approach to how trades are handled.

This section covers the following subjects:

- Short selling: Selling borrowed stock and buying at a lower price level to generate a profit.
- Understanding Level 2: Using Level 2 information in order to determine possible price action based on market maker tables behavior.
- Over-the-Counter Bulletin Boards: Trading the less regulated market, the intricacies and the risks associated with OTCBB trades.
- SEC filings: Performing in-depth research by reading through the required SEC filings of a given company in order to determine fundamental components that could potentially provide a trading edge.
- Position boxing: Entering opposite positions with two separate brokers in order to limit the downside of one of the positions until the price action makes a momentum move.
- Pyramiding positions: Adding to a position by considering the NT RMS settings to increase the position size and maximize potential profits.
- Trading the spread: Entering and exiting a position with a wide spread between the bid and the ask in order to generate profits.
- Finding a niche and developing your strategy: Extending your knowledge and experience in order to develop your own set of rules to trade penny stocks in a profitable manner.

The chapters in this section give you the opportunity to further advance your penny stock trading knowledge and introduce you to more complex ideas in the pennystocking world.

Chapter III.1 - Short Selling

Overview

Getting familiar with the concept of short selling stocks and the intricate set of rules associated with this type of trade.

Goals

The goal of this chapter is to provide you with a proper understanding on how short selling works and what the rules are for performing this type of trade.

At the end of this chapter, you'll know:

- What short selling is
- How to short a stock
- What the dangers of short selling are
- How to enter and exit a short position
- The cost and rules of short selling a stock

What is Short Selling?

Short selling, or "shorting" is the action of borrowing shares from a shareholder through your broker as an interim and then selling them in the stock market as if you would hold them yourself. This action opens the position.

You're then required to buy those shares back in order to return them to the lender. This is known as buying to cover, familiarly known as "covering."

This type of trade is performed when the price of the stock is expected to go down. A trader will short a stock at a high price. If the price drops, the absolute value of the difference becomes a profit. On the other hand, if the price increases, the trader covers at a loss.

The Players

The figure below shows the players involved in a short sell action:

| The Trader | The Broker | The Lender | The (Unhappy) Buyer | The Seller |

Figure III.1.1 - Short Selling players

Each player has an essential role in the process of short selling a stock:

- The trader is usually you
- The broker is the company that provides you with the means of performing a trade
- The lender is the entity that is currently a shareholder of the stock you want to short sell
- The buyer is the entity that will obtain your borrowed shares once you have short sold them
- The seller is the entity you will buy to cover your shares from

In the figures below, a profitable short sell trade is depicted. However, the principle applies to both profiting and losing trades.

The simple explanation

How it Goes

Figure III.1.2 - Step 1 - Short selling a borrowed stock

Figure III.1.3 - Step 2 - Buying to cover a borrowed stock

The Detailed Explanation

The figures below show a more detailed explanation of how the short-selling process is achieved:

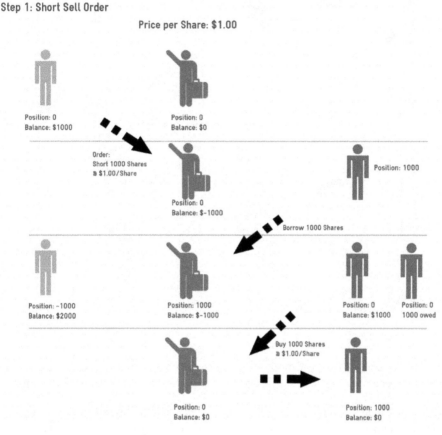

Figure III.1.4 - Step 1 - Short selling a borrowed stock

In simple terms, during the first phase of the short selling process, you are borrowing shares from your broker, who is actually borrowing from a shareholder willing to lend those shares. Then the process works as a regular sell, with the exception that you must at some point return the shares to their rightful owner.

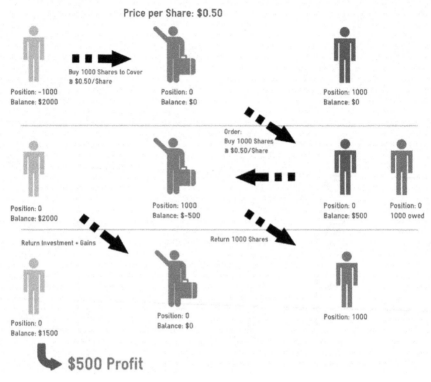

Figure III.1.5 - Step 2 - buying to cover a borrowed stock

The second phase of the short trade is buying to cover, which basically means instructing your broker to buy the shares back on your behalf and return them to the lender.

At this point you keep the negative difference in price (the shares you return are worth less than what you originally sold them for) or you must pay the positive difference (the shares you return are worth more than what you originally sold them for).

This final phase essentially concludes the short selling process.

The Continual Hunt for Shares to Short

One of the main difficulties in performing short sell trades lies in the concept of finding shortable shares.

Unlike traditional buy-and-sell trades, short selling requires a trader to borrow shares in order to be able to short. This implies that there are an even smaller number of shares available for type of transaction, making adding a layer of complexity to the trade.

Shortable shares need to be located by your broker-dealer, and they can either be **easy-to-borrow** or **hard-to-borrow**.

Locating Shares & Regulation SHO

In order for traders to be able to short stocks, their brokers are required to have confidence that they can find shares to borrow. This is one of the rules to which brokers are subjected when it comes to short selling and is established by Regulation SHO.

The rule is as follows:

> *"Locate Requirement: Regulation SHO requires a broker-dealer to have reasonable grounds to believe that the security can be borrowed so that it can be delivered on the date delivery is due before effecting a short sale order in any equity security. This "locate" must be made and documented prior to effecting the short sale." (Commission S. a., 2005)*

Essentially what this means is that a broker must have "reasonable grounds to believe," which is an entirely subjective approach, "that the security can be borrowed." This does not, in fact, require the broker to actually prove that the shares are borrowable, only to have good reasons to believe that they are.

The only market entities actually allowed to engage into short selling without following the "locate" rule stated above are market makers; they are exempt on the grounds that shorting without a "locate" allows them to bring liquidity to the market.

Easy-to-Borrow

Easy-to-borrow shares refers to shares for securities deemed widely available for borrowing because their delivery is assured. This availability is ensured by a high quantity of outstanding shares and easy accessibility.

Easy-to-borrow shares for a given stock appear on the easy-to-borrow list, which simply represents a list of securities that have standing assurances in regards to share availability. This allows firms to perform short selling transactions more easily and removes the necessity to perform a "locate" every time that the stock is requested for a short sale trade. A stock on the Easy-To-Borrow list is assumed to be available, which constitutes "reasonable grounds to believe that the security can be borrowed."

Hard-to-Borrow

Like the name sounds, hard-to-borrow shares represent shares that are difficult to locate, or for which the broker doesn't currently have an inventory available, or has very low availability in its inventory.

The hard-to-borrow list represents a list of securities that are currently not available for the broker to borrow from and an actual "locate" action would be necessary in order to allow traders to perform the short sell transaction. This list is usually only internally available to brokers and not publicly published to traders.

Hard-to-borrow shares, when located by the broker, may be lent to the trader and may be subjected to an additional hard-to-borrow fee on certain short sales.

Entering a Position: Short Selling

The actual process of entering a short sell position varies from broker to broker. The principle is, in essence, similar to a traditional buy order. Instead of buying, you're simply selling and setting your trade parameters accordingly, taking into consideration that "stop" (STP) amounts will be higher than your current price and that in order to generate a profit the price needs to drop.

Some brokers will allow you to perform a short sell by simply selling a security for which you have a 0 position; your position then becomes negative. It is worth noting, however, that some broker platforms have a dedicated short sell button in order to perform these types of transactions.

Figure III.1.6 - Multicharts - AMLH daily chart - Short entry

For more details on entering a position and the necessary parameter, please refer to Chapter II.10.

Exiting a Position: Buying to Cover

Much like selling an open long position initiated with a sell order, closing a short position initiated with a short sell is achieved by performing a "**buy to cover**" order.

Most brokers will simply allow you to buy the necessary number of negative shares (or shares owed) by using the buy order button and setting the order parameters as necessary. Much like opening the short position, some brokers will have a dedicated button to perform the "buy to cover" transaction.

The same risk management rules apply for this type of order.

For more details on exiting a position and the necessary parameter, please refer to Chapter II.10.

Figure III.1.7 - Multicharts - AMLH Daily chart - Buy to cover - short position exit

The Dangers of Short Selling

While trading in itself is inherently about risk management and understanding dangers and risky situations, by adding another layer of complexity, short selling brings its own set of dangers on top of the existing ones for traditional trades.

The Infinite Upside

A traditional buy-and-sell trade involves purchasing shares of a security at a certain price with the expectation of a higher price in the future, with no real mathematical limit to how high the price could go. On the other side, the maximum risk and worst-case scenario associated with that trade would be the price falling down to $0 and losing the whole investment – price for a stock cannot be negative.

This isn't the case for short selling. Since you're entering a position that relies on the price going down, your maximum profit would be limited by the company's worst-case scenario of a $0 price point.

The upside, on the other hand, has no limit. As such, the potential losses are not limited to the investment but could well go beyond that value turning a significant loss into debt.

The reason for this is that there's no limit to how high the price can potentially go, and while it is impossible for a stock to reach infinity, stocks raising ten-fold in price aren't unheard of.

This is where the exit rule of **Cutting Losses Quickly** (Chapter II.10) becomes all the more important. Short selling has no limit on the losing side.

This brings us to the next section: the short squeeze.

Short Squeeze

Considering that there's no limit to how high a stock price can go, short sellers become wary of increasing price action.

A short squeeze is an event relating to positive price action on a stock that is heavily shorted. When the price starts increasing drastically, short sellers get uncomfortable with their positions and cut their losses by covering their positions.

This often causes a chain reaction that results in a continuous increase in price (a result of successive buy orders by short positions) as traders attempt to exit their position by limiting their losses when the price goes up.

A short squeeze can sometimes drive stock momentum and create supernova-type charts that then become potential shorts.

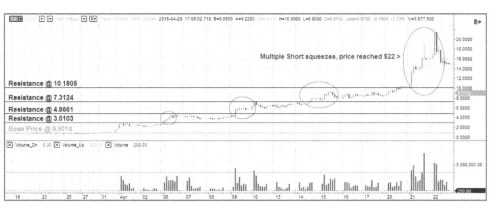

Figure III.1.8 - Multicharts - VLTC 1 hour chart - short squeezes

Forced Buy-in

A forced buy-in is an event where a broker forces a buy-to-cover transaction onto a trader's short sell open position at whatever market price is at the time of the event.

This type of event happens due to another rule of Regulation SHO that states:

> *" "Close-out" Requirement: Regulation SHO imposes additional delivery requirements on broker-dealers for securities in which there are a relatively substantial number of extended delivery failures at a registered clearing agency ("threshold securities"). For instance, with limited exception, Regulation SHO requires brokers and dealers that are participants of a registered clearing agency to take action to "close-out" failure-to-deliver positions ("open fails") in threshold securities that have persisted for 13 consecutive settlement days. Closing out requires the broker or dealer to purchase securities of like kind and quantity. Until the position is closed out, the broker or dealer and any broker or dealer for which it clears transactions (for example, an introducing broker) may not effect further short sales in that threshold security without borrowing or entering into a bona fide agreement to borrow the security (known as the "pre-borrowing" requirement)." (Commission S. a., 2005)*

What this Regulation SHO rule implies is that when brokers fail to deliver shares to buyers during a certain period of time because they're unable to actually locate the shares, they're required to actually add those shares to their inventory by buying and closing the position. This in turn means that brokers are required to close all their client's short positions in order to balance their inventory.

Some brokers will sometimes provide clients with a warning that a forced buy-in may happen in the short term, which gives traders the opportunity to exit their position at their discretion. However, in some cases the forced buy-in will occur without any notice until after it has happened.

SEC Halt

An SEC halt involves the suspension of all trading activity of a given stock by the SEC due to regulatory or non-regulatory reasons.

> *"There are two types of trading halts and delays – regulatory and non-regulatory. The most common regulatory halt and delay happen when a company has pending news that may affect the security's price (a "news pending" halt or delay). By halting or delaying trading, market participants can have time to assess the impact of the news. Another type of regulatory halt happens when a market halts trading in a security when there is uncertainty over whether the security continues to meet the market's listing standards. When a regulatory halt or delay is imposed by a security's primary market, the other U.S. markets that also trade the security honor this halt." (Commission S. a., Trading Halts and Delays, n.d.)*

This basically means that a stock may be halted at any time at the discretion of the SEC when it believes that some events may affect the price of the security. It is intended as a way to protect traders from trading by allowing them to obtain further information on what's happening with a given company.

While this doesn't happen too often, it's usually subjected to stocks that have a high rate of short sellers, such as pump & dumps; this often triggers an SEC investigation.

> *"The SEC does not halt or delay trading in a security for news pending or order imbalances, but it can suspend trading for up to ten days and, if appropriate, take action to revoke a security's registration. For more information about the SEC's authority to suspend trading in a security, please read 'Trading Suspension! When the SEC Suspends Trading in a Stock' in our Fast Answers databank." (Commission S. a., Trading Halts and Delays, n.d.)*

The danger with this type of action is that all trading is suspended for as long as the halt lasts, which means that it's impossible to recover the cash from an open position as long as it remains in effect.

On the other hand, when it comes to shady companies, an SEC halt is usually followed by a significant drop in price.

What is a Short Sell Restriction?

A **short sale restriction** (SSR) is also known as the "alternative uptick rule", or Rule 201 of the SEC's Regulation SHO. It regulates stocks that have dropped more than 10% by subjecting them a short sell rule that prevents short sellers from selling at or below the best bid price.

The rule states the following:

> *"[a] trading center shall establish, maintain, and enforce written policies and procedures reasonably designed to: (i) Prevent the execution or display of a short sale order of a covered security at a price that is less than or equal to the current national best bid if the price of that covered security decreases by 10% or more from the covered security's closing price as determined by the listing market for the covered security as of the end of regular trading hours on the prior day; and (ii) Impose the requirements of paragraph (b)(1)(i) of this section for the remainder of the day and the following day when a national best bid for the covered security is calculated and disseminated on a current and continuing basis by a plan processor pursuant to an effective national market system plan."* (Commission S. a., Amendments to Regulation SHO, 2010)

This rule effectively prevents short sellers from driving the price down at a quick rate. It also ensures that a short sell can only happen after the highest bid is increased, hence the name "uptick rule".

The $2.50 Rule

The $2.50/share rule is only applied by some brokers such as Interactive Brokers. This rule goes into effect when short selling stocks under $1, and states that for every share shorted under $1, the trader must have $2.50/share in account cash value.

This essentially means that if you traded 1,000 shares of a stock at $0.25/share with a market value of $250, your cash account must have at least $2,500 in order to perform that trade.

It's important to keep this fact in mind when attempting to short sell stocks below $1, as it will considerably limit your position sizes.

The Cost of Short Selling

Short selling is similar to a loan: You're borrowing shares from a third party through your broker.

As with any loans, there's an annual interest rate associated with the share loan, which varies from stock to stock.

How interests are calculated also varies from broker to broker, and should be available upon request.

The basic idea is that shortable shares are usually subjected to an annual interest rate on a per share basis. This implies that the total value of your position will be subjected to this interest rate on a daily basis.

This fee is added to broker commissions and regulatory fees.

The basic calculation would be something like this:

$$borrow\ fee\ per\ day = \frac{position\ value \times interest\ rate}{360\ days}$$

Interactive Brokers has an additional rule for stocks priced under \$1, stating that the price per share under \$1 must be rounded to the nearest dollar multiplied by the number of shares in order to get the borrow fee base position value.

This is explained here: http://ibkb.interactivebrokers.com/article/1146

Summary

- Short selling allows a trader to borrow a stock and sell in order to make a profit from a stock with a decreasing price.
- Short selling is entirely reliant on the availability of shares to short in the broker's inventory.
- To enter a short position, it simply requires selling the stock at the desired price. The trade will result in a negative share position.
- To exit a short position, it simply requires buying the stock at the desired price. The trade will result in a 0 share position.
- Short selling is riskier than buying, as a significant losing position will not only bring the investment to a $0 value, but can also create debt by going above the owed value.
- Short selling can be subjected to short squeezes when a great number of short sellers short the same stock and the price increases. This forces every short seller to panic and exit the position, driving the price higher.
- Short sold stocks may be subjected to forced buy-ins, which means that the broker will force a buy-to cover trade at the market value regardless of the trader's current profit/loss position.
- A company's trading may be halted by the SEC for up to 10 sessions for regulatory or non-regulatory purposes when suspicious activity or unusual activity is detected.
- Companies experiencing a 10% drop from the previous close may be subjected to a short sell restriction, also known as the "alternative uptick rule". This prevents traders from shorting a stock at or below the highest bid.
- Some brokers will enforce the $2.50 rule when shorting stocks under $1 per share, which requires traders to have $2.50 for every share shorted that is below $1/share.
- Short sell trades are subjected to borrow fees that vary from stock to stock and from broker to broker.

Questions

1. What is short selling?
   a. Selling a small portion of a long po-
       sition.
   b. Borrowing and selling shares
       providing a negative open position.
   c. Selling a stock while on margin.
   d. None of the above.

2. How do you profit from short selling?
   a. When the price increases the prof-
       its go up.
   b. When the price decreases the prof-
       its go up.

3. What are the dangers of short selling?
   a. There are no shares to short.
   b. The possibility of getting squeezed
       when a breakout occurs.
   c. The possibility of a forced buy-in
       while on a losing state.
   d. Short selling has an "infinite" loss
       potentially putting the trader in
       debt.

4. What is a short sell restriction?
   a. A rule that prevents traders from
       short selling a security.
   b. A rule that limits the number of
       shares that can be shorted by any
       given trader.
   c. A rule that only allows short sell
       orders to be executed on an uptick
       with a price above the highest bid.
   d. A rule that prevents short sellers
       from covering their position.

5. What is the borrow fee?
   a. The fee that is charged when trad-
       ing on margin.
   b. The commissions charged by the
       brokers for each trade.
   c. The fees associated with borrow-
       ing the data feed for real-time in-
       formation.
   d. The fee associated with borrowing
       shares in order to short sell.

6. What is buying to cover?
   a. Closing a short sell position by
       buying back shares.
   b. Buying shares above the highest re-
       sistance.
   c. Buying shares below support.
   d. Buying shares when momentum
       happens.

Homework

- Make a short sell trade with a small position ($50-$100 total position value),
    - o   Let the stock play for a profit or loss of $10 (or close the position if the stock price doesn't show enough movement), and then close your position by buying to cover.
    - o   Stick to stocks with shares available – low volatility and high liquidity.
- Look into shorting strategies for listed stocks (NASDAQ, AMEX, NYSE),
    - o   Chapter IV.3
    - o   Chapter IV.4

Chapter III.2 - Understanding Level 2

Overview

Here, you'll learn what Level 2 is, how it works, and how the information it provides can be used to perform better trades.

Goals

The goal of this chapter is to discover and understand Level 2 and how to leverage the data obtained from it in order to predict price action movements.

At the end of this chapter you'll know:

- What is Level 2
- How to read Level 2
- Walls of buyers and walls of sellers
- How to interpret the information provided by Level 2
- How to potentially predict a stock behavior based on Level 2 information

What is Level 2?

Level 2 (L2) is an enhanced type of data feed that provides a higher level of detail regarding the real-time information of the market for a given stock.

The purpose of Level 2 is to provide an in-depth overview of the order queue currently in line for a given stock. This information can let traders to see how big the awaiting orders at a given price point are and how many aggregated market maker orders there are for each price point.

Unlike the simple time and sales screen, Level 2 offers a higher level of detail at every moment, providing an updated list of orders as they become available on the queue.

Figure III.2.1 below shows the Level 2 monitor for Interactive Brokers platform.

Level 2 is a premium feature offered by brokers or data providers and requires a separate subscription for each of the markets to which one subscribes.

Bid MM Name	Bid Price	Bid Size	Ask MM Name	Ask Price	Ask Size
DRCTEDGE	15.67	10	NSDQ	15.75	2
BYX	15.65	1	ARCA	15.77	1
NSDQ	15.65	9	ARCA	15.79	1
ARCA	15.61	3	DRCTEDGE	15.79	4
BATS	15.56	2	NSDQ	15.79	10
ARCA	15.53	1	BYX	15.80	1
BATS	15.52	1	ARCA	15.82	1
ARCA	15.51	3	BATS	15.88	2
BATS	15.46	1	ARCA	15.90	3
BATS	15.44	1	EDGEA	15.90	3
NSDQ	15.42	50	BATS	15.92	2
ARCA	15.41	1	NSDQ	15.92	1
ARCA	15.40	1	NSDQ	15.95	15
ARCA	15.38	2	NSDQ	15.97	2
BATS	15.38	1	BATS	15.99	1
BATS	15.30	1	NSDQ	15.99	1
ARCA	15.29	1	ARCA	16.00	3
ARCA	15.25	3	ATDF	16.00	4
BATS	15.24	1	NSDQ	16.00	52
NSDQ	15.20	5	UBSS	16.00	28
NSDQ	15.15	5	BATS	16.04	1
NSDQ	15.12	1	NSDQ	16.05	5
ARCA	15.11	1	BATS	16.06	1
ARCA	15.10	5	BATS	16.08	1
ATDF	15.08	3	NSDQ	16.08	2
NSDQ	15.08	2	NSDQ	16.10	3
NSDQ	15.07	10	ARCA	16.17	2

Figure III.2.1 - TWS Level 2 screen for DGLY, size indicated in number of 100s

Level 2 can be used to predict and identify price action behavior based on price queue and order patterns on the monitor.

It's also important to know that the information provided by Level 2 is only a basic indicator of the order queue, but may not reflect actual position sizes, as these can be masked or faked at the time of the order.

In order to increase trading efficiency, Level 2 is normally used in conjunction with the time and sales monitor, which is available as a Level 1 feature.

Definitions

Market Maker

A market maker is a broker-dealer firm that takes the risk of holding a certain number of shares of a given stock or security with the goal of facilitating the trading of that stock. Market makers display buy and sell quotes for a guaranteed number of shares. Upon receiving orders, the market makers sell their own inventory immediately or seek an offsetting order.

In Level 2, market makers are represented by their **market maker ID** (MMID), which usually appears on left side under the MM column, as you'll see in Figure III.2.1.

Bid

In Level 2, the "bid" represents the queue of orders waiting to be processed based on price action. They represent the highest price that buyers are willing to pay for a certain number of shares of a given security.

The list of bids is sorted in descending order based on market availability and is usually located on the left-hand side of the monitor.

Ask

Conversely to the bid, the "ask" represents the queue of sell orders waiting to be processed based on price action and on matching bid.

Contrarily to the "ask", the bid is sorted in ascending order and is usually located on the right-hand side of the monitor.

Size

The size represents the number of shares for any given entry on the bid/ask list. It specifies the number of shares that a trader wants to trade for that given security at the specified price appearing on the L2 monitor.

Always remember that sizes should only be used as a guideline, and understand that they don't necessarily represent actual order sizes. This is because actual order sizes can be faked (a lower size can be shown on the L2 monitor when placing an order) or completely hidden from Level 2.

However, the accurate size information may be available on Level 3, but this isn't a feature that's available to regular traders, and is only an option for market maker firms.

Spread

The spread represents the difference in price between the highest "bid" and the lowest "ask".

Level 2 Indicators

There are various patterns on Level 2 that can be identified in order to potentially predict possible price action or price behavior.

Wall of Buyers

One of the first indicators to take into consideration is the "**wall of buyers**". Figure II.2.2 below shows the typical L2 pattern for the Wall of Buyers at $9.75.

A wall of buyers is usually represented by a large number of buyers at the same price point, or blocks of multiple buyers at the same price points; this creates an aggregated size at a given price point by adding all the sizes together.

Additionally, orders on the "bid" are not cleared while orders on the "ask" continuously disappear from the order queue. This is usually followed by additional "bid" orders being queued on the list.

This is usually indicative that a support point has been reached and that there is interest in obtaining the stock at that price with the expectation of a price increase in the short term.

This type of L2 pattern can usually predict an increase of the price as interest raises for the given security, and the orders on the ask side begin disappearing as a result, driving the price even higher with time.

A prolonged duration wall of buyers is usually a good indicator for entering a long position and can often be the early signs of a potential breakout for a given security.

This indicator, along with fundamental information about the company behind the stock can help predict a price increase, especially when the price point is near a resistance or key resistance line.

MMID	BID	SIZE	MMID	ASK	SIZE
ARCA	9.75	5100	ARCA	9.80	600
EDGX	9.75	2300	EDGX	9.85	1200
BOS	9.75	1200	BATY	9.85	200
BATY	9.75	2600	BATS	9.85	300
EDGA	9.75	200	NSD	9.85	1100
BATS	9.75	200	NSDQ	9.85	1100
NSDQ	9.75	3201	BOS	9.90	800
NSD	9.75	3200	IEXG	9.90	800
IEXG	9.70	800	EDGA	9.95	200
GSCO	9.45	5100	PHL	10.00	300
NITE	9.35	100	GSCO	10.15	5100
PHL	9.20	100	SSUS	10.50	100
ETMM	9.15	100	ETMM	10.50	100

Figure III.2.2 - StocksToTrade L2, wall of buyers for CRBP

A wall of buyers also makes it difficult to short a watched stock, as it reinforces the support line at a certain price level and can potentially discourage sellers from liquidating their existing position.

A wall of buyers serves as an indicator for the following:

- Support created at the wall price line
- Potential breakout on the way
- Potential breakdown fakeout; don't be short

You should know that repeated attempts of a wall of buyers weakens with each iteration, increasing the odds of a potential reversal piercing through the wall price line and potentially resulting in a panic and breakdown.

Wall of Sellers

Conversely to the wall of buyers, the "**wall of sellers**" represents a block or blocks of orders at a certain price point that reinforce a resistance line. Much like the wall of buyers, "ask" orders don't bulge while "bid" orders are cleared as the stock price drops.

Figure III.2.3 shows a good example of a wall of seller at $9.70, having a cumulative size of 10,700 (sum of all the seller sizes at that price) shares.

A wall of sellers usually indicates a potential breakdown or a breakout fake-out. The price points of the wall usually reaffirm the position of the collective mind of the market and keep the price from raising any further.

A wall of sellers indicates the following:

- Resistance created at the wall price line
- Potential breakdown on the way
- Potential breakout fake-out; don't be long

Similarly to the wall of buyers, repeated attempts at maintaining a wall of sellers might result in a spike or breakout, as the will of the market becomes stronger than the wall orders.

MMID	BID	SIZE	MMID	ASK	SIZE
EDGX	9.65	100	EDGX	9.70	2400
ARCA	9.65	300	EDGA	9.70	400
BATY	9.60	100	BOS	9.70	2000
NSD	9.60	500	BATY	9.70	3000
NSDQ	9.60	531	ARCA	9.70	2100
BOS	9.55	800	NSDQ	9.70	300
BATS	9.55	200	NSD	9.70	300
IEXG	9.55	800	IEXG	9.70	200
GSCO	9.45	5100	BATS	9.75	300
NITE	9.35	100	PHL	10.00	300
EDGA	9.25	200	GSCO	10.05	5100

Figure III.2.3 - StocksToTrade L2, CBRP Wall of Sellers

Mexican Standoff

The Mexican standoff L2 pattern is usually characterized by both a wall of buyers and a wall of sellers happening simultaneously.

Stocks experiencing this type of pattern are usually better left alone, as it's difficult to predict future behavior without having the effect of the catalyst guiding the price action.

MMID	BID	SIZE	MMID	ASK	SIZE
BOS	9.75	400	EDGA	9.80	100
BATY	9.75	200	BOS	9.80	900
ARCA	9.75	4700	BATY	9.80	800
EDGX	9.75	700	ARCA	9.80	400
NSD	9.75	1100	NSDQ	9.80	400
BATS	9.75	200	NSD	9.80	400
NSDQ	9.75	1100	BATS	9.80	100
IEXG	9.70	800	EDGX	9.85	1200
GSCO	9.45	5100	IEXG	9.90	800
NITE	9.35	100	PHL	10.00	300
EDGA	9.25	200	GSCO	10.15	5100
PHL	9.20	100	SSUS	10.50	100

Figure III.2.4 - StocksToTrade L2 – CRBP Mexican Standoff L2 Pattern

Figure III.2.4 shows a wall of buyers at $9.75 and a wall of sellers at $9.80, indicating that both buyers are sellers are confident in their hypothesis.

This type of pattern should be avoided without having further confirmation of the potential price action.

Chipping Away and the Cliff Dive

This type of Level 2 pattern is characterized by large orders appearing on the L2 monitor and quickly being cleared in small succession by the opposite side.

MMID	BID	SIZE	MMID	ASK	SIZE
NSDQ	9.85	2200	NSDQ	9.86	735
NSD	9.85	2200	NSD	9.86	700
EDGX	9.85	2100	EDGX	9.86	700
EDGA	9.85	300	BOS	9.86	100
BOS	9.85	100	BATY	9.86	200
BATY	9.85	200	BATS	9.86	800
BATS	9.85	700	ARCA	9.86	500
ARCA	9.85	600	EDGA	9.87	100
PHL	9.85	400	PHL	9.87	100
IEXG	9.82	100	SBSH	9.91	100
GSCO	9.67	9700	GSCO	9.96	9700
MSCO	9.56	100	MSCO	10.16	100

Figure III.2.5 - StocksToTrade L2 - Large order on the bid for OPK

Figure III.2.5 shows 3 large orders on the "bid" in comparison to the order sizes on the "ask". This type of setup is usually indicative of strong support, as buy orders with those quantity sizes are harder to clear by smaller sellers, ensuring that the price is driven up.

When a "chipping away" pattern happens, like in the example above, small sell orders would swarm the large buy orders until cleared, driving the price down.

This type of L2 pattern is usually indicative of a "cliff dive" pattern: When the large orders are cleared, they no longer offer a support or resistance price line, thus offering traders further confidence in the potential price action of the stock and creating momentum.

A cliff dive pattern can be an indicator for:

- Potential breakout or breakdown
- Potential reversal of the price action, good exit indicator
- Best considered around round numbers, due to hard stop losses (this triggers the creation of an automated momentum by using the traders pre-set exit settings for cutting losses)
- It usually works best on speculative stocks

Signs of Possible Manipulation

Stock price manipulation can often be detected by paying attention to the Level 2 monitor. This is usually mostly applicable to pump & dumps, as it's in the best interest of promoters to drive the price of the stock up for the duration of the promotion.

While these patterns may indicate stock price manipulation by entities engaging in trading a given security, such indicators may also represent legitimate traders changing their mind with significant orders.

The manipulation pattern is usually reflected by the price of a stock dropping significantly until a certain price level is reached. Once such a price level is attained, very large orders appear on either the "bid" or the "ask" in order to create artificial support or resistance lines.

These large orders are often maintained and even sometimes chipped away until the price action reverses and reaches an acceptable distance from the manipulation threshold.

The large orders are then removed from the order queue. This process is repeated every time the price drops below the manipulator's threshold.

It's worth noting that when these types of patterns emerge, it's usually better to avoid maintaining a position opposite to the manipulation, due to the uncertainty of how the price action will be affected.

Conclusion

Understanding the dynamic of the Level 2 monitor is an invaluable tool to predict price action behavior based on the order information that is provided by this deeper data subscription.

However, it's necessary to become very experienced in recognizing the L2 patterns in order to become efficient at deciphering the underlying signs that are offered by the various indicators on this monitor.

Level 2 can make the difference between a profitable and a very profitable trade.

Summary

- Level 2 is a real-time order queue monitor for a specific stock.
- Level 2 should be used as a complementary tool and not the only basis for making a trading decision.
- Position sizes displayed in Level 2 can be hidden or faked in order to influence or avoid influencing the price action of a given stock.
- A wall of buyers usually indicates a support line.
  - A wall of buyers may indicate a failure to break down and a potential breakout; don't be short.
  - Repeated attempts at a wall of buyers may indicate a breakdown.
- A wall of sellers usually indicates a resistance line.
  - A wall of buyers might indicate a failure to break out and a potential breakdown; don't be long.
  - Repeated attempts at a wall of buyers may indicate a breakout.
- A Mexican standoff is an unsuitable pattern and trading should be avoided.
- A chipping away pattern may indicate a momentum trend and can be used as an indicator to enter a position when close to a key resistance or support line.
- A cliff dive results from the chipping away pattern followed by a breakout or breakdown.
- Level 2 can reveal stock manipulation when suspicious activity is noticed.
  - Quick appearance and disappearance of very large orders at certain price points in order to ensure a resistance or support line and preventing the price from crossing that threshold.

Questions

1. What is Level 2?
a.   The second resistance level on a stock.
b.   A type of data subscription that provides detailed information about current orders in the form of a list of buyers and sellers.
c.   The list of orders that have been processed including the time and size of the order.
d.   None of the above.

2. What is the spread?
a.   The difference in value between the bid and the ask.
b.   The difference in value between your entry and the ask.
c.   The difference in value between your entry and the bid.
d.   The difference in value between the high and the low.

3. What is a wall of sellers?
a.   A list of orders with increasing prices on the ask window.
b.   A list of orders with different sizes, from different market makers at the same price on the ask window.
c.   A list of order with decreasing prices on the bid window.
d.   A list of orders with different sizes at the same price on the bid widow.

4. What action should you take while being short when a wall of buyers appears?
a.   Add to your position.
b.   Exit your position immediately.
c.   Exit your position as soon as you see the price increasing.
d.   Keep your position if you see the wall of buyers being picked.

5. What are potential signs of price manipulation on L2?
a.   A wall of buyers appearing in order to increase the price.
b.   Very large orders appearing at a certain price point in the bid or ask and disappearing as soon as the price returns to its previous levels.
c.   A wall of sellers with large orders appearing on the ask.
d.   Very large orders on the bid or the ask.

6. What is chipping away?
a.   A wall of buyers or sellers thinning quickly.
b.   Very large orders on the bid or ask quickly decreasing in size and corresponding time and sale entries for executions.
c.   The appearance of a wall of buyers.
d.   The appearance of a wall of sellers.

Homework

- Subscribe to Level 2 data (broker, StocksToTrade).
- For the stocks in your watchlist, look for the following Level 2 signs during the trading session and document how the price is affected by these events:
  - Wall of buyers
  - Wall of sellers
  - Mexican standoff
  - Manipulation

Chapter III.3 - Over-The-Counter (OTC)

Overview

This chapter will help you develop a deep understanding of the intricacies of trading over-the-counter (OTC) stocks and understand the very specific set of trading rules that influence the underlying trading techniques.

Goals

The goal of this chapter is to become intimately knowledgeable with the inner working and processes that dictate the behavior of OTC stocks.

At the end of this chapter you will know:

- The difference in dynamics between listed and OTC stocks
- How to recognize OTC chart patterns and price action
- The dynamic of price action in OTC stocks
- The concepts that dictate the behavior of OTC stocks
- How to prepare in advance for entries and exits on OTC stocks
- How to always have a proper plan and be able to reach quickly when trading OTC stocks

What is OTC?

Over-the-counter stocks, also known as unlisted stocks, can be compared to peer-to-peer file sharing networks, like Bit Torrent, Kazaa, Emule, etc. It's a distributed exchange for stocks with no centralized way of handling trades.

OTC stocks are traded between market makers directly without requiring the intervention of major exchanges to route orders. Market makers and broker-dealers deal directly with each other to complete a trade.

Unlike big markets like NASDAQ, NYSE and AMEX, stocks traded on the OTC are not traded electronically per se. Instead, orders are directly managed by market makers "manually". Also, where the big exchanges rely on a regulated and centralized market to ensure orders are processed in a publicly transparent, standardized, safe and fast manner, OTC stocks do not carry any of those traits when traded. Prices are not disclosed publicly until a trade has been completed.

OTC stocks are usually the stocks of choice for pump & dump promoters, as the companies that exist within its listings are usually of little worth. Very small emerging companies in need of public funding are able to continue healthy operations.

OTC stocks usually represent companies that do not meet the requirements of major exchanges or don't want to pay the major exchange fees.

Stocks listed on the OTC are the true definition of penny stocks, as the price per share is usually around or below the $1.00 price point.

This link provides the references to the official regulations to which OTC stocks are bound: http://www.otcmarkets.com/learn/sec-finra-rules.

Note: OTC does not have after-hours trading; it's exclusively done between 9:30 a.m. and 4 p.m. Eastern time.

Bulletin Board (OTCBB)

OTCBB stocks are a type of OTC listing that regroups companies that have offered their shares publicly to dealers belonging to these listings. Market makers are then directly responsible of ensuring the purchase and resale of a company listed on the OTCBB. All OTCBB stocks are run by the NASDAQ.

Pink Sheets

Pink sheets are part of the OTC listings and companies listed are not bound to the same minimum requirements or even required to file with the SEC. "Pink sheets" are also often used to refer to all stocks managed by OTC Markets, which can often be misleading, as pink sheets (OTCPK) are only a subset of that market.

Pink sheets are a type of OTC stocks and usually represent companies that require public funding without having a proper organization in place.

Pink sheets historically obtained their name from the fact that these types of listings were originally printed on pink paper.

The Gray Market

The gray market is a type of OTC where the dealers may execute orders for preferred customers for a new stock before it is actually opened publicly. Gray markets are usually very hard to trade because not only do they behave like BBs and pink sheets, but they also provide no public quotes to traders.

Gray market stock opportunities don't occur often, but their existence is noteworthy. These are also part of OTC Markets.

The Behavior of OTC Stocks

OTC stocks are bound by an unwritten set of trading rules that affects all traders that dare venture into its realm.

While some legal regulations exist with OTC stocks, they're often not properly enforced and their application is hard to verify, which makes OTC stocks the wild west of Wall Street.

In the sections below, we'll cover some of these unwritten rules that affect the traders who choose to play with OTC stocks.

What an OTC Chart Looks Like

OTC stocks have a very different price action dynamic in comparison to major exchanged. This dynamic results from the fact that OTC stocks belong to a decentralized marketplace where all orders are dealt in a peer-to-peer fashion, making the whole trading process much slower.

This translates in a completely different type of resulting intraday chart when looking at OTC stocks in comparison to NASDAQ or NYSE.

Figure III.3.1 - Multicharts - Appearance of an OTC Stock, 1min chart – THCZ

Figure III.3.1 shows the typical appearance of an OTC stock. Unlike big markets, the price action is not erratic with frequent sudden reversals. These charts usually fit in a "clean" chart category due to the way OTC markets operate.

The figure below shows a steady ramp up, a period of flat price action before ramping down in a consistent manner.

At the Whim of Market Makers

"A "market maker" is a firm that stands ready to buy and sell a particular stock on a regular and continuous basis at a publicly quoted price. You'll most often hear about market makers in the context of the Nasdaq or

other "over the counter" (OTC) markets. Market makers that stand ready to buy and sell stocks listed on an exchange, such as the New York Stock Exchange, are called "third market makers." Many OTC stocks have more than one market-maker." (Commission S. a., Market Maker, n.d.)

OTC stock trading is directly reliant on market makers (MM) processing the orders in a "manual" way. This means that while your platform may allow you to send orders electronically, the processing of these orders may not be done in an automated fashion and may actually require human intervention in order to get it filled.

Market makers are in charge of locating other market makers in order to fill in an order by buying and selling stock inventory to each other.

The general understanding is that market makers are required to fill at least one order at the listed price and size. This would normally work on a first-come-first-served basis in terms of who gets filled. There is, however, no way to ensure that this is the case, and MMs may choose to prioritize some trades over others before filling an order. This often results in unfilled orders at a certain price point for a given size, even if an order is sent and the availability is listed on the Level 2.

The Turtle and the Rabbit

As mentioned in the previous section, OTC orders often require a certain degree of "manual labor" market makers to fill an order. This fact implies that some of the deals are processed by an individual at a computer and could possibly imply a phone transaction with another MM.

Unlike listed stocks (NASDAQ, AMEX, NYSE, etc.), where all trades are automated and all orders are instantly processed by the centralized trading system, OTC offers no such convenience. Consequently, order fill times are considerably slower. Figure III.3.1 shows the result of these delays.

Taking into consideration that trades are managed by humans to a certain extent, orders take a much longer time to be registered in the time and sales and the price action variation changes progressively, preventing it from experiencing the erratic behavior that is often seen in listed stocks.

Think Ahead

One of the most important aspects of trading OTC stocks is having the ability to foresee the price action. In simple terms, traders need to think ahead in order to enter or exit positions.

As you learned in the previous section, trades are managed by people rather than computers. As a result, MMs are subjected to a queue of orders that they need to process in the order they arrive. This very fact implies that every trader attempting to trade a stock must compete for the available shares listed by the MM.

Market makers are then free to choose who to fill and when to fill an order.

Bottom line: When trading OTC stocks, traders must think ahead of the masses in order to enter or exit positions, or risk not having orders filled during spikes or panic.

Trading OTC Stocks

You know that trading OTC stocks require foresight. This is because as momentum increases, order fills become more difficult. MMs are flooded with orders at specific price points battling for their listed shares, yet are only able to accommodate a few orders before adjusting the price point.

Also, the order in which trade orders are processed are completely left to the discretion of the MM. They may choose to fill or not fill your order, even if the shares are available and you were "first" to claim them.

This means that when trading an OTC stock, it's important to have a strong hypothesis, understand the reasons to enter a position, and know exactly when such a position should be exited.

Trying to make such decisions while momentum is in progress will only lead to catastrophic results, as you'll learn in the next section. Timing OTC trades is of the utmost importance.

Figure III.3.2 - Multicharts – THCZ 1min chart - OTC trading

In Figure III.3.2, the red arrow on top shows a potential entry point for a short position. It relies on the expectation that the price will drop in the near future without having total assurance that it will.

A short sell order at that point would get filled rather quickly, while attempting to enter the position while the price is dropping is unlikely to result in a filled order, since numerous traders will attempt to enter such a position while competing for a limited number of shares at that price point for a given size in the MM's inventory.

The same idea applies to the blue arrow on the bottom in Figure III.3.2, where a long position should be expected before the breakout takes place.

Trading OTC stocks requires preparation and information. In order to enter a trade with an OTC stock, you must understand the history of the stock, previous price action, its resistance and support lines, and the fundamental details that can drive the price.

Note: Most pump & dumps are OTC stocks that represent worthless companies. Most OTC stocks you trade will focus on short positions.

Entering an OTC Position

Entering a position in an OTC stock requires preparation and a good hypothesis that justifies the interest in taking either a long or a short position.

The best time to enter an OTC stock position is either during sideway price action with the expectation of a breakout/down, at a time trading volume is limited and orders are quickly filled, or at the last stages of a momentum price event, right before the price reversal happens.

Once volume picks up and momentum starts, market makers are overwhelmed by a mass of traders attempting to enter the position at specific price points. This makes them unable to process all orders, and chances to get a proper entry fill are very unlikely.

It's best to enter a stock during the "calm before the storm" phase.

Exiting an OTC Position

Knowing when to exit an OTC position is far more important than the entry, as you'll learn in the next section.

In a profitable situation, the exit price point can be important, but won't result in losses. In these cases, it's best to exit when either when there's sideway price action, or at the beginning of a reversal move.

In a losing trade, exiting an OTC position quickly is of the utmost importance in order to limit potential losses. Much like for a profitable trade, the best and possibly only time to exit such a position is during sideway price action, or right before a reversal. Attempting to exit while a momentum move is in progress is unlikely, but can be attempted in the following ways:

- Matching a listed ARCA price and size on L2 in order to partially exit the position, as ARCA is an automated MM and exact orders are processed almost instantly.
- Setting a LMT/STP order with a price point below/above (depending on whether you are long or short) the current price that will appear higher on the order queue and will have higher chances of being processed when the price reaches that level.

Always remember that it's very difficult to get orders filled during momentum.

The Dangers of Trading OTC

As you've learned, trading OTC stocks requires a great deal of timing and good hypotheses in order to perform successful trades. This implies that the trader planning on engaging in such a practice is prepared and fully understands the behavior in these types of situations.

However, trading OTC stocks implies a higher risk of potential losses than listed stocks when not prepared.

On the entry side of a trade, the worst that can happen is simply missing a profitable opportunity. This is an acceptable outcome, as there's no loss involved with the trade.

On the other hand, exiting a position requires a lot more attention to the price action and what to expect from a stock.

Attempting to exit a position when a momentum move is happening is usually impossible, which consequently means that a trader with a considerable position will be subjected to an unfavorable price action until volume dies down or until the order gets filled. This may only happen at a much different price point than the RMS absolute stop value established by the trader, thus leading to more considerable losses than originally expected.

As an example, in Figure III.3.2, if a trader entered a long position at the top red arrow price point, he/she would be subjected to most of the down price before obtaining a fill. This is due to the fact that getting orders filled during momentum is very difficult.

It's important to know that even the most experienced traders fall victim to the effects of OTC trading and can experience significant losses.

You should also know that stocks traded in the OTC markets are usually prone to SEC halts, which can suspend all trading of a stock for an undetermined period of time.

Bottom line: Trading OTC stocks without the proper amount of preparation can lead to significant losses and must be executed with great care.

Summary

- OTC stocks follow a much different dynamic than listed stocks.
- OTC markets are a decentralized P2P type of market network.
- OTC orders are not processed instantaneously and a fill at a specific price point is not guaranteed.
- OTC orders are filled at the discretion of market makers, based on availability and order priority.
- Trading OTC stocks requires foresight and preparation.
- It's very difficult to trade OTC stocks when momentum is happening.
- Attempting to exit a losing position in an OTC stock during momentum price action is unlikely to be a possibility and can lead to significant losses.

Questions

1. What is an OTC stock?
  a. A stock traded on a centralized market.
  b. A stock listed on the NASDAQ.
  c. A stock listed on AMEX.
  d. A stock listed on a decentralized market where market makers trade directly with each other.

2. What are some characteristics of OTC stocks?
  a. Orders are executed immediately.
  b. Orders require some "manual" labor on behalf of the market maker.
  c. Orders are not executed immediately. They might require some time – or even possibly not be executed at all.
  d. OTC charts are progressive clean charts.

3. Trading an OTC stock requires
  a. Preparation
  b. Improvisation skills and quick reactions
  c. An understanding of the underlying system
  d. Knowledge that positions can quickly be entered and exited without restriction

4. What are some of the specific dangers of OTC stocks?
  a. Being stuck in an open position without the possibility of exiting while taking losses.
  b. Transaction fees are higher.
  c. Not cutting losses quickly.
  d. None of the above.

Chapter III.4 - SEC Filings

Overview

How to read and interpret the content of SEC filings in order to do in-depth research on stocks.

Goals

The goal of this chapter is to become deeply familiar with reading and interpreting the contents provided by SEC filings.

At the end of this chapter, you'll know:

- What an SEC filing is.
- What filings are the most useful when trading penny stocks.
- How to find relevant information about a company in the filing.
- How to interpret the data contained within the filing.
- How to use this information to perform trading decisions.

Introduction

Knowing how to read SEC filings is an advanced concept that is quite time consuming. While this chapter examines some of the concepts of reading and understanding the contents of SEC filings, it's by no means an exhaustive coverage of learning how to do it.

If you're interested in learning SEC filings in-depth, I urge you to obtain Michael Goode and Timothy Sykes's "How To Read SEC Filings" DVD (Goode & Sykes, 2010) on http://profit.ly.

What is an SEC filing?

An SEC filing is a document required from a publicly traded company to comply with the Securities and Exchange Commission's regulations.

SEC filings allow investors to have a clear view of a company's history and progress in order to make informed decisions on how to further invest in it.

These filings appear in the form of formal periodic reports that are publicly available and have a variety of informational purposes depending on the form being filed.

The SEC is in charge of checking the information contained within these forms in order to ensure that they meet certain requirements.

SEC filings offer investors a very in-depth view of the fundamental information about a company over time.

Where to Find SEC Filings?

There are multiple websites where SEC filings for companies can be found. Here are a few of them:

- EDGAR, the SEC official search for filings: http://www.sec.gov/edgar/searchedgar/companysearch.html
- Yahoo Finance: http://finance.yahoo.com on the right column under "SEC filings" when looking at a stock
- OTC Markets: http://www.otcmarkets.com/ on the right column under "Filings and Disclosure" when looking at a stock

All three sources refer to the official SEC documents.

Additionally, some broker platforms will offer access to the SEC filings directly from the platform itself.

SEC filings are also available electronically, and these electronic versions are easier to comb through when looking for information.

Types of SEC filings

SEC filings are regulatory documents describing the state of a company at the time of filing. There are various types of filings dedicated to this effect that serve different purposes when it comes to providing a company's relevant information.

While all filings provide valuable fundamental data about a given company, only a handful of documents are actually relevant when it comes to pennystocking and performing in-depth research to gain an edge over the market.

Useful SEC Filings in Penny Stocks

When researching companies, you can find information relevant to pennystocking in a handful of SEC documents.

Here are the most relevant to the type of research performed when dealing with these types of securities:

10-K: The Annual Report

The 10-K represents the annual financial report filed by companies at the end of their fourth quarter period – or more precisely, within 90 days of the end of their fiscal year.

The filing date for this document varies from company to company.

The 10-K is a report that provides investors with a comprehensive analysis of the company. This filing provides the detailed financial statements of the company.

The 10-K filing is divided in several sections:

- The "business summary" provides a description for the company's operation, its employees, history, marketing, real estate, business segments, R&D and competition.
- The MD&A, management discussion and analysis offers a description on the company's operations and financial outlook.
- Financial statements, which may include the cash flow, income statements and the balance sheet.
- Other sections of the filing may discuss the company's legal proceedings and the management team.

The 10-K filing is an audited report.

The foreign firm equivalent of the 10-K is the 20-F.

10-Q: The Quarterly Report

This SEC filing is a truncated version of the 10-K that must be filed within 45 days after the end of each fiscal quarter.

This document provides details on the company's latest developments and offers insight on the planned direction the company plans to take.

The sections in this filing are similar to the 10-K and include unaudited financial statements as well as a toned-down version of the 10-K report.

The foreign firm equivalent of the 10-Q is the 6-F.

8-K: Report of Any Other Important Event

The 8-K filing describes important events not included in the 10-K and 10-Q reports. This document is unscheduled and typically issued when a major company event is relevant to investors.

This document addresses events and offers more details and exhibits such as data tables and press releases.

Some of the events that result in the production of an 8-K filing may include:

- Bankruptcy
- Receivership
- Material impairments
- Completion of acquisition
- Disposition of assets
- Departures or appointments of executives
- Other events of importance
- Press releases
- Debt conversion

8-K filings can report multiple events and are usually divided in exhibits.

The foreign firm equivalent of the 8-K is the 6-F.

DEF 14A: Definitive Proxy Statement
The DEF 14A is a filing that provides investors with management salaries and conflicts of interest that may be of interest.

This document is usually filed before a shareholder meeting takes place and must be sent to the SEC before soliciting a vote on corporate matters.

Less Useful SEC Filings

There are a multitude of other forms that must be filed with the SEC, such as:

- Form 4: The purchase or sale of stock by insiders.
- Form 3: Initial filing of ownership.
- Form 5: Annual statement of ownership.
- SC 13G: The purchase or sale of shares by large holders, more specifically those owning more than 5% of the company's shares.
- SC 13D: The purchase or sale of shares by an activist investor, or more specifically an entity wishing to influence the direction of the company.
- /A: This usually indicates an amendment to any of the existing filings (i.e. 10-Q/A).
- NT 10-Q and NT 10-K: Notifications of late filing for a quarterly or a yearly report.
- 10QSB and 10KSB: Similar to the 10-Q and 10-K, applicable to small business and used only for the smallest public companies.
- S-3: The registration of securities, the foreign equivalent is the F-3.
- S-8: The registration of securities for issuing stock option plans for employees.

- Shelf registrations: They allow a company to sell shares without providing an S-3.
- Many other less relevant documents can be found on the EDGAR website.

Combing through the Data

SEC filings are often overwhelming documents containing lots of data regarding the fundamental elements of companies.

Combing through the data takes time, so it's important to know what to look for and what's relevant.

When reading through SEC filings, it's also important to consider all statements in relation to the size or value of a company in order to have a relative perspective of how certain data can affect the worth of the information being considered. In other words, information slightly affecting a $1 billion company may destroy a $10 million one.

Events and information must be put in the right context and the details need to be considered relative to the size and value of the company.

The Structure of a 10-K

The 10-K, as previously defined, is the annual status report for the company. It's a long document that covers all the aspects of the business for the finished fiscal year and contains crucial information for investors.

The 10-K (and similarly the 10-Q, in a less detailed version) is composed of many elements that provide different types of data regarding the company in question.

The various sections are described on the SEC website (Commission S. a., How to Read a 10-K, n.d.).

The 10-K is structured as follows:

- An index describing the sections of the document.
- Part I
  - Item 1 – "**Business**" is description of the business and how it operates, including its business strategy, products, services, marketing, intellectual property, recent events, etc.
  - Item 1A – "**Risk Factors**", which often describes the competition but may also contain some other juicy details that may affect operations. It does not, however, focus on how to counter these risks.

- o Item 1B – "**Unresolved Staff Comments**" is usually dedicated to respond to comments from the SEC staff on previously filed reports that weren't resolved after a certain time.
- o Item 2 – "**Properties**" pertains to the information about the properties, locations, plants or other important physical properties.
- o Item 3 – "**Legal Proceedings**" focuses on pending lawsuits, legal proceedings or other types of litigation.
- o Item 4 – This item doesn't currently offer any information and is reserved by the SEC for future use.

- Part II
  - o Item 5 – "**Market Registrant's Common Equity, Related Stockholder Matters and Issuer Purchases of Equity Securities**" is about the company's equity securities that may include market information, number of shareholders, stock repurchases by the business, dividends, or similar information.
  - o Item 6 – "**Selected Financial Data**" represents certain financial data for the company over the last five years.
  - o Item 7 – "**Management's Discussion and Analysis of Financial Condition and Results of Operations**" pertains to the company's perspective over the business results of the past financial year. Also known as the MD&A, it allows a company to tell its story.
  - o Item 7A – "**Quantitative and Qualitative Disclosures about Market Risk**" is the information regarding the company's exposure to market risk. In other words, risks of the stock market that may affect the company's operation.
  - o Item 8 – "**Financial Statements and Supplementary Data**" primarily focuses on the company's audited financial statements. This information is presented according to the accounting standards, conventions and rules known as the Generally Accepted Accounting Principles (GAAP). This section includes:
    - Income statements
    - Balance sheets
    - Cash flow statements
    - Shareholder equity
  - o Item 9 – "**Changes in and Disagreements with Accountants on Accounting and Financial Disclosure**" discusses any disagreements arising with accountants if there has been a change in accountants.
  - o Item 9A – "**Controls and Procedures**" provides the information about the company's controls and procedures to handle internal financial reporting.

- o Item 9B – **"Other Information"** provides information that is required to be reported on a different form but was not yet reported.
- Part III
  - o Item 10 – **"Directors, Executive Officers and Corporate Governance"** includes the information about the experience and background of the company's directors and executive officers, as well as the business code of ethics, and any relevant qualification information for directors and committees of the board.
  - o Item 11 – **"Executive Compensation"** provides a disclosure about the compensation provided to the top executive officers, and compensation policies over the past year.
  - o Item 12 – **"Security Ownership of Certain Beneficial Owners and Management and Related Stockholder Matters"** provides information about the number of shares owned by the company's officers, directors and large shareholders. Also includes details about equity compensation plans.
  - o Item 13 – **"Certain Relationships and Related Transactions, and Director Independence"** provides information in regards to the relationships and transactions between the business and its officers, directors, and their respective family members.
  - o Item 14 – **"Principal Accountant Fees and Services"** is used to disclose the fees paid to accounting firms for their services during the year. However, this information is usually included in the DEF 14A form, "proxy statement" and this item would simply reference to that form.
- Part IV
  - o Item 15 – **"Exhibits, Financial Statement Schedules"** provides a list of exhibits and financial statements included with the 10-K, and includes:
    - Company bylaws
    - Copies of material contracts
    - List of the companies' subsidiaries
    - Etc.

What to Look For

When dealing with penny stocks, combing through SEC filings is about finding discrepancies in financial statements, outstanding debts, insider deals that may adversely affect shareholders, and so on.

All this information is publicly available and hidden under a large amount of data regarding the current state of the company being researched.

Financial Statements

In order to understand SEC filings such as the 10-Q and the 10-K, you must know how to read financial statements like balance sheets, cash flow and income statements. The financial information is built upon the Generally Accepted Accounting Principles (GAAP). Ensure that you're familiar with these rules when doing SEC filing research.

Understanding the company's business is always important prior to plunging into the financial information. Fundamental analysis can help understand how certain numbers come to be.

Financial statements can hide all the juicy details about a company's financial health. Understanding the math behind it can help uncover discrepancies or hidden expenses that may reflect other dubious events.

> *"Most audit reports express an 'unqualified opinion' that the financial statements fairly present the company's financial position in conformity with GAAP. If, however, an auditor expresses a 'qualified opinion' or a 'disclaimer of opinion', investors should look carefully at what kept the auditor from expressing an unqualified opinion. Likewise, investors should carefully evaluate material weaknesses disclosed on internal controls over financial reporting." (Commission S. a., How to Read a 10-K, n.d.)*

The above quote is a hint by the SEC to look for the results of auditor reports on 10-K forms to find interesting data.

Faking financial data isn't an easy task, so it's important to pay attention to how numbers balance between the balance sheet and the income statements. This type of information is usually a good indicator that something questionable is happening.

> *" 'Changes in and Disagreements with Accountants on Accounting and Financial Disclosure' requires a company, if there has been a change in its accountants, to discuss any disagreements it had with those accountants. Many investors view this disclosure as a red flag." (Commission S. a., How to Read a 10-K, n.d.)*

It also brings the attention to Item 9 on the 10-K. Disagreements between accountants can be an interesting indicator, when looking for dirt.

Legal Events

Look for the results of legal events, as this type of information can reflect ongoing lawsuits that can, in certain cases, bring a company to bankruptcy.

Understanding how the legal proceedings affect the company can help further understand its health and potential outcome.

Risk Factors

Finding this type of data can be tricky and can't simply be categorized, as it represents the risk factors for the company. As such, this type of information varies from company to company and requires some fundamental understanding of the underlying business.

Risk factors are usually a good way to discover potential issues that the business faces or will face in the near future that could affect operations, finances, etc.

Excessive Debt Due in the Short Term

Owing excessive debt and having a payment due date in the short term can reveal that the company is in serious trouble in terms of finances.

This usually indicates that the underlying company is unable to generate enough income to clear the debt, which consequently points to the fact that the business might end up filing for bankruptcy and having its assets liquidated among the creditors and largest shareholders.

Be sure to learn the primary beneficiaries in the case of the liquidation of the company's assets and find out how this affects holders of publicly traded shares.

Other Indicators

A multitude of indicators can be found in the SEC filings to discover potential issues with a company. Here are some things you should look for when performing in-depth SEC filings research:

- Going concerns that indicate a company isn't doing well usually represent a red flag. Applicable to most P&Ds.
- Name changes usually indicate reverse mergers. Essentially, reverse mergers allow private companies to become public without raising capital. Investopedia offers a great explanation on reverse mergers (Dumon, n.d.).

- Number of outstanding shares and calculated market capitalization (outstanding shares multiplied by the stock price per share).
- Acquisitions and how the acquired companies relate to the acquiring company.
- Dramatic increase in asset value. Can indicate a reverse merger.
- Entries in the balance sheet providing complex or confusing names.
- Research shares other than common stock.
- Debt conversion costs should be investigated.

Simply put, find where the money comes from and where it's going.

Using the Data to Make Trade Decisions

Digging through SEC filings is a time-consuming research activity that requires you to study and analyze the most intricate details contained within a company's reports.

The main purpose of performing such an in-depth analysis is to validate information that's already suspected in order to further reinforce a trading hypothesis. It is, however, important that you know when to stop looking into a company, as the time spent may not yield any profitable result.

Making trade decisions based on the data contained within SEC filings pertains to understanding how the fundamental data may affect the stock price.

For example, quickly recognizing a company that announces majestic future events but doesn't have a strong financial or legal basis to prove these advances can indicate a potential pump & dump (whether it's compensated or not is a completely different subject).

The result of the in-depth research performed by looking into SEC filings is intended to determine whether a company has real worth and if its statements can be taken seriously.

More importantly, such research can help predict potential price action behavior by giving an edge to traders who understand the underlying business operations and how these operations compare to the basic information that is publicly available to those who don't perform such research activity.

Diving into SEC filings can help you make the following assessment and decisions:

- Determine if a company is worthy. Is it a potential long position?
- Determine if a company is dubious or performing questionable financial activities. Is it a potential short?

- Determine if a stock with an overextended price action has a justified catalyst to push traders to continue buying.
- Determine if a company's press release on financial matters, contracts or agreements have any concrete backing rather than just artificially pumping interest.
- Determine who owns the shares of the company and how that may affect the price.
  - Is it being funded by toxic financing such as PIPEs (Private Investment in Public Equity)?
  - Is it being used for a pump & dump?
- Determine if the company is potentially suspicious. Will it get halted? Is it a potential short position?
- Determine if the cash flow statements are representative of the company's actual operations and if the values make financial sense.
- Determine if hidden expenses are questionable.
- Determine if company's officers have previously been part of questionable businesses, or if they have been in litigations that may affect the company or represent a conflict of interest. Is it a potential short?

Summary

- SEC filings are required by the SEC for public companies.
- SEC filings disclose all the necessary information required for investors to make decisions.
- There are multiple SEC filings. The most important are:
  - 10-K, annual report
  - 10-Q, quarter report
  - 8-K, report of important events
  - DEF 14A, proxy statements
- Researching SEC Filings is a complementary tool for reinforcing trade hypotheses.
- SEC filing research should never be used alone to perform trade decisions.
- Look for red flags in SEC filings.
- Learn to identify the reasons and facts found in SEC filings that can influence stock prices.
- SEC filings contain factual information. Compare them to promotions and press releases to get the big picture and reinforce your hypothesis.
- Bad companies may perform well in the market for a certain period of time.

Questions

1. What is an SEC filing?

a. A major media network news release providing detailed information about a stock.

b. A form filed with the US Securities and Exchange Commissions to update the current status of the company.

c. A form filed with the US Patent Office to protect intellectual property.

d. None of the above.

2. What is a 10-K?

a. A quarterly financial report

b. The report of a company event

c. A yearly financial report

d. A definitive proxy statement

3. What is a 10-Q?

a. A quarterly financial report

b. The report of a company event

c. A yearly financial report

d. A definitive proxy statement

4. What is an 8-K?

a. A quarterly financial report

b. The report of a company event

c. A yearly financial report

d. A definitive proxy statement

5. What elements are important to consider in a 10-K?

a. Financial statement

b. Important company events

c. Proxy statements

d. Excessive debt due soon

Homework

- For every stock on your watchlist, take the time to comb over the available SEC filings and see which are relevant to the price action.
  - Document the reaction to stocks with the release of 10-Q, 10-K and 8-K.

Chapter III.5 - Position Boxing

Overview

Here, you'll learn the concept of position boxing in order to counter the downside of a potential play, while ensuring the retention of shares to short for a given stock that has low availability.

Goals

The goal of this chapter is to teach you how to box a position in order to perform a short sell trade with an instrument that has low short share availability.

Short Selling and the Hunt for Shares

Chapter III.1 focused on the various intricacies of short sell trades. One of the important points you learned was the sometimes difficult nature of obtaining shares to borrow for a short sell trade.

As previously explained, shortable shares rely on the broker-dealer's inventory; however, in some cases these shares are quickly used by other traders and shorting a stock when momentum happens becomes impossible.

"Hunting" for shares in this type of situation becomes necessary when you want to take a short position in order to generate profit, but this needs to be much in advance. As a result, entering a potential short too early can result in a short squeeze situation, forcing you to exit the position with significant losses.

A Tale of Two Brokers

In order to remedy this type of situation, a solution can be applied: boxing a position. The very concept of boxing a position relies on having multiple stockbroker accounts to perform trades – ideally two or more.

Having two or more brokers allows you to take multiple differing positions on the same stock without affecting the position sizes at other brokers.

Boxing the Position

Boxing a position takes into account the concept that shares for a given stock are hard to borrow or difficult to find at a given broker, meaning that these shares need to be reserved in advance in order to be able to trade them. Reserving shares isn't always possible, so it's therefore necessary to enter the short position whenever the shares are available. This is often unsuitable when the stock price is still expected to rise before crashing.

The concept of boxing the position is:

- Taking a short position with Broker 1.
- And taking a similarly sized long position with Broker 2. This position may be a bigger size if you expect a prolonged upside on this trade.

This first step ensures that the current total value of your position is balanced close to 0, meaning that a move in either direction will result in neither a profit nor a loss when both positions are exited at the same time.

Once the stock is ready to crash, resulting in a price drop of the stock, you then close your long position with broker 2, leaving only the short position open with broker 1.

You can then simply close the short position with broker 1, as he/she normally would according to the chosen trading strategy.

Figures III.5.1 through III.5.4 show the process of position boxing.

The Trader   Broker 1   Broker 2

Figure III.5.1 - The players

Figure III.5.1 shows the players in this process, namely the trader, broker 1 and broker 2.

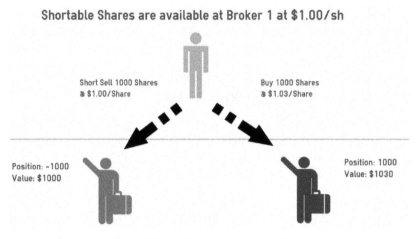

Figure III.5.2 - Entries with both brokers

Figure III.5.2 shows the position boxing entry process, which implies that the trader takes both a short (based on availability) and long with similarly sized positions. The figure above depicts both positions as being 1,000 shares; however, the trader could have taken a larger position in order to increase potential gains on the upside.

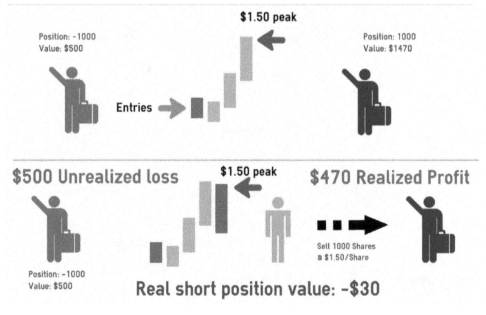

Figure III.5.3 - First exit with Broker 2 when the trader expects the price to break down

Figure III.5.3 shows the trader exiting the long position. This is typically done once the trader has determined through the various strategy indicators that the stock price is about to drop.

In exiting the position, the trader realizes the profit on the upside, compensating for the short sell trade's unrealized losses up to this point.

Prior to exiting the position, the combined cash value of both positions was close to $0. As soon as the trader exits the long position, this essentially corresponds to a typical short sell entry. With no counterbalancing trade, this position is now ready to either generate a real profit on the down side or an actual loss on the up side.

Figure III.5.4 below depicts a typical buy-to-cover exit for a short position. In this fictional case, the profit is considered to be $970, for a $1/share drop from its highs. This profit is ensured by the fact that the long position compensated for the losses of the short position. Consequently, the short position actually becomes an actual position when the trader exits the long position.

Buy to Cover 1000 Shares a $0.50/Share

$970 Realized Profit

$0.50 bottom

Figure III.5.4 - Typical buy to cover exit with broker 2 for a profit

Note that the final account differences in brokers 1 and 2 will respectively be +$500 and +$470 .The cumulative profit of both positions results in a profitable trade.

The Dangers of Position Boxing

Position boxing requires proper timing in order to enter both broker positions almost simultaneously with two different broker accounts. This means having the proper experience to minimize the time required to get those orders filled while experiencing a very little price variation between both entries (entry price on broker 1 should be very close to the entry price on broker 2).

Additionally, all the dangers of short selling are still applicable, namely forced buy-ins and SEC halts of the stock.

These dangers must be taken into consideration when boxing a position, as the financial risk is technically doubled even though both positions balance one another to a $0 market value.

Summary

- Position boxing is used when shares to short for a given security are scarce.
- It's also used when it's necessary to maintain a balance between the prior to committing to a position.
- Position boxing can improve the efficiency of short positions.
- Two or more brokers are necessary in order to box a position.
- The dangers of position boxing are the same as those for short selling.
- Position boxing allows you to "reserve" shortable shares for a given security in order to perform a trade when the stock is ready for a drop.

Questions

1. What is position boxing?
a. Placing a price bracket on a trader in order to preset the exit at profit and the exit at loss.
b. It allows the trader to take both a long and short position simultaneously on the same stock on different brokers.
c. It consists buying and selling shares simultaneously with the same broker.
d. None of the above.

2. How many brokers are involved in position boxing?
a. 1
b. 2
c. 3
d. 4 or more

3. What are some of the dangers of position boxing?
a. The same that exist for OTC stocks.
b. The same that apply to short selling.
c. The same that apply to buying securities.
d. None of the above.

4. What's the purpose of position boxing?
a. Allowing the trader to enter a short position before it is ready to crash without taking capital losses.
b. To profit both from the long and short positions.
c. To circumvent the hunt for shares to short and avoid being unable to short the stock when it crashes.
d. To ensure that the profits and losses are always in balance.

Homework

Note: this assignment is only intended for those with more than one broker account.

- Trade a small position ($50-$100) on each account in opposite directions:
  - 1 short position.
  - 1 equivalent long position.
  - Let the price move for a time and document the profit/loss on both accounts.
  - Close the long position (sell your open shares) and let the short position follow the stock.
  - Exit the position at a profit or loss of $10 (or close the position if there's no price movement that provides the magnitude of gain/loss). Document your results.
  - Pick a stock with low volatility and high liquidity.
- Gain experience.

Chapter III.6 - Pyramiding Positions

Overview

All about the concept of pyramiding positions, also known as adding to a position.

Goals

The goal of this chapter is to teach you to know when to add to a position and when to add to your position in order to maximize your potential profits.

At the end of this chapter, you'll know:

- The rules for adding to a position.
- How big your added position should be.
- Your new absolute stop.
- How to add multiple times and determining the necessary values.

Introduction

When trading, some plays might turn out better than originally expected, making a base investment less profitable – and it could be with a larger position. Pyramiding positions – or adding to a position – takes advantage of a favorable stock price action and increases the potential profits for that series of trades.

I adapted the theory behind this strategy based on the concept of trend following pyramiding positions introduced by the Turtle Experiment (Covel, 2009), and applied it to penny stocks.

This relies on the NT risk management strategy presented in Chapter II.4 and uses the concepts of **risk unit** (U) and **average true range** (N) in order to determine position sizes, entries and stops.

Warning

Adding to an existing position implies increasing your position size in order to generate more profit on a given trade. This chapter is included in the Advanced Concepts section, as taking larger positions is a bigger risk, with potentially bigger losses in unfavorable scenarios.

Pyramiding positions requires understanding the process, but also experience and discipline in order to cut losses quickly and exit positions at a moment's notice.

This type of strategy is better suited to listed stocks rather than OTCs due to the speed of execution and the effects that this can have on entering or exiting positions.

The Numbers

The pyramiding positions technique relies on a couple of concepts established in Chapter II.4, with the NT RMS.

When considering adding to a position, you must consider the following parameters:

- Total equity: E
- Average true range: N
- Risk unit %: p
- Risk unit $: U
- The absolute stop multiplier: x
- The addition threshold multiplier: m

The risk unit is the same as established in the NT RMS and should be adjusted with the evolution of the total equity value (which includes realized and unrealized profits/losses).

Pyramid Limits

While pyramiding positions can be a very profitable strategy, it's advisable to limit the number of entry additions to 5 risk units.

This limits the amount of cash that is dedicated to a single position.

Example:

Equity: $10,000
Risk unit: 2%

Risk unit value: $200

For a stock having an N of $0.50 and a stock price of $5.00/share, you can take a position of 400 shares with a maximum risk of $200.

The position value at 400 shares would be $2,000.

Adding to a position five times with a risk unit of 2% with a stock price of $5+ implies a total position value of over $10,000, which is equivalent to your total equity.

Taking a position that occupies a 100% of your capital is unacceptable, as it can blow up the account if something goes wrong.

Always consider this fact when using this technique for adding to your position.

Adding to Your Position

Adding to your position using the pyramiding technique implies recalculating the N, U, and stops for each new position taken in the concerned security.

We'll look at an example below.

The exit (established by the RMS) and addition multipliers also need to be taken into consideration, and remain constant throughout the whole pyramiding process.

The first step is the original entry into the position. RMS basics are covered in Chapter II.4.

Steps two through five operate based on adjusted trader's equity and N based on the stock price action, profit and loss, which then determines the new absolute stops and subsequent entries if necessary.

The entry prices for steps 2-5 are determined as follows:

$$EP = base\ price + (step\# - 1) \times m \times N$$

This essentially means performing the product of the entry multiplier, the current step number minus 1 and the average true range, then adding this value to the base entry price to obtain the entry price for the current step.

Fictional Case Study

Let's look at an example of how this technique for pyramiding entries works. It assumes a fictional long position on a non-existent stock in order to present the details of the technique in a more practical manner. Additionally, we'll assume that the price of the stock follows a constantly increasing pattern for the duration of the example. However, the absolute stops described below should serve as an example of when to fully exit the position when that value is crossed following a reversal.

Step 1 – Basic Long Entry
For the purpose of this example, the following parameters will be established:

- Base equity: $E = \$10,000.00$
- Risk unit: $p = 1\%$
- Absolute stop multiplier: $x = 1$
- Entry multiplier: $m = 0.5$

This provides us with the Risk unit $ value as being

$$U = \$100.00$$

We assume the starting point of the stock as having the following values:

- Current price and 1st step entry price: $2.50
- Average true range: $N = \$0.50$

An entry at the current price with the current N value implies the following position size for a long position:

$$P = floor\left(\frac{\$100}{0.50}\right) = 200 \; shares$$
$$Position \; value \; \$P = 200 \times \$2.50 = \$500.00$$

Additionally, we calculate our first stop to be:

$$S_1 = x \times N = 1 \times \$0.50 = \$0.50$$
$$S_1 = \$2.50 - \$0.50 = \$2.00$$

Our first absolute stop is therefore set at $2.00 for a $100 loss if the price drops.

Table III.6.1 summarizes the current state of the trader's position:

Table III.6.1 - Pyramid entry Step 1 - initial position

Unit #	Entry price	# Shares	Stop price	P/L	RtOE[6]
1	$2.50	200	$2.00	$0.00	1%

Step 2 – First Addition

The second entry point is determined as follows:

$$EP_2 = entry \; price + (step\# - 1) \times m \times N$$
$$EP_2 = \$2.50 + (2 - 1) \times 0.5 \times 0.5 = \$2.50 + \times 1 \times 0.25$$
$$EP_2 = \$2.50 + 0.25 = \$2.75$$

---

[6] Risk to Original Equity

The current stock price is $2.75, resulting in the following values:

- Equity: $E = \$10,050.00$
- Risk unit: $U = \$10,050.00 \times 1\% = \$100.50$
- Adjusted stop price: $S_2 = \$2.75 - \$0.50 = \$2.25$
- Second entry position size: $P_2 = floor\left(\frac{100.50}{0.5}\right) = 201\ shares$
- Position value: $\$P_2 = 201 \times \$2.75 = \$552.75$

Table III.6.2 - Pyramid entry Step 2 - first addition

Unit #	Entry price	# Shares	Stop price	P/L	RtOE
1	$2.50	200	$2.25	$50.00	0.5%
2	$2.75	201	$2.25	$0.00	1%
Total:		401		$50.00	1.5%

Step 3 – Second Addition
The second entry point is determined as follows:

$$EP_3 = entry\ price + (step\# - 1) \times m \times N$$
$$EP_3 = \$2.50 + (3 - 1) \times 0.5 \times 0.5 = \$2.50 + \times 2 \times 0.25$$
$$EP_3 = \$2.50 + 0.50 = \$3.00$$

The current stock price is $2.75, resulting in the following values:

- Equity: $E = \$10,150.25$
- Risk unit: $U = \$10,150.25 \times 1\% = \$101.50$
- Adjusted stop price: $S_3 = \$3.00 - \$0.50 = \$2.50$
- Third entry position size: $P_3 = floor\left(\frac{101.50}{0.5}\right) = 203\ shares$
- Position value: $\$P_3 = 203 \times \$3.00 = \$609.00$

Table III.6.3 - Pyramid entry Step 3 - second addition

Unit #	Entry price	# Shares	Stop price	P/L	RtOE
1	$2.50	200	$2.50	$100.00	0%
2	$2.75	201	$2.50	$50.00	0.5%
3	$3.00	203	$2.50	$0.00	1.01%
Total:		604		$50.00	1.51%

Step 4 – Third Addition

The fourth entry point is determined as follows:

$$EP_4 = entry\ price + (step\# - 1) \times m \times N$$
$$EP_4 = \$2.50 + (4 - 1) \times 0.5 \times 0.5 = \$2.50 + \times 3 \times 0.25$$
$$EP_4 = \$2.50 + 0.75 = \$3.25$$

The current stock price is $2.75, resulting in the following values:

- Equity: $E = \$10,301.50$
- Risk unit: $U = \$10,301.50 \times 1\% = \$103.01$
- Updated ATR: $N = \$0.60$
- Adjusted stop price: $S_4 = \$3.25 - \$0.60 = \$2.65$
- Fourth entry position size: $P_4 = floor\left(\frac{103.01}{0.6}\right) = 171\ shares$
- Position value: $\$P_4 = 171 \times \$3.25 = \$555.75$

Table III.6.4 - Pyramid entry Step 4 - third addition

Unit #	Entry price	# Shares	Stop price	P/L	RtOE
1	$2.50	200	$2.65	$150.00	0%
2	$2.75	201	$2.65	$100.50	0.20%
3	$3.00	203	$2.65	$50.75	0.61%
4	$3.25	171	$2.65	$0.00	1.02%
Total:		775		$301.25	1.83%

Step 5 – Fourth and Last Addition

The fifth entry point is determined as follows:

$$EP_5 = entry\ price + (step\# - 1) \times m \times N$$
$$EP_5 = \$2.50 + (5 - 1) \times 0.5 \times 0.5 = \$2.50 + \times 4 \times 0.25$$
$$EP_5 = \$2.50 + 1.00 = \$3.50$$

The current stock price is $2.75, resulting in the following values:

- Equity: $E = \$10,533.75$
- Risk unit: $U = \$10,533.75 \times 1\% = \$105.33$
- Adjusted stop price: $S_5 = \$3.55 - \$0.60 = \$2.50$
- Fifth entry position size: $P_5 = floor\left(\frac{105.33}{0.6}\right) = 175\ shares$
- Position value: $\$P_5 = 175 \times \$3.55 = \$621.25$

Table III.6.5 - Pyramid entry Step 5 - 4th and last addition

Unit #	Entry price	# Shares	Stop price	P/L	RtOE
1	$2.50	200	$2.95	$210.00	0%
2	$2.75	201	$2.95	$160.80	0%
3	$3.00	203	$2.95	$111.65	0.10%
4	$3.25	171	$2.95	$51.30	0.51%
5	$3.55	175	$2.95	$0.00	1.05%
Total:		950		533.75	1.66%

Total cumulative entry position value @ $3.55:

$$TEPV = 500 + 552.75 + 609 + 555.75 + 621.25 = \$2,838.75$$

The total cumulative investment for each of the positions taken in this example is $2,838.75, assuming a profit of $533.75, by maintaining all the positions at the $3.55 price point per share.

If the price continued to rise, so would the profits of each of your steps, progressively eliminating the total risk to equity. Conversely, with an absolute stop set at $2.95, the maximum loss would be of $166.00 at step 5, which is already covered by the gains in steps 1 and 2.

Summary

- Pyramiding positions is an advanced concept to add to an existing position in order to maximize profits.
- Pyramiding can be risky, as it implies increasing the position size.
- A five-step limit should be set when pyramiding positions in order to limit the total amount of equity being invested.
- This technique relies on the NT RMS described in Chapter II.4 and the values defined therein.

Homework

- Look for stocks with the potential to break out and enter a position ($50-$100 total position value).
    - Use the pyramiding rules to add to your position when the threshold is reached.
    - Exit the position when the highest step absolute stop is reached.
    - Stick to your RMS rules.
    - Document your results.

Chapter III.7 - Trading the Spread

Overview

Here, you'll learn the concept of trading the spread, which allows you to profit from medium volume stocks that are subjected to a wide difference between the "bid" and the "ask".

Goals

The goal of this chapter is to teach you a technique to profit from stocks that experience very little price change due to a stalemate in trading resulting from a wide price gap between buyers and sellers.

At the end of this chapter, you'll know:

- How to uncover potential candidates for this type of play.
- How to enter and exit position relying on this technique.
- The potential dangers of trading the spread.

Introduction

Trading the spread is a technique that relies essentially on taking advantage of the difference between what buyers are willing to pay for a stock and what sellers want to receive.

Becoming successful at this advanced technique requires experience and patience. More importantly, it's not the type of play that comes to you often, but it can potentially be profitable since it can be repeated as many times as the stock allows it.

Trading the spread is directly dependent on a wide difference between the "bid" and the "ask" prices, usually looking for anything above a $0.15 gap for stocks priced under $10.00.

Trading the spread also relies on having access to Level 2 real time-data in order to have a proper overview of how buyers and sellers stand up to each other. More precisely, identify the presence of walls of buyers and sellers present to reinforce the hypothesis that this technique may be successfully applied.

Understanding the Spread

The spread is usually the result of mid- and low-volume stocks where both buyers and sellers remain firm on their order prices, dramatically reducing the immediate volatility of the stock.

MMID	BID	SIZE	MMID	ASK	SIZE
PHL	14.75	600	PHL	14.85	500
NYE	14.75	1400	NYE	14.85	700
NSDQ	14.75	996	NSDQ	14.85	800
NSD	14.75	900	NSD	14.85	800
IEXG	14.75	100	EDGA	14.85	1700
EDGX	14.75	600	BOS	14.85	1900
EDGA	14.75	400	BATY	14.85	12300
BOS	14.75	600	BATS	14.85	500
BATY	14.75	800	ARCA	14.85	1600
BATS	14.75	500	EDGX	14.90	500
ARCA	14.75	600	GSCO	15.20	1900
GSCO	14.50	1900	MSCO	15.35	100
MSCO	14.35	100	XGWD	15.40	100

Figure III.7.1 – StocksToTrade - WAIR $0.10 Spread on L2

Figure III.7.1 shows a $0.10 spread between the "bid" and the "ask" at similar position size orders.

In terms of charts, this usually means very little movement over time in price action, hence revealing a low volatility stock. This can also often be associated with a low liquidity stock.

Stocks with a wide spread often have a volume under 200,000 shares on the day.

Finding Interesting Stocks

There are a couple of ways to find stocks to which this technique could be applicable.

The first way is "manual". You'll have to use a real-time screener/scanner to look for stocks with a spread, determine the spread visually, and mentally calculate the difference between "bid" and "ask" for each of the stocks on your scanner, and then determine those that meet your criteria.

The second option, which is currently the only way to perform this type of filtration, is by creating a StocksToTrade filter that looks for a spread above a certain value.

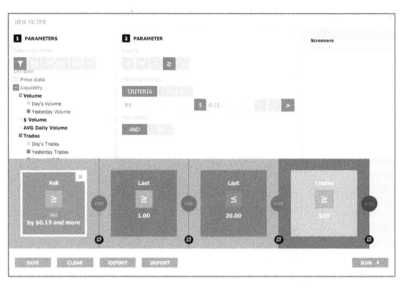

Figure III.7.2 - StocksToTrade - Filter to look for a spread greater than $0.15

Figure III.7.2 shows the scanner builder that allows you to create a real-time filter in order to find stocks that have an "ask" price greater than the "bid" price by $0.15. Once you run the filter, you obtain the desired results and can look further into whether any of those plays are of any interest for this technique.

Time	Symbol	Company ...	Last	Bid	Spread	Ask	% Chg	Net Change	Volume	Trades
12:15:43	UPLMQ	Ultra Petroleu...	4.48	4.70	0.18	4.88	-6.08 %	-0.29	225,171	315
12:02:12	MRZLF	Mirasol Resour...	1.25	1.22	0.18	1.40	-4.53 %	-0.06	75,203	140
12:13:06	ETX	Eaton Vance M...	18.641	18.65	0.18	18.83	-2.40 %	-0.439	62,257	306
12:15:41	SND	Smart Sand Inc.	11.04	11.04	0.18	11.22	-2.82 %	-0.32	17,000	133
12:15:04	ESSA	ESSA Bancorp ...	14.455	14.37	0.17	14.54	+0.80 %	0.115	12,429	104
12:10:56	USAC	USA Compressi...	18.13	18.05	0.17	18.22	+0.78 %	0.14	31,137	170
12:02:12	SVT	Servotronics Inc.	9.46	9.30	0.17	9.47	-1.42 %	-0.136	43,121	173
12:15:45	DEST	Destination Mat...	8.22	8.21	0.17	8.38	-0.48 %	-0.04	26,071	204
11:42:32	ACST	Acasti Pharma ...	1.36	1.26	0.17	1.43	-1.45 %	-0.02	61,861	209
12:15:56	FRTA	Forterra Inc.	18.77	18.69	0.16	18.85	+1.96 %	0.36	1,039,836	4,358
12:10:56	SYX	Systemax Inc.	8.99	8.55	0.16	8.71	-1.60 %	-0.14	19,071	139
12:12:48	CRSP	CRISPR Thera...	17.60	17.50	0.16	17.66	+0.57 %	0.10	33,498	156
12:12:29	EXTN	Exterran Corpo...	16.81	16.80	0.16	16.96	-3.45 %	-0.60	57,297	559
12:10:56	DMLP	Dorchester Min...	15.30	15.25	0.15	15.40	0.00 %	0.00	24,229	105

Figure III.7.3 - StocksToTrade - Spread filter results

Figure III.7.3 shows the results of the filter above during trading hours. It shows all the stocks currently matching a spread wider than $0.15, and also matching a price between $0.10 and $12, and a volume greater than 250,000.

Trading the Spread

Now that we've established what to look for, we can move to the specifics on how to trade stocks with a wide spread.

We'll use Figure III.7.4 as an example reference for how to trade this type of technique.

The basic concept is:

- Take a long or short position respectively higher or lower than the current bid or ask.
- Wait until your order is filled at that price.
- Close your position below or above the current ask/bid.
- Wait for your order to be filled.

Trading the spread strongly relies on patience, as the orders may take some time to get filled, and rely on some traders trying to open or close their positions at the price you're posting.

In some instances, the orders may not be filled at all.

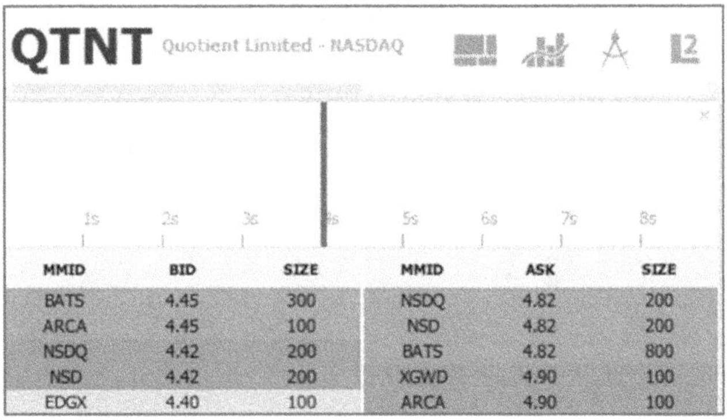

MMID	BID	SIZE	MMID	ASK	SIZE
BATS	4.45	300	NSDQ	4.82	200
ARCA	4.45	100	NSD	4.82	200
NSDQ	4.42	200	BATS	4.82	800
NSD	4.42	200	XGWD	4.90	100
EDGX	4.40	100	ARCA	4.90	100

Figure III.7.4 - StocksToTrade - QTNT with a $0.45 spread

Based on Figure III.7.4, you could trade the spread as follows:

- Take a 100 share long position above the current bid: for example, $4.46.
- Wait until the order is filled.

Once the order is filled you can immediately send a closing order:

- Close the 100-share long position by selling at $4.81, for example.
- Wait until the order is filled.

Once the closing order is filled, the technique is complete. The end result is a $0.35/share profit without relying on any advanced technical analysis or catalyst, but instead entirely depending on the status quo of the stock price.

Dangers of Trading the Spread

While trading the spread can be a profitable and repeatable technique, it's not without its dangers. Timothy Sykes often warns about these dangers.

Just like every stock, a stock fitting into this type of play is also subjected to fundamental factors that may affect the price one way or another. This basically means that a stock may have very little volatility for an extended period of time, only to meet a situation where it encounters a breakout/down event.

This can result in losses for spread traders unable to exit their positions quickly enough before any large move and needs to be considered when trading the spread.

Additionally, due to the very nature of this technique, orders may not get filled for extended periods of time, if at all, which may force you to exit a position at or below the entry price, considerably limiting the profitability of such a technique.

You must take all these factors into account in order to do well with this technique.

Summary

- Trading the spread is an advanced, risky trading technique.
- Trading the spread relies on a good knowledge of Level 2 (See Chapter III.2).
- Trading the spread takes advantage of the difference of price between "bid" and "ask".
- Trading the spread works best with low/medium volatility/liquidity stocks.
- Trading the spread can be done by taking entries either long or short respectively above the "bid" or below the "ask".
- Trading the spread exits can be selling below the "ask" for a long position or above the "bid" for a short position.
- Trading the spread requires patience, as orders are not executed immediately and depend on buyer/seller interest at the posted price points.
- Orders using this technique aren't guaranteed to be filled, and you may need to exit the position at a loss.
- Trading the spread can be dangerous if the stock encounters momentum through an unexpected catalyst of fundamental factor that may affect price action and volume.

Chapter III.8 - Finding a Niche and Developing your Strategy

Overview

A look at the necessary concepts to help you find a trading niche and develop your own trading strategy.

Introduction

This is the final chapter of the course, and I've saved the best for last. This is the part where we discuss how you will, uniquely, become a self-sufficient and self-reliant trader.

All the previous chapters leading to here have built upon a vast wealth of information and provided you with all the necessary tools to be able to think by yourself. While you might have completed the course in a relatively short time, there's still much experience to be gained.

This chapter aims to provide you with the guidelines you need to help you find your own trading path from this point on.

Section IV presents some of the most popular sample trading strategies, but they're by no means the only ones – and certainly not absolute cash cows in all situations. Use them as a baseline for developing your own.

Where to Start?

Developing your strategy is about building upon all the trading concepts and ideas that we've covered throughout this course.

The only place you can really start is by learning the material in a way that it becomes embedded in your subconscious and allows you to successfully perform trades without having a second thought. Studying past trades, both good and bad, from Timothy Sykes and his millionaire students will be helpful in your educational process.

Studying, constantly improving by expanding your knowledge base, and becoming comfortable with these rules and theories is the is the starting point to developing your own way of handling your own trades.

Martial artists are taught to learn thousands of techniques over many years. Some of these techniques are repeated thousands of times in order to assimilate them as a reflex. A martial artist only becomes a true master once he/she is able to move from the "external techniques" to the "internal techniques". This is also known as self-discovery, and relies on knowing yourself to further improve.

Never Stop Learning

Trading, much like anything else, is about a continuous state of learning. The market evolves like any aging creature. New rules are added; new events affect its core behavior.

Constant learning and continuously adapting to these changes is mandatory in order for you to become a successful and self-sufficient trader. The most successful traders understand that in order to continue peak performance, you must keep on learning every step of the way.

Those who fail to learn and adapt, relying on obsolete techniques, ultimately end up victims of a fast-paced, constantly evolving and growing market.

Find your Niche

Finding a trading niche is about experience. It's not something that can be achieved by novice traders, as it requires a large trade history and experience with the market to discover what works and what doesn't.

Finding your niche starts with tracking your trading results, as you learned in Chapter I.6. More specifically, it's very important to track the performance of every strategy you've traded.

Over time, you'll realize that you're more successful with certain types of plays and less with others. Finding your niche ultimately relies on optimizing your trading strategies based on the results you obtain from your past performance.

This will eventually dictate which plays are best for you, which are the most comfortable, and which you should truly focus on.

Experiment & Track Your Results

As you build upon finding your niche, you'll start experimenting with new approaches on your entries, exits and performance.

This approach is very similar to the scientific process, which is basically as follows:

- Define the question.
- Gather your information and resources.
- Build a hypothesis for your trades.
- Experiment based on your hypothesis and collect the data obtained.
- Analyze the data.
- Interpret the date and draw conclusions that will serve as the basis for new hypotheses.
- Publish your results.

This process allows you to build upon existing knowledge in order to find new and novel approaches to tackle penny stocks.

Develop Your Trading Strategy

The final step is developing your own trading strategy based on all that you've learned. This process can take months or years of continuous trading.

It's important to keep in mind that the most successful traders – whether they're self-taught or they learned from a guru – all ended up developing their own strategies and stopped relying on the opinions of others to perform their trades.

Each has a certain level of leadership attitude that allows them to have conviction in the trades they perform, and never follow the trades of others.

Developing your strategy is about finding your niche, experimenting with different entry and exit approaches, trying different risk management strategies, and ultimately determining what works best for you.

Trading is a very personal endeavor. While in the beginning it might look more like a group effort, and could seem like you're following on the steps of more experienced traders, ultimately trading is done for yourself and no other.

Every trader is different. And much like DNA, every trading strategy is truly unique, even when it starts off as a copy of every other strategy in the field.

> *"Don't get set into one form, adapt it and build your own, and let it grow, be like water. Empty your mind; be formless, shapeless, like water. Now you put water in a cup, it becomes the cup. You put water into a bottle it becomes the bottle. You put it in a teapot it becomes the teapot. Now water can flow or it can crash. Be water, my friend."* – **Bruce Lee** *(Lee & Little, Bruce Lee: A Warrior's Journey, 2000)*

Conclusion

From this point on, you'll start your journey to become a self-sufficient trader by progressively assimilating all of the concepts covered throughout this manual.

The next section focuses mainly on existing, well-established, strategies that have been proven to be successful over time. Use them as the basis for your day-to-day trading as well as for building your own strategies.

Finally, if you really want to dedicate yourself to pennystocking and think you have a good chance at becoming successful at it, I strongly encourage you to apply for Timothy Sykes's Millionaire Challenge at http://tim.ly/sykesmc (let them know you read this course). The curriculum, live trading, Q&A webinars, and other information included in the Challenge have already created several millionaires from scratch. You could be one of them.

Tim's Challenge program represents a great way of learning with experienced traders and mentors who can help guide you throughout every step of your journey. Besides Tim, you also get direct access to other experienced traders and great mentors, especially Michael Goode (Reaper) and Mark Croock, both of whom show great patience with novice traders and always offer useful insight with every question asked.

Recommended Learning Material and Newsletters

Throughout this course you've learned a lot of information about trading penny stocks, definitions, basic and advanced techniques, do's and don'ts, etc. But you're far from done learning. Trading is a continuous process of assimilating new information, new techniques, and new rules that fit to every single situation and allow you to develop experience and confidence.

This final section offers some of the material that greatly helped me in my pennystocking education, and helps me continuously improve my skills as a trader.

Timothy Sykes Millionaire Challenge Program

Apply here http://tim.ly/sykesmc. Fair warning: they reject many applicants due to a lack of dedication, due to the program including prolonged personal interaction with both Timothy Sykes and several of his millionaire and upcoming millionaire students.

The Millionaire Challenge program is oriented toward dedicated students who want to take their trading to the next level and truly want to become self-proficient traders. So if you aren't prepared to study harder than you've ever studied before, this program isn't right for you.

More importantly, Tim's Challenge offers a wealth of information and support that can't be found anywhere else. While this course covers the core concepts, the Millionaire Challenge offers access to millionaire mentors, weekly webinars from very successful traders, access to trading chats and a vast library of video lessons.

Additionally, Challenge students receive the most significant DVDs produced by Timothy Sykes.

It's worth repeating that while Tim's Challenge program offers great support to its students, it also requires a deeper level of commitment to learning and following the rules in order to pave the way to becoming a successful trader.

If you're truly interested by the Millionaire Challenge Program, contact admin@timothysykes.com and let them know you've read this book for a little leg up on your competition

The Newsletters

The Millionaire Challenge program may not be for everyone, but you can still have access to a vast wealth of information that you won't find anywhere else through the newsletters – and their associated perks – offered by Timothy Sykes. See http://timothysykes.com/plans for more details.

Tim Alerts

Tim Alerts is the most basic newsletter subscription on profit.ly. It provides a daily watchlist of potential stock plays.

Subscribers also have access to the trading chat, which provides great tips and alerts of stocks encountering momentum in real time, with usually over 1,000 traders in the chatroom daily.

Many of Timothy Sykes's successful students participate in the chat.

Moreover, Tim Alerts provides real-time alerts on every trade that Timothy Sykes makes during the live session. This is a great learning tool to understand entries and exits based on many of the triggers that we've covered during this course.

Those just starting out and wanting a simple overview of penny stocks as well as a very solid watchlist should definitely subscribe to this service.

Here's the link to subscribe: http://timothysykes.com/plans

Pennystocking Silver

Pennystocking Silver takes the Tim Alerts subscription up a notch, also offering access to the full educational library of hundreds of hours of video lessons. The library currently has over 2,100 videos accessible on demand from Profit.ly.

Many of the invaluable video lessons feature specific case studies for stock events – good and bad – that can happen on any given day. This is premium viewing for dedicated students.

You can subscribe here: http://timothysykes.com/plans.

The DVDs

Newsletters are great learning tools when it comes to live trading and following the markets in real time.

On the other hand, DVDs are the very basis upon which this course has been built. And while this course contains all of the elements covered in the DVDs, the DVDs take a more in-depth approach into each of the elements we've covered in this course.

I advise any reader considering trading as a serious wealth-building tool to get all of these DVDs and watch them. Use the link http://timothysykes.com/store for special discounts.

- Pennystocking
  - The DVD that started it all. A must-watch for any serious pennystocking trader. Detailed coverage of chart patterns and the original strategy.
- Pennystocking Part Deux
  - Follows up on the original Pennystocking DVD and updates the original patterns and strategies.
- How to Make Millions
  - One of the most comprehensive DVDs on penny stock trading. Comprised of over 35 hours of material, with contributions from many successful traders.
- Trading Tickers
  - The official DVD of Tim Grittani, Timothy Sykes's #1 student. Covers all the steps of Grittani's successful trading process, and how he makes profitable trading decisions.
- Pennystocking Framework
  - Detailed coverage of the 7-step framework from Chapter IV.7. Extensive chart examples that cover the full process in this strategy.
- ShortStocking
  - The basis for Chapter III.1, ShortStocking covers short selling stocks in great depth and explains all the intricacies associated with the process.
- Spikeability
  - The latest DVD in Timothy Sykes's collection. Covers the experience gained in 15 years of dealing with pump & dumps and supernovae.
- Tim Tactics
  - Focuses on the process surrounding the trading process. Covers the various steps used by Timothy Sykes to perform daily research, daily routine and the actual process of trading. This set of videos offers great value in terms of learning how to perform tasks outside of the trading process.
- Learn Level 2
  - This DVD covers the contents of Chapter III.2 in greater depth. Provides 6 hours of learning material focused entirely on deciphering and understanding the intricacies of Level 2. It takes the L2 knowledge to a different Level.

The Books

Along with the books I recommended earlier in the course, here are a few others. While not directly related to our course material, they provide a great overview of the necessary state of mind and required environment to perform well, and some of the basic concepts required to become a successful trader.

All of these are available on Amazon.

- The Psychology of Trading – Brett N. Steenbarger
- How Yoga Works – Michael Roach
- The Complete Turtle Trader – Michael W. Covel
- An American Hedge Fund – Timothy Sykes

Summary

- Learn and deeply assimilate all the contents offered in this course.
- Adapt to the evolving market and never stop learning new things.
- Find your niche by discovering the trading actions that work best for you and learn from these.
- Optimize your trading strategy by understanding your performance and tracking your record.
- Define new trading hypotheses based on your performance.
- Experiment with new trading approaches and track your results.
- Develop your own strategy based on your results.
- Look into the recommended material; they're worth your time and your money.
- *"Be water, my friend."*

Section IV - Sample Pennystocking Strategies

This section is dedicated to presenting the most popular pennystocking strategies that can help you successfully trade stocks for a profit.

Each of these strategies has been tested time and time again, and proven to work by numerous successful traders. They're the result of many years of experimentation.

Each strategy focuses on a different approach to penny stocks, and demonstrates the basis for what novice traders should focus on when starting out and attempting to generate profits.

Remember, these strategies still need to be complemented with all the knowledge you acquired in this course, and should never be attempted without having performed the proper amount of research on a given security, or without considering the various technical and fundamental factors that affect the stock market at any given time.

Chapter IV.1 - Buy Earnings & Contract Winners

Strategy: Buy Earnings & Contract Winners (BECW)
Difficulty: Easy (listed stocks)/Medium (OTC)
Orientation: Long
Suitability: Novice traders

Introduction

Buying earnings and contract winners is one of the most basic and yet most profitable pennystocking strategies.

This strategy relies on finding stocks that are subjected to catalysts that will strongly impact the price action.

What to look for

The interesting stocks for this type of play are usually represented by companies that offer real products and are backed by proper business models.

The ideal price range per share is usually between $1 and $15.

These types of plays are usually found by following the market reactions on contract win news and earnings. Attempting to predict price action without having a strong hypothesis and supporting technical factors will often not yield any profitable results.

StocksToTrade offers a great way to find these kinds of stocks by looking at pre-market/intraday 4% winners with earnings or news. Figure IV.1.1 shows the results of such a filter that provides a good overview of matching stocks.

You can further filter down your results based on your price range, desired volume, number of trades, etc.

In the case of earnings, it's worth knowing the company's history and how the market has previously reacted to this type of catalyst. On the other hand, contract winners rely more on the essence of the contract itself and how it will impact the core business of the stock it represents.

BECW stocks are usually characterized by a strong increase in volume and price. If the catalyst is announced before the market open, this can result in a morning spike.

Time	Symbol	Company ...	Last	Bid	Spread	Ask	% Chg	Net Change	Volume	Trades
12:26:01	CRBP	Corbus Pharm..	9.775	9.75	0.05	9.80	+67.09 %	3.925	8,519,374	24,954
12:24:03	KEEKF	Keek Inc	1.07	0.00	0.00	0.00	+45.32 %	0.3337	107,430	88
12:15:18	GRWG	GrowGeneratio..	2.96	2.29	0.01	2.30	+28.70 %	0.66	71,955	146
12:24:03	OGRMF	OrganiGram H..	2.87	2.27	0.10	2.37	+24.24 %	0.56	435,930	592
12:17:29	SLGD	Scotts Liquid G...	1.30	0.0001	7.9999	8.00	+23.81 %	0.25	45,830	41
12:19:41	ESDI	Eastside Distill..	1.85	0.01	79.99	80.00	+23.33 %	0.35	7,700	12
12:15:18	ACAN	Americann Inc	1.60	0.0001	10.9999	11.00	+20.72 %	0.2746	55,050	64
12:25:38	TWMJF	Canopy Growt..	8.33	6.51	0.41	6.92	+20.38 %	1.41	548,421	1,367
11:11:57	EFLVF	Electrovaya Inc	1.62	0.00	0.00	0.00	+20.00 %	0.27	22,750	33
12:26:14	OBCI	Ocean Bio-Che...	3.3889	3.34	0.11	3.45	+18.08 %	0.5189	1,019,644	2,996
12:26:01	MTL	Mechel PAO A..	6.36	6.33	0.03	6.36	+16.70 %	0.91	961,228	2,959
09:51:08	EYTH	Eco Energy Te..	7.00	4.00	2.00	6.00	+16.67 %	1.00	200	3
12:26:02	DGII	Digi Internatio...	13.55	13.55	0.05	13.60	+16.31 %	1.90	540,650	2,908
12:25:40	CANN	General Canna..	3.93	3.30	0.45	3.75	+12.93 %	0.45	389,671	741
10:21:43	CBHMF	Cobham Plc Ord	2.02	1.90	0.30	2.20	+12.85 %	0.23	8,620	2
12:24:03	KSHB	Kush Bottles Inc	3.30	0.02	4.20	4.22	+12.63 %	0.37	255,313	466
12:24:03	UNTS	Unifie Croncea	2.9801	2.98	0.01	2.99	+11.61 %	0.3101	260,923	578

Figure IV.1.1 - StocksToTrade - 4% gainers with news, filings and earnings

As was mentioned, be wary of past price action to similar events, and also keep in mind the general state of the market, as it may have an impact on the overall performance of the stock in question.

How It Works

In order to play a BCEW type of strategy, you must know some of the technical factors about the stock. These elements should be of interest:

- 52w high
- 52w low
- Key resistance and support
- Current price vs. resistance and support
- Past behavior on contract wins and earnings

Knowing these elements allows you to form a sound hypothesis on how the stock could potentially move based on the currently available information and how it was perceived by the will of the market in the past.

Entry Signal

A BCEW play is characterized by a significant increase in volume and price following the announcement of the catalyst.

When the price is near a resistance or support line, it usually indicates that the stock might experience a breakout and the start of a momentum trend. An overnight catalyst announcement or pre-open for the next session could be a precursor to a morning spike.

In order to profit from BCEW plays, it's best to notice the catalyst as close as possible to its announcement and perform a buy order early in the momentum price action.

Exit Signal

A profitable exit on this type of play depends on your RMS. Based on the stock, its fundamental factors, and its price action, you may wish to have a pre-set profit target, or wait for signs of price reversal before closing your position.

Your exit will be based on your hypothesis and how you expect the stock to behave in the short and mid terms.

More specifically to the BCEW plays, if you expect the price to continue to rise, it's usually wise to keep the position open as long as possible. On the other hand, if the stock has a history of a limited upside, or the sector is experiencing a virtual resistance point, it's best to evaluate a maximum upside and exit the position once this threshold is attained.

Keep in mind resistance lines and the reaction to the catalyst.

Case Study

For the purpose of getting a good idea on how a BCEW strategy applies, we'll look at a company called Digital Ally Inc., also known as **DGLY**.

Digital Ally Inc. is a great example of the true potential of this type of play and how it's important to understand the market in order to profit from these types of opportunities.

In terms of price action and duration, plays like DGLY are very rare. They are the "11" on the volume knob... the cherry on the cake... the best of the best. Plays like this one don't happen very often and shouldn't be considered in any way as the norm for a BCEW strategy play.

Context

On August 9, 2014, Michael Brown was shot and killed by a police office in Ferguson, Missouri. The circumstances surrounding the shooting of this 18-year-old black man resulted in massive protests and civil unrest throughout the U.S. and abroad. This event led to a very heated debate about law enforcement and their relationship with African Americans.

As a result of the protests, law enforcement agencies were forced to look into measures to increase accountability for the actions of their officers. One of these approaches was the acquisition of specialized wearable video equipment.

Digital Ally Inc. is the manufacturer of specialized video equipment for law enforcement. One such product is the FirstVU HD Body Camera.

On August 14, 2014, DGLY released an 8-K Form (Form 8-K for DIGITAL ALLY INC, 2014) for the result of operations that was not included in their 10-Q (see Chapter III.4 for more details on the SEC filings) following a press release on Aug 13:

> *"Digital Ally, Inc. (NASDAQ: DGLY), which develops, manufactures and markets advanced video surveillance products for law enforcement, homeland security and commercial applications, today announced its operating results for the second quarter and first half of 2014. An investor conference call is scheduled for 11:15 a.m. EDT tomorrow, August 14, 2014 (see details below)." (Digital Ally, Inc. Announces Second Quarter Operating Results, 2014)*

On August 20, 2014, a press release about increased interest in their products by law enforcement was published.

> *"Digital Ally, Inc. (NASDAQ: DGLY), which develops, manufactures and markets advanced video surveillance products for law enforcement, homeland security and commercial applications, today announced that the number of inquiries that it has received from law enforcement agencies interested in its FirstVU HD Officer-Worn Video System has increased dramatically since the national media began covering the civil unrest in Ferguson, Missouri." (Inquiries Regarding Digital Ally's FirstVU HD Body Camera Increase Dramatically During Past Week in Response to Civil Unrest in Ferguson, Missouri, 2014)*

The following week was marked by the release of an 8-K filing for an entry into a definitive agreement for a $4M private placement, implying the private acquisition of shares by a private investor. (Form 8-K for DIGITAL ALLY INC, 2014)

On August 28, a DGLY press release announced a contract for $1.1M from the state police of Michigan:

"Digital Ally, Inc. (NASDAQ: DGLY) ("the Company"), which develops, manufactures and markets advanced video surveillance products for law enforcement, homeland security and commercial applications, today announced the receipt of an order valued at more than $1.1 million from the State of Michigan." (Digital Ally Receives Order From State Police Of Michigan Valued at More Than $1.1 Million, 2014)

The combination of these events led to 11 trading days of continuous momentum for DGLY, pushing the stock price 10 times its starting value, as we'll cover in the next section.

Price Action

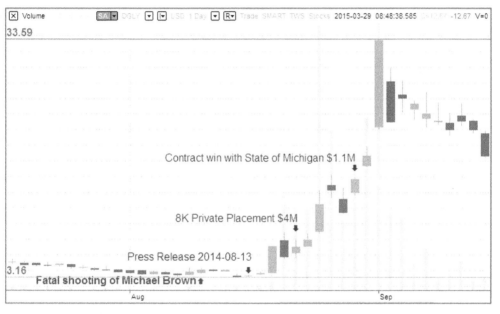

Figure IV.1.2 - Multicharts - DGLY price action contract win

Figure IV.1.2 shows the price action of DGLY in correspondence with the various events that produced a ten-fold price increase in a relatively short period of time.

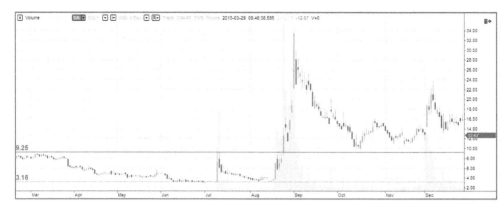

Figure IV.1.3 - Multicharts - DGLY key support and resistance prior to momentum

Figure IV.1.3 shows six months prior to the momentum move for DGLY. Before any of the events described in the previous section, the key support for this stock was set around $3.00, making it a safe bet to open a long position around this price point with minimal down side.

Conversely, key resistance, based on past behavior, could be established around $9 per share.

It's important to notice that DGLY experienced a spike in mid-July, but didn't hold its gains.

All this information, coupled with the news, provides great indicators of what could be expected from the price action: a strong support at $3 and a potential breakout above $9.

Figure IV.1.4 - Multicharts - DGLY Intraday 2014-08-14 to 2014-08-20

Figure IV.1.4 shows a potential entry point, using as reference around $5.17. The figure above shows an increase of volume around 14h58 and the technical breakout at 15h20.

Around market opening, the price increases from $3.72 at open to $4.98 at 10h44, a $1.36 increase. This happens following the press release regarding increased interest from law enforcement for their line of wearable products.

Figure IV.1.5 - Multicharts - DGLY contract announcement on the 28th of August

Figure IV.1.5 shows the reaction to the announcement of the $1.1M contract given to DGLY by the state of Michigan. Notice the gap-up in price from the previous day. This is the result of an early morning announcement and some premarket activity driving the price way above previous close.

Throughout the day, the stock price increased around $2/share, from $13.99 at the session opening to $15.69 at day close. The momentum remained throughout the following days as traders became aware of this stock.

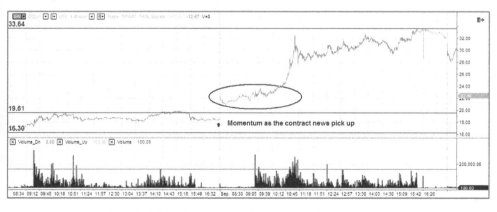

Figure IV.1.6 - Multicharts - DGLY momentum breakout on contract

Figure IV.1.6 is the continuation of Figure IV.1.5. As interest gathered around this stock, price spiked to a high of $33.50, almost a $20 price increase from the announcement two days before.

Potential Profit for Long Positions

A stock like DGLY, given the context and the fact that is was supported by a contract, news, and financial information, was an ideal play for short-term profits while holding for multiple days.

The most defining factor for this stock was the news behind the surge and what created a favorable environment for this stock to thrive.

While plays like DGLY are rare in terms of potential profits, it provides a good overview of what the reaction to a contract win or earnings can offer to traders in terms of profitability.

Chapter IV.2 - Buy Dips

Strategy: Buy dips (BD)
Difficulty: Medium
Orientation: Long
Suitability: Intermediate traders

Introduction

Buying dips builds upon the previous strategy of buying contracts and earnings winners. As the price peaks, shareholders lock profits by selling their shares, thus driving the price down.

This provides a new opportunity for traders to enter a potentially profitable position by understanding that while many shareholders lock their profits, many others look for a renewed opportunity to enter the stock at a price lower than the peak.

This type of situation starts with a peak, then a drop in price – the "dip" – followed by a "bounce" that often retraces the dip and sometimes results in a breakout event.

What to Look For

Much like for the BCEW strategy, the BD strategy relies on finding stocks with a reaction to earnings or contract news.

Please refer to the "What to Look For" section in Chapter IV.1, as it describes essentially the same requirements that the BCEW strategy has that are also necessary to the BD strategy.

Additionally, BD plays are strongly reliant on support and key support lines for the concerned stocks.

How It Works

In order to play a BCEW type of strategy, you must know some of the technical factors about the stock. These elements should be of interest:

- 52w high
- 52w low
- Key support and intraday support
- Current price vs. resistance and support
- Past behavior on contract wins and earnings

Knowing these elements allows you to form a sound hypothesis on how the stock could potentially move based on currently available information and how it was perceived by the will of the market in the past.

Entry Signal

Entry for a DB strategy strongly relies on support and key support lines for a given stock.

While the BCEW relies on an early knowledge of the catalyst in question, the BD strategy requires watching how the price behaves near the support or key support. In simpler terms, a support line that is not crossed is usually a good signal for entering a BD position, as it strengthens the price line for the stock and prevents a potential breakdown resulting from the lack of interest.

Also, conversely to the BCEW strategy that relies on price action and volume, the BD relies on more fundamental factors that may influence the price action. In other words, knowing the worth of the news and the company, coupled with the knowledge of a strong support line, represents a sound entry signal for BD strategy position.

Exit Signal

A profitable exit on this type of play depends on your RMS. Based on the stock, its fundamental factors, and its price action, you may wish to have a pre-set profit target or wait for signs of price reversal before closing your position.

Your exit will be based on your hypothesis and how you expect the stock to behave in the short and mid terms.

More specifically to the BD plays, if you expect the price to continue rising, it's usually wise to keep the position open as long as possible. On the other hand, if the stock has a history of a limited upside, or the sector is experiencing a virtual resistance point, it's best to evaluate a maximum upside and exit the position once this threshold has been attained.

Keep in mind resistance lines and the reaction to the catalyst.

Case Study

To get a good idea on how a BD strategy works, let's look at a company called RADA Electronic Industries Ltd., also known as **RADA**.

RADA, unlike stocks like DGLY and VLTC, does not offer an extreme price range. It shows a good example of the type of price action that can be expected from stocks that provide a similar type of chart. More importantly, it shows a good example for the dip buy strategy.

Context

On March 23, 2015, RADA announced that it was selected for Lockheed Martin's Laser Weapons Program.

The announcement was followed by a spike and subsequent drop in price. The price displayed a parabolic move based on the news as a catalyst.

Price Action

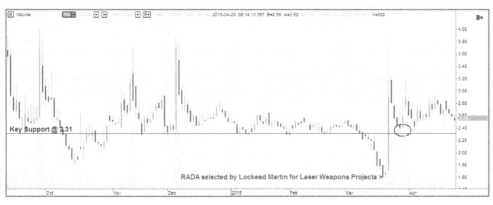

Figure IV.2.1 - Multicharts - RADA daily chart - key support and post-Supernova dip

Figure IV.2.1 shows the multi-month daily chart for RADA with an emphasis on a key support trend line around $2.31. This support line is important, as it shows that the stock has consistently failed to drop below that Level until the unjustified March 3 to March 19 drop.

On March 23, RADA made the Lockheed Martin announcement, which created a short-lived parabolic type of price action, immediately followed by a drop.

Figure IV.2.2 shows the 10-minute chart of those events:

Figure IV.2.2 - Multicharts - RADA 10 minute chart – dip

The figure above shows the price action near key support and the sideway action during this period before breaking out as a result of the dip. This occurs as traders attempt to gain from the reduced price following the morning spike on March 23.

Additionally, being so close to the key support level reinforces the belief among traders that the stock is unlikely to drop below that point, as was seen in Figure IV.2.1.

Potential Profit for Long Positions

Buying dips is directly reliant on understanding the characteristics of the stock being watched. For RADA, understanding the relationship between its current price levels and past behavior was crucial for various reasons. RADA displayed past behavior of spikes followed by bounces. More importantly, RADA's price during the past year always seemed to return to around $2.31.

These factors can be used as an indicator for the potential behavior when hyperbolic moves happen, which might signal when it could be appropriate to buy on dips.

Figure IV.2.3 below shows the potential entries that a trader could have made on RADA make in order to profit long from a dip, following a hyperbolic move.

Figure IV.2.3 - Multicharts - RADA 10 minute chart - potential dip entries

Unlike DGLY (discussed in the Case Study of Chapter IV.1) and VLTC (Case Study Chapter IV.3), RADA offers a between $0.30 and $0.80 profit per share on a good entry.

Chapter IV.3 - Short Overextended Stocks

Strategy: Short overextended stocks (SOS)
Difficulty: Medium (listed stocks)/Hard (OTC)
Orientation: Short (Chapter III.1)
Suitability: Intermediate traders

Introduction

The shorting overextended stocks strategy focuses on stocks that have had a major increase in price without necessarily having a sound catalyst to back the price hike.

This is usually the result of speculation from traders or simply the fact that traders take a position on a stock that shows volume and price action based uniquely on technical factors.

What to Look For

The SOS strategy is about looking for stocks that show a major increase in price in a short period of time, matching a supernova (Chapter II.6) type of chart, while not having a good reason for experiencing such an overextension of the price.

This type of strategy applies to stocks of any price, ideally with high liquidity (100K+ volume on the day) and volatility.

Stocks suitable for SOS plays are usually represented by companies that don't have proper businesses in place and don't offer good products or services. This can be further investigated by looking at the SEC filings (Chapter III.4).

The main indicator for these stocks is the obvious lack of a proper catalyst that could be attributed to a rise in price: no earnings, no contract wins, and no news to justify such a move.

Stocks for an SOS play usually spike 5%-10% in the early morning, or have been uptrending for a certain number of days. However, they don't show any news that would normally create such a reaction.

How It Works

In order to play a SOS type of strategy, it's important to know some of the technical factors about the stock. These elements should be of interest:

- 52w high
- 52w low
- Key support and intraday support
- Key resistance and intraday resistance
- Current price vs. resistance and support
- Past behavior on the stock
- Recent average price point and chart pattern

Knowing these elements allows the trader to form a sound hypothesis on how the stock could potentially move based on the currently available information and how it was perceived by the will of the market in the past.

Additionally, digging into the SEC filings to find out the financial health of the company and the actual worth of its products/services reaffirms the speculation that the stock will eventually crash.

Entry Signal

Entries for these types of plays are hard to evaluate, as they rely on traders realizing that the stock they're trading actually represents a worthless company. Each of these types of plays will have their own particularity in terms of price action.

SOS plays rely on constantly watching the price action and noticing signs of reversal of the price, which may indicate a potential breakdown. This is based upon intraday support and resistance.

When the stock is ready to crack and the Level 2 shows a wall of sellers, this is usually an indicator of a good time to short sell the stock.

Additionally, this type of play can be done by using a boxing position strategy (Chapter III.5) in order to ensure balance until the stock price is ready to crack, which may increase the potential for profit.

Exit Signal

A profitable exit on this type of play depends on your RMS. Based on the stock, its fundamental factors, and its price action, you may wish to have a pre-set profit target, or wait for signs of price reversal before closing your position.

Your exit will be based on your hypothesis and how you expect the stock to behave in the short and mid terms.

More specifically to the SOS plays, you'll need to consider support and key support lines as potential stops for the drop in price.

If the stock has historically been able to be maintained at a support line, there's a great chance that it might fail to drop below that price point, unless there are fundamental factors to support that behavior.

Case Study

For the purpose of getting a good idea on how a SOS strategy applies, we'll use a company called Voltari Corporation, also known as **VLTC**.

Voltari Corporation is another extreme example of the true volatility that exists within the realm of penny stocks and how this volatility can be exploited in order to generate a profit.

Much like DGLY, VLTC is a play that doesn't occur often and shouldn't be considered the norm when it comes to an overextended stock or an SOS strategy.

Context

On March 31, 2015, billionaire investor Carl Icahn increased his stake in VLTC to 52%, acquiring around 4 million additional shares of Voltari Corporation at a price of $1.36. He previously owned 29.8% of the company.

Following this announcement, VLTC was progressively picked up by social media and gained the attention of traders.

This trend lasted about three weeks before reaching its peak at $21.75 per share from its $1.01 starting point.

Price Action

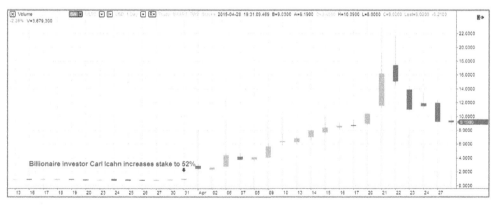

Figure IV.3.1 - Multicharts - VLTC daily chart - Carl Icahn takes increases stake in VLTC

Over the course of the next 14 sessions following the Carl Icahn announcement on March 31, VLTC encountered a 2,100% price increase from its starting point.

During that time, the stock was subjected to much social speculation about the behavior of the price action, which led the market to consecutively trick traders into shorting the stock, only to squeeze them out of their positions shortly after. This contributed to pushing the price all the way to $21.75.

Figure IV.3.2 - Multicharts - VLTC 45 minute chart - price action intra day

Figure IV.3.2 shows the progressive increase in price and the moments where it is estimated that the short squeezes had taken place. Each of the intraday resistance levels was crossed, resulting in a breakout condition.

Additionally, the figure above shows a period of consolidation following each breakout/drop instance – reminding us of our stair-stepper chart pattern.

The culmination of this process resulted in a total change of $20.74/share over the course of 16 trading sessions.

This peak represents an extreme overextension of the price action given the actual company and the news supporting it. In essence, traders expected cracks at multiple levels during the ramp-up leading to the supernova.

The hyperbolic movement then became indicative of the inevitable crash and significant drop in price that ensued the massive rise.

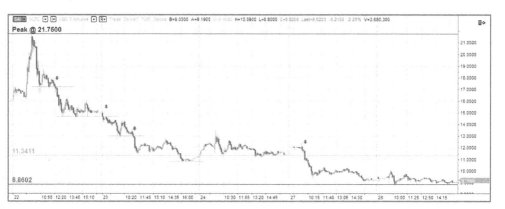

Figure IV.3.3 - Multicharts - VLTC 5 minute chart - cliff dive and support breakdowns

Figure IV.3.3 shows the immediate retrace of the supernova move that drove the price to its peak, followed by a series of minor bounces unable to hold their levels. This, in turn, resulted in a succession of support breakdowns.

As of May 2015, the price has dropped around $11/share from its highs, within five trading sessions.

Potential Profit for Short Positions

VLTC is the perfect example of an overextended stock – a victim of its own success. The high demand for its shares from long positions, coupled with the recurring expectation of a crash from short sellers, resulted in an unsustainably high price point for a stock priced below $1 only weeks prior.

Figure IV.3.4 shows potential short entry points for such a stock. In essence, each significant sign of reversal was considered as a potential signal for shorting a stock. However, attempting to predict the peak is the reason behind the repeated short squeeze events that occurred.

Figure IV.3.4 - Multicharts - VLTC 5 minute chart - short entries

Ultimately VLTC provided a great opportunity for short sellers to generate great profit by shorting into a parabolic move.

Chapter IV.4 - Short Bounces

Strategy: Short bounces (SB)
Difficulty: Hard
Orientation: Short (Chapter III.1)
Suitability: Advanced traders

Introduction

Shorting bounces is the converse action to buying a dip. A bounce is usually the result of an overextended stock crashing (dip) before experiencing a bounce type of behavior. This is characterized by the definition of a resistance line at which traders attempt to short sell shares at a higher price than the peak, expecting a drop in the price.

A SB play is usually applied to stocks that are overextended without a proper catalyst to back up a positive price action, as seen in Chapter IV.3.

What to Look For

The search criteria for stocks suitable for an SB play is essentially the same as that covered for the SOS strategy in Chapter IV.3.

Additionally, stocks that fall into this strategy have already experienced a price drop, a price increase at a support line, and might be close to a breakdown reversal at the bounce's peak.

How It Works

In order to play a SB type of strategy it's important to know some of the technical factors about the stock. These elements should be of interest:

- 52w high
- 52w low
- Intraday support
- Key resistance and intraday resistance
- Current price vs. resistance and support
- Past behavior of the stock
- Recent average price point and chart pattern

Knowing these elements allows the trader to form a sound hypothesis on how the stock could potentially move based on the currently available information and how it was perceived by the will of the market in the past.

Additionally, digging into the SEC filings to find out the financial health of the company and the actual worth of its products/services reaffirms the speculation that the stock will eventually crash.

Entry Signal

Entry for a SB strategy relies on resistance and key resistance levels for the given stock. It's important to watch the stock closely for an up-trending price action that tops, but does not cross resistance lines.

This type of behavior is indicative a potential breakdown after a bounce.

Exit Signal

A profitable exit off this type of play depends on your RMS. Based on the stock, its fundamental factors, and its price action, you may wish to have a pre-set profit target, or wait for signs of price reversal before closing your position.

Your exit will be based on your hypothesis and how you expect the stock to behave in the short and mid terms.

More specifically to the SB plays, you'll need to consider key support lines as potential stops for the drop in price.

If the stock has historically been able to be maintained at a support line, there is a great chance that it might fail to drop below that price point, unless there are fundamental factors to support that behavior.

Case Study

For the purpose of getting a good idea on how an SB strategy applies, we'll examine a company called Lifevantage Corp., also known as **LFVN**.

This company provides a realistic example on shorting a bounce for a stock with regular price action, without being subjected to extreme overextensions, unlike DGLY or VLTC.

Context

Over the course of 2014, LFVN maintained a constant range of price never dropping below $1.10. On February 2, 2014, LFVN announced an executive leadership change. The reaction to this news was an immediate drop in price that lasted multiple days.

Figure IV.4.1 shows the daily one-year chart for LFVN, which illustrates the state of the company before the announcement.

Figure IV.4.1 - Multicharts - LFVN 1 year daily chart - price state

On February 4, LFVN released both its 10-Q (Quarterly report) and 8-K (Report of an Event; in this case, results of financial operations), and this provided the necessary catalyst for the stock to bounce.

Price Action

Following the Feb 2 announcement, the stock price dipped from $1.27 down to a low of $0.76 within the course of three days, following a cliff dive type of price action.

A good quarterly report released on Feb 4 provided the necessary catalyst for traders to gain interest in a lower priced stock with the potential to reach its previous level from its current low point.

Figure IV.4.2 illustrates this behavior and the appearance of a catalyst induced bounce.

Figure IV.4.2 - Muticharts - LFVN daily chart – events

A more detailed overview of the price action can be seen in Figure IV.4.3, depicting a 45-minute chart of these events:

Figure IV.4.3 - Multicharts - LFVN 45 minute chart – bounce

The figure above shows a clear retrace of the drop reaching around 75% of its previous value. This is typically a good indicator for a bounce, as this type of price action has a tendency to bounce between 50% and 80%.

Following the bounce, the stock inevitably succumbed to the effect of the original news as the effect of the earnings and financial report finally faded.

Potential Profit for Short Positions

Figure IV.4.4 - Multicharts - LFVN 45 minute chart - possible entries

Figure IV.4.4 shows clear resistance at around $1.16 with short-term sideway action. This usually indicates a potential move, and considering the news, odds were against a possible breakout.

With this in mind, possible profitable entries could have been taken between $1.15 and $1.09 in order to short this stock profitably.

Short-term short positions would be able to generate between $0.15 and $0.20 per share, while holding this stock short for a couple of weeks could have yielded about $0.40.

Short Bounces

Chapter IV.5 - Buy Pump & Dumps

Strategy: Buy Pump & Dumps (BPD)
Difficulty: Medium/Hard
Orientation: Long
Suitability: Intermediate traders

Introduction

Pump and dumps are one of the original pillars of profitable trades in pennystocking. While the rules of the game may have changed over time, pump & dumps are still a good way to profit.

You'll find a detailed description of pumps & dumps in Chapter II.8.

What to Look For

The BPD strategy is entirely based on promoted stocks. The basis of this strategy relies on identifying stocks that are being actively promoted by stock promoters.

This implies subscriptions to promoters' lists and being able to differentiate promoters with a good performance record when it comes to driving a stock price up from those who do a poor job at getting their subscribers to buy their stocks.

How It Works

The BPD strategy's basis is in recognizing good promoters and knowing when promotions will start.

Promoters are known to tease traders with upcoming promotions; this allows the promoters to hype the stock before it's even announced.

Entry Signal

A BPD strategy requires a trader to enter a long position early in the pump. This usually implies buying the stock of a reputable stock promoter as soon as the stock promotion announces the security to trade.

Since most P&Ds are OTC stocks, entry timing is an important factor, which is why it's necessary to enter these positions early. When the price starts gaining momentum, a good entry may no longer be a possibility, as you learned in Chapter III.3.

Exit Signal

A profitable exit on this type of play depends on your RMS. Based on the stock, its fundamental factors, and its price action, you may wish to have a pre-set profit target, or wait for signs of price reversal before closing your position.

Your exit will be based on your hypothesis and how you expect the stock to behave in the short and mid terms.

More specifically to the BPD plays, you must consider price action, volume and L2 information.

When a stock starts showing signs of slowing down or reversal, it's important to properly time your exit in order to avoid being caught in the downside momentum.

Also, avoid remaining for long periods of time (more than a day or two) in a P&D long position, as given the untrustworthy nature of P&D stocks, the stock may be halted.

Case Study

For the purpose of this case study, we'll use a stock promotion for Telupay International Inc., also known as TLPY.

Context

On February 18, 2015, StockTips teased its subscribers about an upcoming pick. StockTips is a well-known promoter that performs relatively well whenever its promotions are running.

Figure IV.5.1 shows a screenshot of the teaser email sent by StockTips to create hype about its upcoming pick.

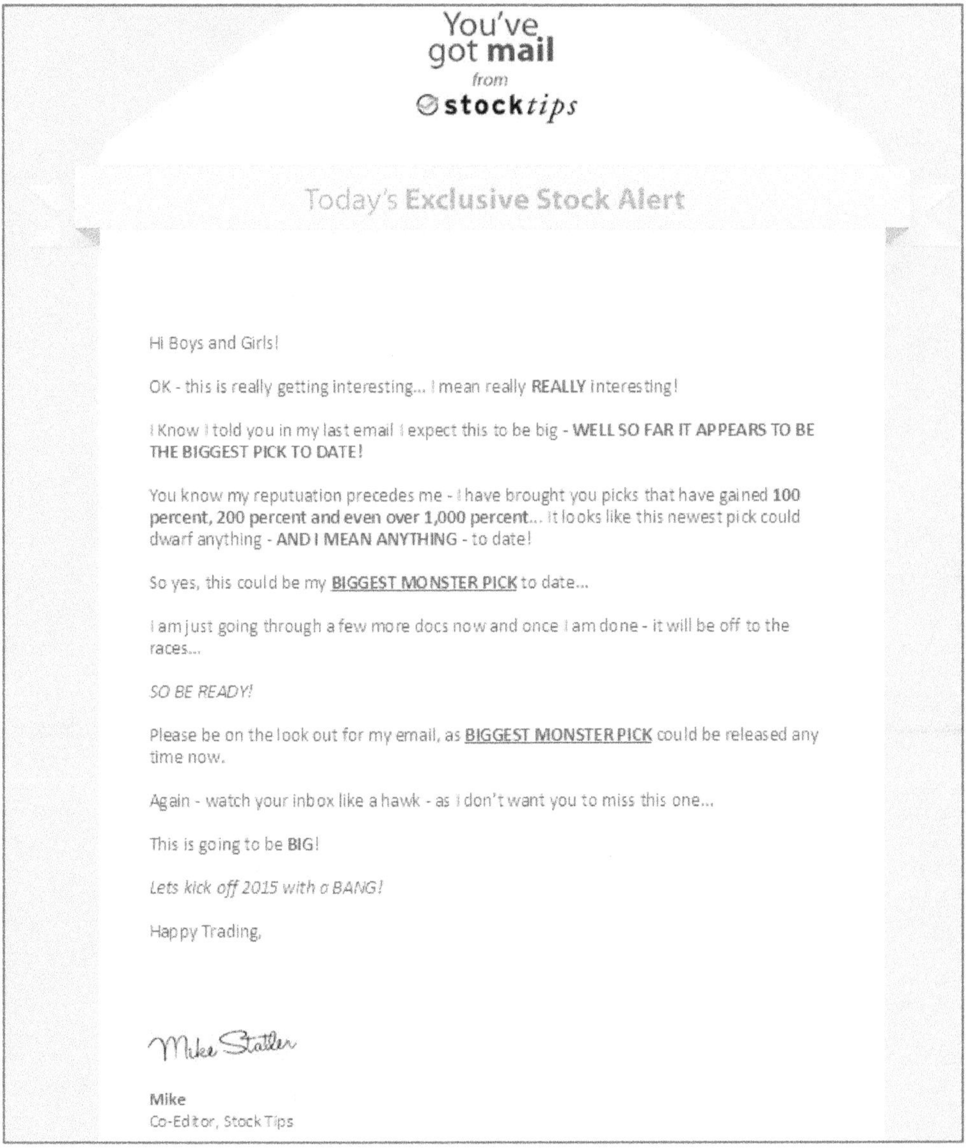

You've
got **mail**
from
⊘**stock**_tips_

Today's **Exclusive Stock Alert**

Hi Boys and Girls!

OK - this is really getting interesting... I mean really **REALLY** interesting!

I Know I told you in my last email I expect this to be big - **WELL SO FAR IT APPEARS TO BE THE BIGGEST PICK TO DATE!**

You know my reputuation precedes me - I have brought you picks that have gained **100 percent, 200 percent and even over 1,000 percent**... It looks like this newest pick could dwarf anything - **AND I MEAN ANYTHING** - to date!

So yes, this could be my **BIGGEST MONSTER PICK** to date...

I am just going through a few more docs now and once I am done - it will be off to the races...

SO BE READY!

Please be on the look out for my email, as **BIGGEST MONSTER PICK** could be released any time now.

Again - watch your inbox like a hawk - as I don't want you to miss this one...

This is going to be **BIG!**

Lets kick off 2015 with a BANG!

Happy Trading,

Mike Statler

Mike
Co-Editor, Stock Tips

Figure IV.5.1 - Email excerpt - Stocktips teaser

Following that announcement, StockTips sent out another teaser on March 5, as depicted in Figure IV.5.2:

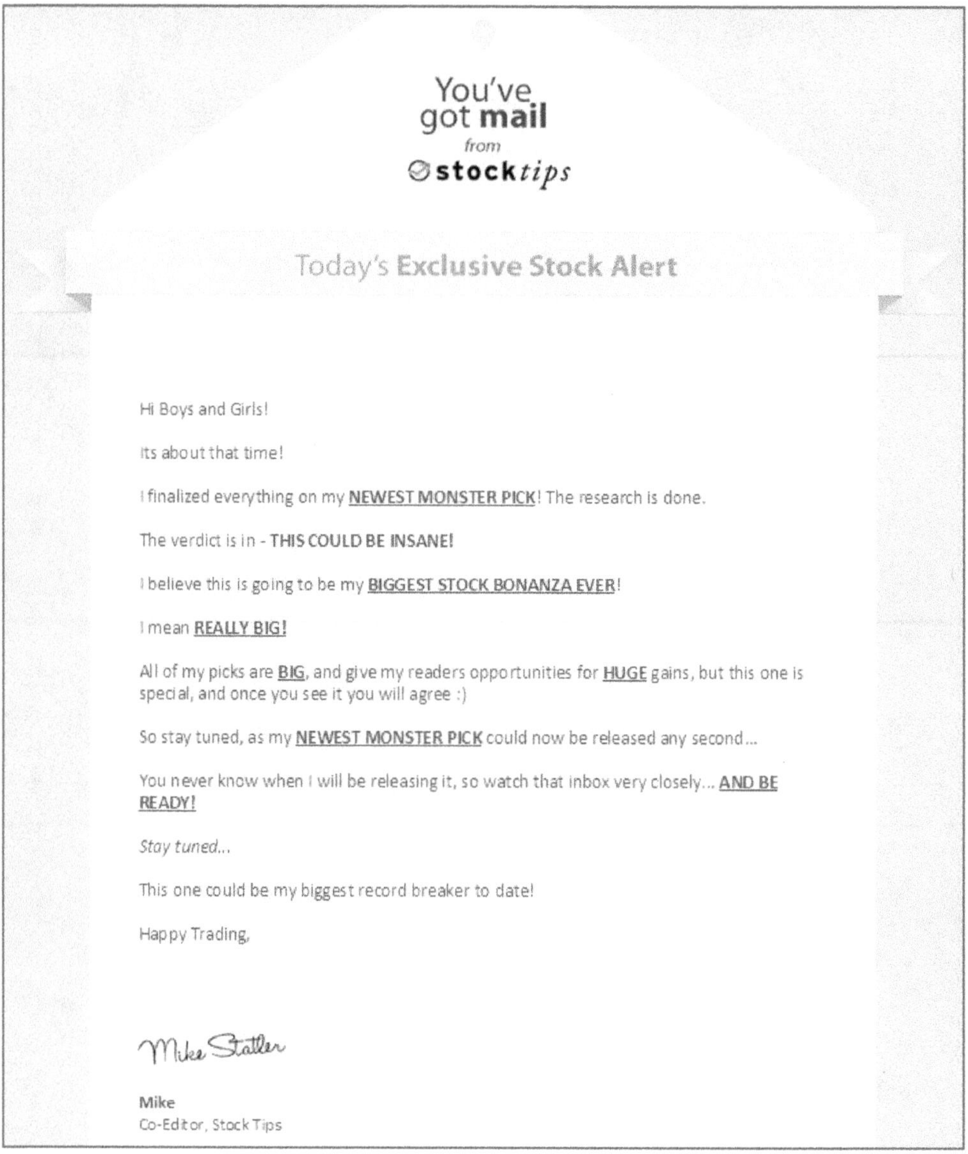

You've
got **mail**
from
stocktips

Today's **Exclusive Stock Alert**

Hi Boys and Girls!

Its about that time!

I finalized everything on my **NEWEST MONSTER PICK**! The research is done.

The verdict is in - **THIS COULD BE INSANE!**

I believe this is going to be my **BIGGEST STOCK BONANZA EVER**!

I mean **REALLY BIG!**

All of my picks are **BIG**, and give my readers opportunities for **HUGE** gains, but this one is special, and once you see it you will agree :)

So stay tuned, as my **NEWEST MONSTER PICK** could now be released any second...

You never know when I will be releasing it, so watch that inbox very closely... **AND BE READY!**

Stay tuned...

This one could be my biggest record breaker to date!

Happy Trading,

Mike Statler

Mike
Co-Editor, Stock Tips

Figure IV.5.2 - Stocktips teaser 2

Finally, on March 6, StockTips announced its pick, as shown in Figure IV.5.3:

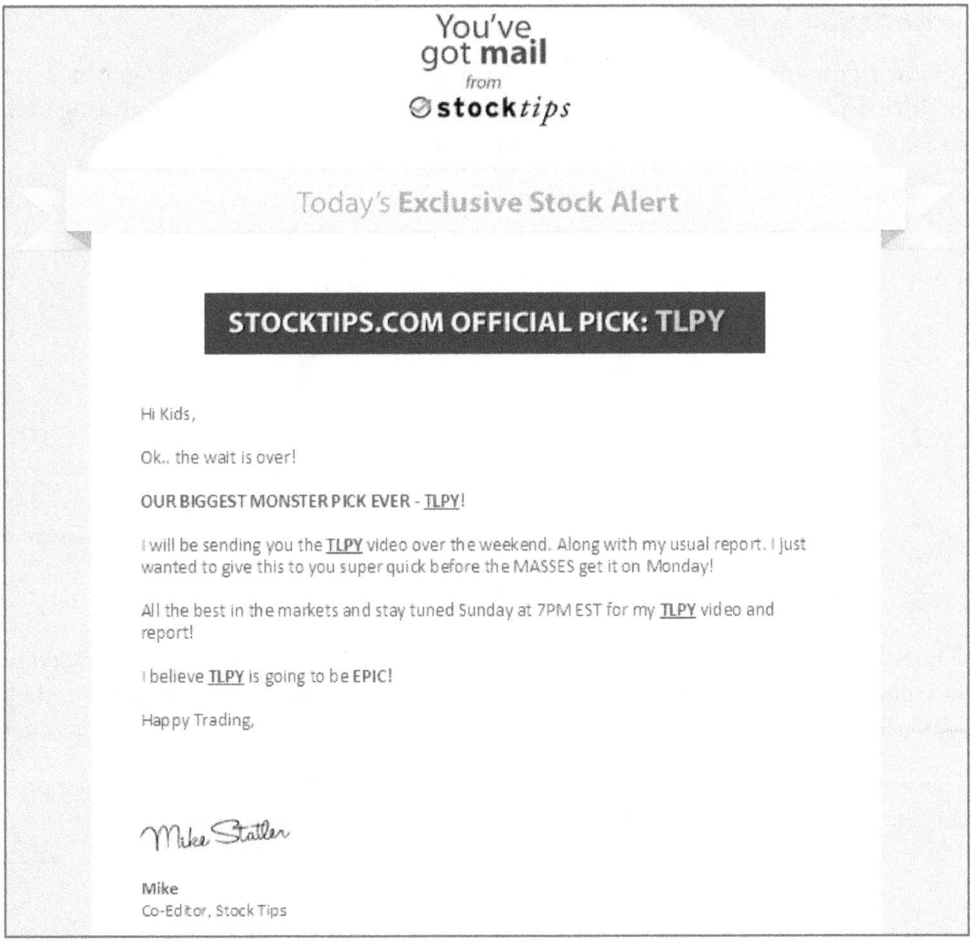

You've
got **mail**
from
⊘ **stock***tips*

Today's **Exclusive Stock Alert**

STOCKTIPS.COM OFFICIAL PICK: TLPY

Hi Kids,

Ok.. the wait is over!

OUR BIGGEST MONSTER PICK EVER - TLPY!

I will be sending you the TLPY video over the weekend. Along with my usual report. I just wanted to give this to you super quick before the MASSES get it on Monday!

All the best in the markets and stay tuned Sunday at 7PM EST for my TLPY video and report!

I believe TLPY is going to be EPIC!

Happy Trading,

Mike Statler

Mike
Co-Editor, Stock Tips

Figure IV.5.3 - Stocktips announcement for TPLY

The price action following this announcement will be discussed in the following section. A well-known promoter, StockTips proved over the years to do a good job pumping its stocks. This translates in supernova-like chart patterns.

StockTips then sent daily emails reinforcing the promotion, attempting to drive the stock price even higher from March 6 to March 9. No more emails on this security where received after this date.

Price Action

Following the announcement of the StockTips pick, TPLY experienced a rapid increase in price, from $0.12 to $0.22. This was then met by a small dip to $0.19, bouncing back to $0.27 on the second day before starting to fade.

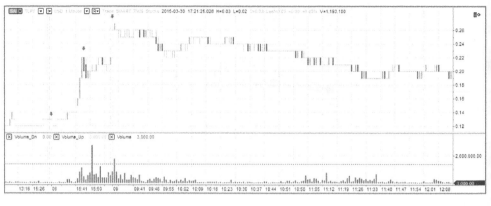

Figure IV.5.4 - TPLY days 1 and 2 of the P&D

Figure IV.5.4 shows the start of the pump on March 6, 2015, at open. A strong increase in volume can be noticed mid-day on the first day as the mails start being noticed by subscribers.

Day two is marked by an additional spike before finally starting to fade. The mailer promotion officially ran from March 6 to March 9, achieving a 130% price increase.

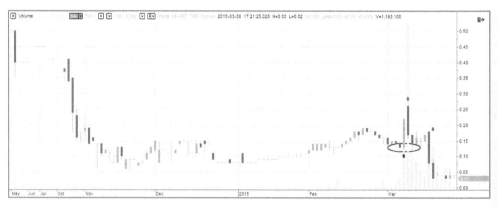

Figure IV.5.5 - TPLY daily chart

Figure IV.5.5 shows the daily chart for TPLY, showing the initial spike on March 6, the second high on March 7, and finally fading from that point on.

Notice in the figure above that the price dropped below the promotion's starting point by the time the promoter stopped promoting the stock.

Potential Profit for Long Positions

BPD plays are plays that require experience and very good timing skill. Moreover, they rely on proper knowledge of the capacity of a promoter to push a stock price up. Very few promoters are able to show this kind of performance when pumping a stock.

Considering this, BPD plays can be very profitable by knowing that a reputable promoter is able to drive a stock over 100%. More importantly, these are easy profits if properly prepared and played well, since these types of plays are fast moving and extremely predictable.

Entries in these types of stocks should be timed very early in the promotion. Usually a successful entry will be done moments after the promoter's announcement of the stock in their promotion. You also must remember that it's unsafe to keep such a long position for the duration of the promotion and attempt to wait for the peak, as the SEC can halt these companies because they often don't respect regulations.

Chapter IV.6 - Short Pump & Dumps

Strategy: Short Pump & Dumps (SPD)
Difficulty: Medium/Hard
Orientation: Short (Chapter III.1)
Suitability: Intermediate/Advanced traders

Introduction

Shorting pump and dumps is truly the heart of the original pennystocking strategy. Even though the availability of good promoters has died down over the years, there are still some promotions that are worth the time and can offer some very profitable opportunities.

SPD plays are the other side of the BPD strategy. Instead of betting odds on the upside, which can potentially reach new heights with every promotional email, the downside is ensured after a certain period of time.

What to Look For

The research parameters for the SPD play are exactly the same as the BPD strategy described in Chapter IV.5. A pump & dump stock can be profitable in both the upside and downside if played properly.

How It Works

Being on the short side of a P&D requires experience and timing. More importantly, it may require the use of the position boxing technique, as described in Chapter III.5.

The reason for this, as described in both Chapters III.1 and III.5, is that availability of shares to short for these types of shares is often scarce and may require a trader to enter a position much sooner than the readiness of the price to crack and dive.

Entry Signal

Entering a short position for an SPD strategy considers price reversal after the stock price has been overextended for a certain period of time. A price reversal is often followed by the "dump" phase of the promotion, which results in a significant drop in price.

Keep in mind that the promoters may continue pumping the stock following a price reversal and the seeming start of a "dump".

Exit Signal

The beauty of a P&D is the fact that considering the shady type of company represented by the stock at hand, the price has little to no chance of recovery. This essentially means that you can ride a position in an SPD strategy stock all the way to the bottom.

Of course, as for every position taken, your RMS applies and you must respect your absolute stop rules. That being said, once a promotion is over, this is often not necessary.

Case Study

For the purpose of this case study, we'll look at a promotion pushed by ElitePennyStocks and StockTip Magazine on American Leisure Holdings, Inc., also known as AMLH.

This stock was very heavily promoted, prompting numerous emails per day for a longer-than-usual promotion.

Context

A couple of weeks prior to the promotion start, ElitePennyStocks sent a mailer campaign that stating that they would announce their next pick on January 20, 2015.

A few weeks later, StockTip finally launched their campaign for AMLH. The campaign ran for a full month, from January 20, 2015 to February 17, 2015.

Both StockTip and ElitePennyStocks participated in the promotion of this pump & dump by sending emails on a daily basis.

Figure IV.6.1 shows an excerpt of the first mailer sent out by StockTip in order to promote AMLH and entice gullible investors into buying this as an investment opportunity.

Figure IV.6.1 - Stocktips mailer excerpt for AMLH

The subsequent weeks were filled with daily emails – constant reminders of how well this stock would do.

Price Action

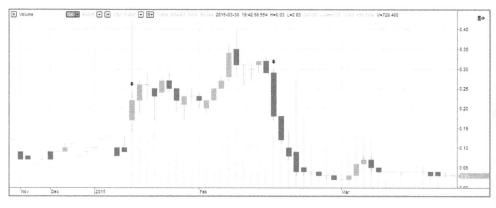

Figure IV.6.2 - Multicharts - AMLH daily chart of P&D from Jan 20, 2015

Figure IV.6.2 shows the behavior of this promotion and how it performed over the course of mailer campaign.

The stock started at $0.10/share on January 16. At the start of the promotion, the price gapped up to $0.14 and crossed the $0.20 mark by the end of the day, doubling the price per share.

Over the course of the promotion, the stock reached a high of $0.40; that's four times its starting price.

The AMLH promotion was a long one. Typically, paid promotions last a couple of weeks. However, the duration of the actual promotion is entirely at the discretion of the promoters and "The Smartest Man in the Room" (see Chapter II.8).

As you see in the picture above, as soon as the promotion ended on February 17, the stock price dropped considerably.

Potential Profit for Short Positions

Profiting for a P&D on the short side can often mean ensured profits if timed properly. Considering that the only reason that stocks such as AMLH have such a dramatic increase in price is the paid promotion that supports it, it's usually safe to assume that the price will drop quickly, with little chance of recovery.

In fact, Figure IV.6.2 actually shows the price of AMLH dropping way below its pre-promo price, ending at $0.03 per share.

The difficult part about shorting a P&D such as AMLH lies in the timing and the availability of shares to short.

In the specific case of AMLH, share availability was scarce midway through the pump. This usually means that it is necessary to box the position in order to be able to profit from it (see Chapter III.5).

Additionally, timing this stock was difficult, especially for those not boxing their position. Midway through the pump, it seemed as if it would end; however, the promoters ran more campaign series, sending the stock soaring from the mid-0.20s to a high of $0.40. This essentially resulted in a massive short squeeze, driving the price up fast.

Finally, the stock was unable to maintain its $0.40 price level and started tanking while the promotion was still active and traders became more aware of the worthlessness of the company.

Notice here that shorting a P&D requires experience, understanding of how OTC stocks work and how promoters operate in order to pump their stocks. More importantly, it's crucial to remember that timing is important for such a play, and boxing positions like these usually reduces the difficulty of this kind of trade by ensuring an early entry into the position without sustaining considerable losses on the upside.

Chapter IV.7 - Timothy Sykes's 7-Step Pennystocking Framework

Strategy: 7-Step Pennystocking Framework (7SPSF)
Difficulty: Medium/Hard
Orientation: Long & Short
Suitability: Intermediate/Advanced traders

Introduction

The 7-Step Pennystocking Framework is a strategy developed by Timothy Sykes and originally introduced at the Fourth Annual Pennystocking Conference in Las Vegas in 2011 (Sykes & et al., Pennystocking Framework, 2012). This strategy focuses on various approaches intended to exploit pump and dumps (Chapter II.8) at the various phases of the promotion.

What to Look For

This framework is divided into identifying seven states on a pump & dump type of stock. Most successful P&D promotions go through these states and this behavior has remained constant over the years.

It's important to understand the underlying reasons behind each step rather than just memorizing how the pattern on the chart looks. Understanding why a P&D phase fits in each of these steps is crucial to exploiting this strategy at its best.

How It Works

Pump & dumps have seven identifiable steps that define potential behavior. You must consider, however, that these steps are not sequential and some may be omitted or repeated.

The 7-Step Framework is a combination of the individual strategies described in Chapters IV.2, IV.3, IV.4, IV.5 and IV.6, adapted specifically to the context of a promotion.

This framework is not an exact science and requires traders to possess a degree of adaptability in order to play the position best.

Step 1: The Pre-pump, Early Pump

The early pump stage requires a certain type of knowledge about the stock being promoted, or an early entry into the stock, having done proper research that would justify a hypothesis of a stock being pumped in the short term.

Having this knowledge about the upcoming promotion requires you to hold the stock for an extended period of time, ranging from multiple days to possibly months before the pump starts. Additionally, a trader could enter on the very start of the promotion in order to get in at the lowest possible price.

This purpose of this step is to attempt to predict a hyperbolic price movement resulting in a supernova in the short-midterm.

Step 1 of the framework can offer big profits when a hypothesis is right, but does require a lot of research and isn't guaranteed to yield a result. Moreover, traders must possess a significant amount of patience in order to deal with this phase of the P&D.

Step 2: The Ramp

The second step of the framework is characterized by a significant increase in trading volume while keeping the price action sideways before a breakout occurs.

This phase is marked by the anticipation of the supernova as traders start speculating on the possibility of the spike.

Chatter about the stock on social media and in forums and chatrooms significantly increases during this phase, as traders try to ascertain how they should play the stock and if it's a position worth taking. Volume can be directly correlated to the social perception as the price slowly increases with public interest.

This phase may last some days or weeks before a breakout finally occurs.

Step 3: The Supernova

As seen in Chapter II.6, the supernova is characterized by a hyperbolic price action and a significant increase in trading volume. The stock officially breaks out as the promotion gets underway and the promotional material starts reaching traders.

Step 3 is the best time to have a long position in a P&D, as prices can spike significantly (400%-1,000% for successful promotions). However, due to the very nature of the pattern, the price action is very quick, and consequently a risky position to have if not watched very closely for a price reversal.

Traders can expect to make between 100% and 1,000% within a couple of minutes, hours or days.

Step 4: The Cliff Dive

The fourth step of the framework is marked by a price reversal on the supernova and a significant drop in price from its highs. This usually occurs after a period of overextension as the pump promotion stops, or as traders start realizing the worthlessness of the company being traded.

A cliff dive is best played as a short position, and these types of movements are best entered before the actual reversal of the price action. Boxing the position (Chapter III.5) is worth considering here to help reserve shares to short, as these become rare with a cliff dive underway. If boxing your position, make sure to close your long position quickly to avoid getting caught in the middle of the crash.

Step 5: Dip Buying

This phase takes the essence of the strategy discussed in Chapter IV.2, and is based on buying the P&D as interest remains after a significant drop in price with a hypothesis of a potential bounce.

This step of the framework can be risky if the bounce fails, so you must be ready to exit the position quickly in order to avoid losses.

Step 5 is best played with the help of tools such as L2 and technical analysis in order to be able to predict what the trend lines (support and resistance) are, as well as the potential behavior in the short term.

This step is also usually marked by an increase in price due to short squeezes (discussed in Chapter III.1), which usually drives the bounce to its peak. This is beneficial to short-term long positions.

Step 6: The Dead Pump Bounce

This step focuses on shorting the bounces when they occur. A bounce, depending on the promotion, can reach previous highs or surpass them, offering great shorting opportunities as the price increases from significant drops.

Bounces can have a duration ranging from hours to days; however, bounces can also fail and not offer a peak – or even skip it altogether.

Bounces offer great shorting opportunities.

Step 7: The Long Kiss Goodnight

When the promotion is over, the price action of the P&D is characterized by a steady decline in price, slowly reverting back to the pre-pump price point and sometimes even below.

During this phase of the framework, bounces may occur, which may force or scare short position holders to exit their positions prematurely.

The long kiss goodnight step requires patience since it's focused on taking a longer-term short position in a declining stock.

The advantage of shorting at this point is the availability of shares to short; however, the profitable side may be limited, as the significant drops have already happened.

Case Studies

These case studies focus mainly on pump & dump charts, and indicate the steps of the framework applicable to each of the examples shown below.

The trading rules and strategies discussed throughout this course still apply to each of these steps, since the 7-Step Pennystocking Framework is a combination of multiple strategies and techniques.

The 7-Step Pennystocking framework is illustrated in Figures IV.7.1 through IV.7.8.

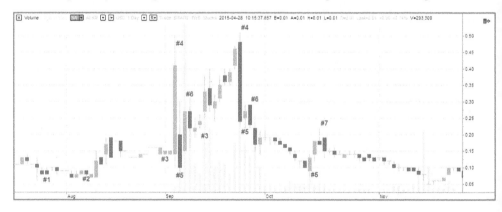

Figure IV.7.1 - Multicharts - ALKM

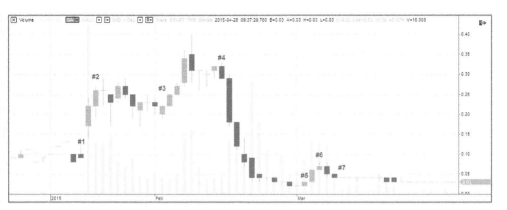

Figure IV.7.2 - Multicharts - AMLH

Figure IV.7.3 - Multicharts - CANF

Figure IV.7.4 - Multicharts - CLRX

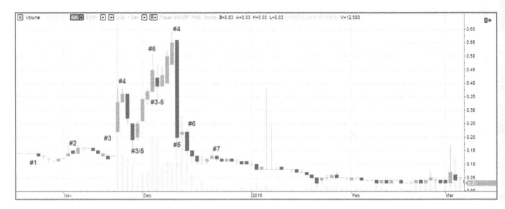

Figure IV.7.5 - Multicharts - ECRY

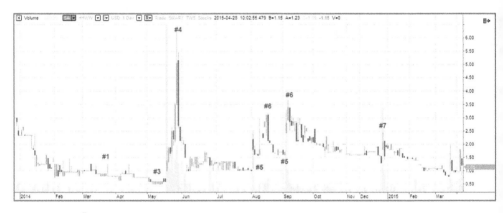

Figure IV.7.6 - Multicharts - HHWW

Figure IV.7.7 - Multicharts - NMED

Figure IV.7.8 - Multicharts - TAPM

Table of figures

Appendix I: Answers to Questions & Exercises

Questions

Chapter I.6:   1c – 2b – 3b – 4c,d,e,f – 5h

Chapter II.3:   1d – 2c – 3a,b,d – 4b – 5c – 6c

Chapter II.4 :   1b,2 - 2a,c - 3b - 4c - 5 e, 5f

Chapter II.5 :   1a - 2b - 3c - 4a

Chapter II.6 :   1b - 2a - 3b - 4b,c - 5b - 6c

Chapter II.7 :   1d - 2b - 3b - 4a,d - 5d

Chapter II.8 :   1c,d - 2c - 3b,c - 4b,c,d - 5a - 6d

Chapter II.9 :   1b - 2a - 3e - 4a,b,d - 5d - 6b,c

Chapter II.10:   1c - 2a,b - 3a - 4a - 5b

Chapter II.11:   1c,d – 2d – 3c – 4d - 5b – 6c

Chapter III.1:   1b - 2b - 3b,c,d - 4c - 5d - 6a

Chapter III.2:   1b - 2a - 3b - 4c,d - 5b - 6b

Chapter III.3 :   1d - 2b,c,d - 3a,c - 4a

Chapter III.4 :   1b - 2c - 3a - 4b - 5a,d

Chapter III.5:   1b - 2b - 3b - 4a

Exercises

Chapter II.4

Exercise 1

With an upside of 0.75 and a downside of 0.23 we can calculate the risk reward ratio as follows:

$$R^3 = 1:round\left(\frac{upside}{downside}\right) = 1:round\left(\frac{0.75}{0.23}\right) = 1:round(3.26) = 1:3$$

Exercise 2

We can establish the following:

$E = \$27{,}593.49$

$p = 1.5\% = 0.015$

$N = \$0.25$

$x = 1$

We can then calculate the Risk Unit as follows:

$U = \$27{,}593.49 \times 0.015 = \$413.90$

We can then evaluate the position size as follows:

$$P = floor\left(\frac{U}{x \times N}\right) = floor\left(\frac{\$413.90}{1 \times \$0.25}\right) = floor(1{,}655.60) = 1{,}600$$

Additionally, given a $2.63 price entry, a 1N stop and an ATR of $0.25 the absolute stop for a long position would be set at:

$Stop = 2.63 - 1 \times 0.25 = 2.38$

Conversely, for a short position:

$Stop = 2.63 + 1 \times 0.25 = 2.88$

Finally, the total position value at entry would be calculated as follows:

$$P\$ = 1600 \times \$2.63 = \$4{,}208.00$$

Chapter II.5

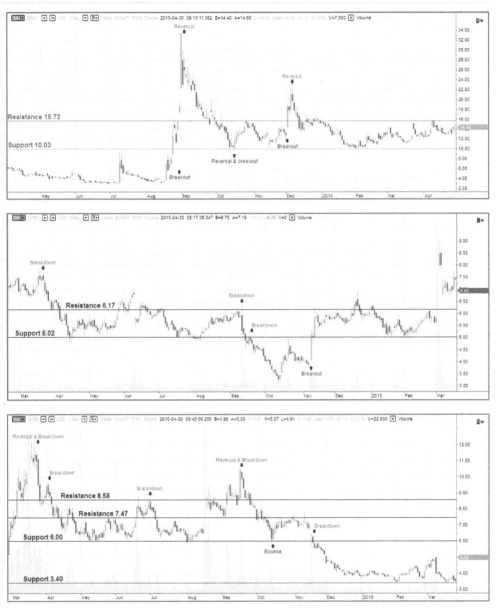

Exercises

Bibliography

Commission, S. a. (2005, 04 11). *Division of Market Regulation: Key Points About Regulation SHO*. Retrieved from https://www.sec.gov/spotlight/keyregshoissues.htm

Commission, S. a. (2010, 05 10). Amendments to Regulation SHO . *RIN 3235-AK35*. Retrieved from http://www.sec.gov/rules/final/2010/34-61595.pdf

Commission, S. a. (n.d.). *How to Read a 10-K*. Retrieved from http://www.sec.gov/answers/reada10k.htm

Commission, S. a. (n.d.). *Market Maker*. Retrieved from http://www.sec.gov/answers/mktmaker.htm

Commission, S. a. (n.d.). *Pattern Day Trader*. Retrieved from http://www.sec.gov/answers/patterndaytrader.htm

Commission, S. a. (n.d.). *Trading Halts and Delays*. Retrieved from http://www.sec.gov/answers/tradinghalt.htm

Covel, M. W. (2009). *The Complete Turtle Trader*. HarperBusiness.

Digital Ally Receives Order From State Police Of Michigan Valued at More Than $1.1 Million. (2014, August 28). Retrieved from Yahoo Finance: http://finance.yahoo.com/news/digital-ally-receives-order-state-113000674.html

Digital Ally, Inc. Announces Second Quarter Operating Results. (2014, August 13). Retrieved from Yahoo Finance: http://finance.yahoo.com/news/digital-ally-inc-announces-second-220457511.html

Dumon, M. (n.d.). *Reverse Mergers: The Pros And Cons*. Retrieved from Investopedia: http://www.investopedia.com/articles/stocks/09/introduction-reverse-mergers.asp

Form 8-K for DIGITAL ALLY INC. (2014, August 27). Retrieved from Yahoo Finance: http://biz.yahoo.com/e/140827/dgly8-k.html

Form 8-K for DIGITAL ALLY INC. (2014, August 14). Retrieved from Yahoo Finance: http://biz.yahoo.com/e/140814/dgly8-k.html

Goode, M., & Sykes, T. (2010). How to read SEC Filings. Bullship Press.

Inquiries Regarding Digital Ally's First VU HD Body Camera Increase Dramatically During Past Week in Response to Civil Unrest in Ferguson, Missouri. (2014, August 20). Retrieved from Yahoo Finance: http://finance.yahoo.com/news/inquiries-regarding-digital-allys-firstvu-113000017.html

Lee, B. (1971, December 9). The Lost Interview. (P. Burton, Interviewer)

Lee, B., & Little, J. (Directors). (2000). *Bruce Lee: A Warrior's Journey* [Motion Picture].

Runup, B. (n.d.). Retrieved from Bio Runup: http://www.biorunup.com

Sykes, T. (2010). PennyStocking. BullShip Press.

Sykes, T., & et al. (2011). The New Rules of Pennystocking. BullshipShip Press.

Sykes, T., & et al. (2012). Pennystocking Framework. Millionaire Media LLC.